Yet With A Steady Beat

Stony the road we trod, Bitter the chast'ning rod,
Felt in the days when hope unborn had died;
Yet with a steady beat, Have not our weary feet
Come to the place for which our fathers sighed?
We have come over a way that with tears has been watered;
We have come, treading our path through the blood of the slaughtered.
Out from the gloomy past, Till now we stand at last
Where the white gleam of our bright star is cast.

JAMES WELDON JOHNSON (1871–1938)

Harold T. Lewis is rector of Calvary Episcopal Church, Pittsburgh, Pennsylvania. Formerly staff officer for black ministries at the Episcopal Church Center in New York, he has taught at the Mercer School of Theology and New York Theological Seminary. He was coordinator of the second international Conference on Afro-Anglicanism in Cape Town, South Africa, in 1995.

HAROLD
T. LEWIS

Yet With A Steady Beat

THE AFRICAN AMERICAN STRUGGLE FOR RECOGNITION IN THE EPISCOPAL CHURCH

TRINITY PRESS INTERNATIONAL
Valley Forge, Pennsylvania

Trinity Press International, P.O. Box 851, Valley Forge, PA 19482-0851

Library of Congress Cataloging-in-Publication Data

Lewis, Harold T.

Yet with a steady beat : the African American struggle for recognition in the Episcopal Church / Harold T. Lewis. – 1st ed.

p. cm.

Includes bibliographical references and index.

ISBN 1-56338-130-3 (pbk. : alk. paper)

1. Afro-American Episcopalians–History. 2. Episcopal Church–History. 3. Episcopal Church–Membership. 4. Anglican Communion–United States–History. 5. Anglican Communion–United States–Membership. I. Title.

BX5979.L49 1995

283'.73'08996073–dc20 95-46837

CIP

Printed in the United States of America

96 97 98 99 10 9 8 7 6 5 4 3 2

To
George Freeman Bragg Jr.
1863–1940
Priest, Historiographer, Exemplar

Contents

Part Four
INTERPRETERS OF THE GOSPEL

Acknowledgments

I am deeply indebted to Dr. Werner Ustorf, professor of mission in the University of Birmingham, for taking me under his wing and for his missiological guidance; and to Dr. Randall Burkett, associate director of the W. E. B. Du Bois Institute for Afro-American Research at Harvard University, for his historical guidance; and to both of them for keeping my feet to the fire when I waxed more homiletic than academic. I have benefited richly from this unique transatlantic team of advisors. Thanks are also due to the Reverend Dr. J. Carleton Hayden, Episcopal chaplain to Howard University, for his suggestions and comments, and for his prolific contributions to the field, which greatly aided my research.

My studies could not have been undertaken without the financial assistance of the Episcopal Church Foundation, and more particularly, William G. Andersen Jr., its executive director, for his interest in and support of my research; the Right Reverend Orris G. Walker Jr., bishop of Long Island, for his generous scholarship assistance; and the Very Reverend Lloyd A. Lewis Jr., dean of the Mercer School of Theology, for providing a grant from the Faculty Assistance Fund.

I am grateful for the assistance given by the librarians and staffs at the University of Birmingham Library; the Sterling Memorial and Divinity School Libraries at Yale University; the St. Mark's Library at the General Theological Seminary; the Bishop Payne Library at the Virginia Theological Seminary; the Library of the Episcopal Theological Seminary of the Southwest; the Library of the George Mercer School of Theology; the Henry Knox Sherrill Resource Center at the Episcopal Church Center in New York City; and the Schomburg Center for Afro-American Research and Culture in New York City. Special appreciation is expressed to Mark Duffy, archivist at the Episcopal Church Archives in Austin, Texas, and to his staff for their invaluable help in providing me access to primary sources.

A word of thanks is also expressed to Michael Beary of the University of Arkansas for rekindling my interest in and providing me with information about Bishop Edward Thomas Demby; and to the Reverend Paul Minor, associate at Grace Church in New York City, who furnished me with information about Jonathan Wainwright from the parish archives. I am grateful to Bishop John Burgess for sharing a wealth of information with me, especially about West Indian clergy, as well as for the many sermons and addresses he has delivered throughout his long ministry, which in many ways have chronicled the struggle of black Episcopalians. My profound gratitude is expressed to Bishops Quintin Primo and Walter Dennis and the Reverend Dr. Austin Cooper, for supplying me information about the founding of the Union of Black Episcopalians; and to the Reverend Canon Thomas W. S. Logan Sr., unofficial historiographer of black Episcopalians, for affording me access to his extensive files and memorabilia.

Marc Stephen Jones, formerly my program associate at the Episcopal Church Center in New York, and my son, Justin Craig Lewis, are to be commended for their computer expertise, which greatly aided me in the preparation of this work. To the staffs of St. Andrew's Hall, the Episcopal Theological Seminary of the Southwest, and the Episcopal Divinity School is expressed my appreciation for the ministry of hospitality extended to me during the periods I spent in Birmingham, Austin, and Cambridge respectively.

Finally, my loving appreciation is expressed to my wife, Claudette Richards Lewis, for her comments, her invaluable skills as a proofreader and editor, and for her support, patience, and understanding during the period of my research and writing.

Introduction

The African American Struggle for Recognition in the Episcopal Church

No alien race, no foreign shore, no child unsought, unknown.

—H. H. TWEEDY (HYMN TEXT, 1929)

"If a black man is anything but a Baptist or a Methodist, someone has been tampering with his religion." Attributed to Booker T. Washington, the aphorism is a popular one in certain African American ecumenical circles. It betrays a commonly held belief that there is something incongruous about being black and Episcopalian. Because, as one historian put it, "it surprises many to know that there are such people as Negro Episcopalians,"[1] the term "black Episcopalian" approaches the status of oxymoron. This is certainly corroborated by the literature on the black church. During the past half century, several books have been published that address the place of religion in the lives of black Americans, and that analyze the impact of the black church as an institution on the history of the United States. In virtually all of these volumes, there is scant mention of black Episcopalians. In fact, C. Eric Lincoln specifically excludes black Episcopalians from his recent study of the black church.[2]

If it were not for the fact of the historical relationship between Richard Allen and Absalom Jones, two Methodist lay preachers who were prominent in the decades following the American Revolution, black Episcopalians might receive virtually no recognition at all. E. Franklin Frazier's treatment is typical and, moreover, in its inaccuracy betrays an attitude all too prevalent among historians, especially among those belonging to black denominations, who tend to minimize the significance of black Episcopalians and their impact on American church history. In describing the eviction of the two men from the gallery of St. George's Methodist Church in Philadelphia, he writes:

> After Richard Allen and Absalom Jones organized the Free African Society, they differed as to whether Negroes should model their church

> organization after the Methodist or after the Protestant Episcopal Church. Allen was of the opinion that the Methodist form of worship was more suited to the religious needs and form of worship to which the Negroes had become accustomed. As a consequence of this difference between Jones and Allen, Jones organized the African Protestant Episcopal Church of St. Thomas, but the majority of the Negroes who had seceded from the white church followed Allen.... The movement begun by Allen ... spread to other cities where the so-called African Methodist Episcopal Church was set up.[3]

Since Frazier relates that the ejection of Jones and Allen came at a time "when the number of Negroes attending St. George's Methodist Church increased,"[4] it is clear that the removal of the two men and their fellow black worshipers was racially motivated. Ann Lammers suggests that the increase in black membership at St. George's resulted in an "increase of white anxiety and resentment."[5] Such an interpretation is expanded and explicated by Forrest Wood in his comment on the incident. He observes:

> The bitter debates over slavery ... actually obfuscated the more fundamental issue of *racism*.... When the Reverend Hamilton insisted [in the late 1880s] that "race preference and prejudice has built a wall between the two races," he was only reflecting a Methodist opinion that could be traced back at least a century. When, in 1787, ... black worshipers were pulled from their knees while praying in St. George's Methodist Church in Philadelphia, and ... ordered to the back of the sanctuary, they left and vowed never to return.... It triggered one of the most significant movements in American social and religious history: the emergence of the black church.[6]

Apart from the blacks' alleged preference for the "plain" worship of Methodism, a motivation for Allen's followers was clearly a desire to be in control of their own religious institution. That being the case, Frazier's tacit question is: Why would any blacks, having been mistreated by white Christians, cast their lot with another group of white Christians? If indeed it is true, as James Cone suggests, that "the black church in America was founded on the belief that God condemned slavery and that Christian freedom meant political emancipation,"[7] it becomes axiomatic that blacks, given a choice, would be less inclined to affiliate with the church of their oppressors.

The overwhelming majority, of course, did not. Most black Christians in the United States are spiritual sons and daughters of Allen. Lincoln claims that "seven major black denominations account for more than 80 percent of black religious affiliation in the United States."[8] With these facts, historical, theological, and political, it is easy to see why black Episcopalians often find themselves in a defensive posture. Their authenticity and even their integrity as Christians are almost routinely brought into question. They must answer allegations of "Uncle Tom-ism." They have been accused of selling their spiritual birthright for a mess of pottage of rather dubious nutritional value. John Melville Burgess, retired bishop of Massachusetts and the first black priest elected a diocesan bishop in the United States, once recalled: "I personally have experienced the ostracism of being a member of a minority religious group, having doubts cast upon the validity of my Christian faith and experience, of being the butt of jokes about liturgy and ritual."[9] In short, black Episcopalians, who number somewhere between 4 and 6 percent of all Episcopalians,[10] are often made to feel that they must provide a justification for their membership in — not to mention their loyalty to — a church that has consistently been identified in the United States with the power elite. The Episcopal Church has been a church in which "Afro-American members [have been] limited by a racial monopoly of power and the duplication in the life of the Church of [societal] patterns of racial segregation and discrimination."[11] Kortright Davis addresses the problem in this way:

> To be British and Anglican goes as a hand in a glove, but to be Black and Anglican seems to require both explanation and adjustment. Black people are always susceptible to the problem of having to explain why they are associated with styles of belief and patterns of social behavior which do not readily reflect their ethnic antecedents or *natural* tendencies. Anglicanism, it is said, is cold, stiff, formal, hierarchical — it lacks the warmth, flexibility, informality and communality of Africanism. How can both be placed together in any harmonious and lasting way? Is it not a commonly accepted norm that blacks should be Baptists?[12]

The riddle has traditionally been answered in sociological terms. Conventional wisdom holds that the affiliation of African Americans to the Episcopal Church is inextricably connected to matters of class and status. Blacks are said to be members of the Episcopal Church for one of two reasons: either they were born into it, or they sought it out because it is the church "to belong to" when climbing the proverbial social ladder. In other words, blacks' motivations for membership are said to mirror those of their white counterparts. There is no paucity of literature (or oral history) that would lend credence to such a view. Even George Freeman Bragg Jr., the preeminent historiographer of black Episcopalians who speaks of the "dominance of education, culture and refinement" among early black Episcopalians, seems to admit as much.[13] Another black priest-historian comments that "the appeal of the [Episcopal] Church has been directed more to the urban and better educated groups in the north,"[14] and further comments that "the Negro congregations of the Episcopal Church have been composed of what might be termed the upper classes. At least in general they represented a more exclusive group than the independent church organized and controlled by Negroes alone."[15]

Striking a similar chord, J. Carleton Hayden, an expert on the history of black Episcopalians, writes that "in many places black congregations gained a reputation for social exclusiveness. Some congregations, notably in Charleston, Savannah, St. Louis, and Detroit, were identified with light-skinned families known as the 'blue vein' society."[16] Wallace Thurman, writing about religious life in Harlem in the 1920s, describes St. Philip's as "the religious sanctum of the socially elect and wealthy Negroes [whose] congregation is largely mulatto [and whose] Parish House serves as one of the most ambitious and important social centers in Harlem."[17] Similarly, Bishop Burgess comments: "We have enjoyed the fiction that being an Episcopalian lifted us out of the ordinary black community. The 'blue-vein church' has more or less disappeared among us... but the church still has been an exclusive social club for many of our members."[18]

Willard Gatewood, in his recent study of the black elite, devotes more pages to black Episcopalians than to any other religious grouping of African Americans. He states:

> The ranks of the black Episcopalians included a disproportionately large number of the most respected "old families," professional people, and others whose education and affluence often set them apart from other blacks. The small number of black Episcopalians (amounting to only 15,000 by 1903) also contributed to an image of exclusiveness.... Although the degree to which congregations exhibited social exclusiveness varied from parish to parish, the idea of Episcopalians being "the select few" was sufficiently widespread to prompt upwardly mobile blacks to transfer their allegiance from Baptist and Methodist denominations to the Episcopal Church.[19]

It is not our intention in the following pages to discredit such views, but to suggest that they alone cannot account for the dedication and unfeigned loyalty that blacks have shown to the Episcopal Church for 200 years. At base, then, we believe that there are profoundly theological reasons for such loyalty, and that these reasons are grounded in a belief on the part of black Episcopalians that the Episcopal Church is a catholic institution. By "catholic," black Episcopalians have understood the Church to be

> universal, that is, a church for all people, not one limited to any period, race or culture.... This catholicity meant that the church was pre-slavery

and therefore pre-racism. Its formularies, practices and constitutions were divine and in place before racial inequality.[20]

Black Episcopalians' belief in the Church as a catholic institution is eloquently expressed in the words of a sermon preached by John Love, a priest and medical missionary who worked in Haiti under James Theodore Holly, the first black bishop in the Episcopal Church:[21]

> To be like him (that is, Jesus) [the church] must embody a religion essentially the same in any age, grand and enduring, a religion which changes not however the world may change... like the Holy Gospel, not for a day but for all time, not for one individual but for all classes and conditions of men.[22]

The thought is echoed in an address delivered by Dr. Anna Julia Cooper to a group of black clergy in 1886, in which she proclaimed:

> We believe in the Holy Catholic Church. We believe that however gigantic and apparently remote the consummation, the Church will go on conquering and to conquer till the kingdom of this world, *not excepting* the black man and the black woman... shall have become the kingdoms of the Lord and of His Christ.[23]

This recurrent theme of catholicity was addressed at a black clergy conference held in Washington in 1977, at which the late Bishop John Walker queried: "Is it possible for black people to maintain integrity and identity within a 'white' church?"[24] Two years later, at a convocation of black Episcopal theologians, the Reverend Van Bird asked, "What does it mean to be a Christian witness in a racist church?" and "How can Black Episcopalians become agents of utopian religion in church and society?"[25] Neither Bishop Walker nor Dr. Bird claimed to be raising new issues. They were addressing perennial concerns of African Americans who confess and call themselves Episcopalians, and who have historically claimed their rightful place as full-fledged members of the Episcopal Church, and have taken it at its official word that it "espouses and adheres to a theory and tradition that membership is open to all persons who accept its doctrine, discipline and worship."[26] Bragg cites this statistic with unabashed pride:

> The Episcopal Church is the only Christian body of note, covering the entire country, with representative assemblies. In this respect, it is in a class by itself. There is only *one* Episcopal Church. It knows neither north nor south, east or west, race or color. The American Episcopal Church until now has most positively refused to recognize the "color-line" in its canons and general laws, and in considering what the church has done or has not done, this fact must constantly be borne in mind.[27]

Recognizing that "there are no racial prohibitions or exclusions in the national constitution, canons or by-laws, nor in those of the majority of the dioceses,"[28] black Episcopalians, when confronted with attitudes, policies, and behavior that have attempted and, in many cases, succeeded in marginalizing, disenfranchising, or ostracizing them, have historically attributed such actions to the shortcomings of their perpetrators, and not to the intrinsic nature of the institution. Bishop Holly appealed to such reasoning when he encouraged black Episcopal clergy not to desert "the church of our love" since it was "the sovereign will and power of Almighty God that preserves grace in the Church in spite of unworthy administrators."[29]

What is more, black Episcopalians have consistently held the Church's feet to the fire, and reminded it when its actions have been inconsistent with the principles it has espoused. In so doing, black Episcopalians have consistently called the Church to be true to its catholic principles even when it had abandoned them, or had run the risk of abandoning them. As Eleanor Harrison observes:

> Not only have African Americans demanded full incorporation in the Episcopal Church . . . they have also forced the church to balance its pietism with their [black] propheticism. Throughout their history, they have impelled the church to define the extent of its catholicity and answer the question: what does incorporation *actually* mean in terms of equality, status and power? African American Episcopalians have challenged the definitions that the Episcopal Church has generally given, calling white Episcopalians to recognize that genuine catholic fellowship requires and demands *full* incorporation and *full* equality.[30]

A notable example of such a challenge is contained in a memorial to General Convention prepared by the Conference of Church Workers among Colored People in 1906:

> With all fairness and frankness of speech, the real issue cannot be evaded. The people represented by your petitioners are citizens of the United States, having a share in the Government under which they live. We cannot reasonably expect such persons to accept membership in a Church which denies them a share in the ecclesiastical government, which, in honor-bound, they must sustain and bear true allegiance. We claim that ours is a Catholic Church, and yet, in its highest legislative body, the exclusions of members of our race as parts of the Catholic entity would seem a silent but expressive contradiction of such an all-embracing claim.[31]

More recently, Bishop Burgess underscored the same point:

> For conscience sake we Black Episcopalians must understand that we are legitimate, not only in the eyes of our brothers and sisters in the so-called

> black denominations but to white Episcopalians as well. It is important since the church needs us more than we need it. Black members help to keep the church honest, to give substance to the firmly held dogma that *we are church and not sect. A separate black church is no serious alternative.* To back away from the fight to be full-fledged members of the church in every level of its life would be to remove from the church the very reason for its existence, to declare that in Christ there are ever new and eternal possibilities for *all* the people of God.[32]

This emphasis on the Church's catholicity is not an insignificant contribution to the life of the Church, given that the Episcopal Church claims through membership in the Anglican Communion to be part of the historic catholic church;[33] upholds the doctrine of apostolic succession;[34] and maintains that "Protestant" in its official title does not refer to "Reformation-Protestant" but is intended to mean "non-Papist."[35] Yet it remains, in the American scheme of things, a Protestant denomination, indeed the quintessential Protestant denomination. To most Americans, the first image conjured up by the acronym WASP (White Anglo-Saxon Protestant) is the Episcopalian.

It is to this protestant context that black Episcopalians have historically provided a catholic corrective:

> The Episcopal Church, as a founding member of the protestant establishment, is one of the principal religious institutions which tend to legitimate the current American social order. It is pre-eminently a form of ideological religion. How can black Episcopalians become agents of utopian religion in church and society?... Black Episcopalians... are ... strategically located in a theological sense to offer... a periodical corrective.... Not only can black and Anglican traditions coexist; they do exist in a potentially creative and constructive tension.... While in the "House of Pharaoh," black Episcopalians have the opportunity to be a catalytic force to puncture the shell of its ideological religion.[36]

It should be mentioned that the situation in which black Episcopalians find themselves is not peculiar to the American experience. Just as Dr. Bird could cite the unique opportunities for mission afforded black Episcopalians within the context of an often inimical American society, so black Anglicans elsewhere have relied on a broader, catholic vision of the church as the linchpin that has kept them within the fold of Anglicanism, despite the fact that its historical trappings are culturally alien. John Pobee, in an address before the Conference on Afro-Anglicanism in 1985, posed a question that he answered in terms of the catholicity of a previously very British Anglicanism now enriched by the diverse cultures of the Third World:

> How can an African, a Ghanaian from Ghana, who led the way to the modern phase of African nationalism... continue to be part of Anglicanism, which is every bit British, if not English, the established religion of the former colonial master, Great Britain, who "ruled the waves"?... The growth rate [of Anglicanism] outside the British Isles is higher than in them.... Anglicanism, whatever its historical origins and makeup, is a communion, a mosaic, one part of which is "Afro" with an identity of its own, and that Anglicanism is no longer only British or for that matter, Caucasian.... Thus, Afro-Anglicanism... must be authentic in its theology, structures, values and general ethos and orientation, in short in its context of mission.[37]

To understand the movement among black Episcopalians in an even broader historical and missiological perspective, we would further suggest that it conforms to a universal pattern in which those in every clime to whom the Gospel has been brought — the "missionized" — have interpreted the Gospel in light of their peculiar needs. Black Episcopalians are among the "diaspora descendants" of black Africans who, according to Richard Gray, have understood that "the Gospel carries implications which transcend the understanding of those who proclaim it."[38] Afro-Caribbeans and African Americans, like all other blacks, have been "a particular type of people who have had the distinction of being the only ones in history whose claims of being human have been systematically called into question." This has manifested itself in an "indefatigable attempt... to transform the meaning of slavery and oppression, poverty and dependence, failure and weakness, into powerful signs of promise, achievement, fulfillment and historical emancipation."[39]

Indeed, black Episcopalians have given new definition to this concept. Many early black leaders not only maintained that *fides anglicana* was not inimical to blacks, but that it was especially suited to them and, properly seen, was an instrument of their uplift. Thus, the Reverend Shelton Hale Bishop, rector of St. Philip's, Harlem, from 1933 to 1955, could write: "The genius of the [Episcopal] Church may be described as composed of two elements: First, sane and thoroughly moralized religion; secondly, the ideal of the Church Catholic. And these two elements constitute the primary religious need of the Negro people."[40] Bishop Holly declared (interestingly enough, to a group of black clergy in the Diocese of Virginia who were concerned about the curtailment of certain of their ecclesiastical privileges):

> The African race must find in the Churches of the Anglican Communion the powerful lever, which under God, will elevate them to the full stature of their Christian manhood. That race is under a dark and heavy

> cloud of spiritual ignorance. It is only the entrance of God's word that giveth light. That saving word of inspiration... can be heard in its purity in those churches in the Scriptural order of the liturgical services, in greater abundance, and by a clearer and more systematic presentation of the whole mystery of Godliness, than in any other or all other churches under the sun.[41]

In the following chapters, we shall attempt a theological history of black Episcopalians from 1623, the date of the baptism of the first slaves at Jamestown, Virginia, through 1968, the date of the "involuntary retirement"[42] of the Reverend Dr. Tollie LeRoy Caution as Secretary for Negro Work and Associate Secretary of the Division of Domestic Mission in the Home Department at the Episcopal Church headquarters in New York, an event that in turn served as a catalyst in the formation of the Union of Black Clergy and Laity (later the Union of Black Episcopalians) in the same year. Part One (chapters 1–4) will treat the period from colonial times through the end of the Civil War, during which blacks were, for the most part (although by no means exclusively), "receivers of the Gospel," that is, the objects of Anglican missionary endeavor. Part Two (chapters 5–7) will deal with an era, roughly the period between the Civil War and World War I, during which blacks assumed greater missionary initiative and became "sowers of the Gospel" in their own right. Part Three (chapters 8–9), whose timeframe is the first half of the twentieth century, will recount the events through which black Episcopalians became "contenders for the Gospel," striving for equality (principally through the efforts of the Conference for Church Workers among Colored People and the "deputies for colored work") and fighting to solidify their power base in the Church. In the final section (chapter 10), we shall look at how black Episcopalians, who discovered that there was a complementarity between their catholic witness and the theology of the civil rights movement, became "interpreters of the Gospel."

It is our hope that the reader will discern in this progression that black Episcopalians have achieved a virtual metamorphosis, that is, from a condition in which the Gospel was used as an instrument of their oppression and control to a circumstance in which the Gospel has been understood to be the instrument not only of their liberation and empowerment, but also of the liberation of all members of the Church from oppression and racism. This study does not lend itself to a neat, concise conclusion drawn from the analysis of the hard data of a discrete historical period. The conclusion, therefore, will in some ways be like an epilogue, in which we reflect on the findings in light of ongoing developments in the life of black Episcopalians between 1968 and the present.

This study will endeavor to show that the controversies, the struggles, and the tensions that have existed between blacks and whites in the Episcopal Church have stemmed less from racial differences, per se, than from ideological and theological ones, which in turn are reflective of a distinctively different ecclesiology. Arnold Hamilton Maloney, a black Episcopal priest born in Trinidad and a 1910 graduate of the General Theological Seminary,[43] neatly capsulized the differences between white and black religious systems. His remarks presage the thinking of liberation and third world theologians of the 1960s who, writing theology from "below,"[44] draw distinctions between the church as a chaplaincy to the status quo and the church as an advocate for the oppressed:

> The "white church" and the "colored church" are not the same thing. They represent two distinct psychological phenomena. In the former, the people congregate to render "service." ... They pay God a call to offer their help in the difficult problem of *guiding the course of the world.* They make God their debtor. They bring Him down to them. To the latter, the church is a "meeting place." It is here that the talent for racial leadership is developed. It is here that the literary and dramatic faculties of the race have the freedom of range to revel in the more refined and ennobling regions of art. It is here that the problems of home and of the community are threshed out. It is from this social meeting place that the souls of Negroes soar up "to meet their God in the skies."[45]

Historically, the white power structure within the Episcopal Church has viewed blacks as intended objects of one missionary strategy or another. Blacks have been seen as a group to be missionized, worked among, brought (sometimes conditionally) into, and at times kept out of, the fold — in short, treated as an anomaly, an oddity, a separate group, tangential to the mainstream, over whom some form of control should be maintained. To this end, the Society for the Propagation of the Gospel, the Protestant Episcopal Freedman's Commission to Colored People, the Commission on Work among Colored People, the American Church Institute for Negroes, the Commission on Negro Work, and most recently, the Office of Black Ministries, have been special agencies established for the purpose of ministering to blacks in successive periods in the Church's life. From 1878 to 1951, a separate seminary, the Bishop Payne Divinity School, existed for the purpose of preparing black men for the ordained ministry. Similarly, archdeacons and suffragan bishops for colored work, field agents and secretaries for Negro work, and staff officers have been seen as the point men expected to be the liaisons, interpreters, and ombudsmen between the Church at large and the "Negro masses."

Commissions and committees, such as the Joint Commission on Negro Work, the Committee on Racial Minorities, the Bi-racial Sub-Committee on Negro Work, and more recently, the Commission on Racism, *inter alia,* which have considered such matters as the racial episcopate, the "status of the Negro," and the deployment of black clergy, have been established by the General Convention, the House of Bishops, diocesan conventions and the Executive Council, all of which have viewed the black membership of the Episcopal Church as a special case. These and other bodies have produced scores of documents, most of which have attempted to justify the exclusion of blacks from one aspect of the Church's life or another (such as Bishop Gibson's letter to the planters in Virginia reassuring them that baptism was not tantamount to manumission; or the infamous "Sewanee canon," which sought to establish Negro missionary districts under white episcopal leadership). Others, such as Bishop Randolph's 1889 address to the Diocese of Virginia instituting a separate "colored convocation" in the diocese, have either justified or apologized for the Church's mistreatment of blacks.

Nor has the Church always shown signs of learning from its experiences. It appears that the members of each generation must wrestle anew with the same issues with which their forebears struggled. While the language has undergone cosmetic changes, data are often presented as if they were fresh discoveries, a practice that gives new definition to "reinventing the wheel." Thus the findings of the committee responsible for preparing a racial audit for the 70th General Convention of the Episcopal Church in 1991 can draw conclusions remarkably similar to the findings of the Joint Commission on the Status of the Negro presented to the 51st General Convention in 1934.[46]

We shall attempt to show that, conversely, the theological and ideological position of black Episcopalians has always been that they are, by virtue of the Church's being a catholic institution, part and parcel of the membership of the Church, for whom no sort of special, patronizing treatment is deemed necessary. (The position of black Episcopalians in some ways was summed up in a statement by George Freeman Bragg Jr., in which he said that when the Church began to treat her Negro priests as men and not children, she would reap the harvest among the race, but that until then she would just be marking time.)[47] As members of the Episcopal Church, blacks have believed themselves to be entitled to all the rights and privileges of membership, and have never tired of reminding the Church when it refused to accord them their due. The form of the protest, however, has almost never been predicated on a perception of themselves as the aggrieved party; rather, blacks have simply reminded the Church that its actions have been inconsistent with its own standards, incompatible with what it claimed that it stood for. In this vein, Bishop Burgess could proclaim, "We are children of Absalom Jones. We have identified with him in his desire to recognize seriously the Church as one, holy, catholic and apostolic, and make it fulfill those notes of its character on every level in its struggle and existence."[48] The strategy has been shown to be efficacious on several occasions, because the Episcopal Church, hoisted by its own petard, has often been prodded into doing the honorable thing, in order that it might at least appear to safeguard its integrity.

While the Church at large was establishing agencies to address the "Negro problem," black Episcopalians were forming self-help organizations and caucuses. From these platforms, they could, in a united voice, challenge the Church to be true to its catholic principles. As early as 1856, James Theodore Holly, then rector of St. Luke's, New Haven, founded the Convocation of the Protestant Episcopal Society for Promoting the Extension of the Church among Colored People, whose original membership was comprised of four black clergy and seven congregations. "With their female auxiliary, the Good Angels, they fought the exclusion of blacks from the Episcopal seminaries[49] and took a stand against slavery."[50] In the wake of the failure of the Freedman's Commission, the Society for the Promotion of Church Work among the Colored People was formed for the reestablishment of a national program for evangelism.[51] It was short-lived. In 1883, Alexander Crummell, rector of St. Luke's, Washington, D.C., and senior black priest in the Episcopal Church at the time, organized his brother clergy and founded the Conference of Church Workers among Colored People (hereinafter CCWACP), a forerunner of today's Union of Black Episcopalians.[52] In the 1960s, impatient with the Church's progress in racial matters, black clergy banded once again, this time under the banner of the "Ad Hoc Committee concerned with racial inequities existing in the Protestant Episcopal Church," and had several meetings with the presiding bishop, on whom they laid specific demands.

A historian has observed that "black Episcopalians' history is not a particularly successful one, but it has its fascination."[53] We would like to suggest that by any measure of success, black Episcopalians, with tenacity, assiduousness, and dedication, have overcome formidable odds, and have made invaluable contributions to the life and mission of the Episcopal Church. In that success story is the fascination; and we hope in the following pages to share both the story and the fascination with our readers. By subjecting the data (consisting of, but not limited to sermons, articles in church periodicals, the proceedings of diocesan and General Conventions, the records of the CCWACP, and other sources) to analyses both ecclesiological and missiological, we hope to demonstrate that black Episcopalians' sense of catholicity not only helped them to achieve their rightful place in the Church's life, but did much to affect the nature and direction of the Church's mission. We shall also compare the missionary strategies and policies employed in the Episcopal Church's mission and outreach to blacks with parallel developments among people of color elsewhere in the Anglican Communion, especially in Africa and the West Indies. Because of this comprehensive and systematic approach, we believe that this book embodies the first major study of black Episcopalians since 1922, when George Freeman Bragg Jr. published *History of the Afro-American Group in the Episcopal Church.*

As a student of hymnody and a composer of hymns, the author has always been fascinated by hymns as conveyors of the theologies of the periods in which they were written.[54] Victorian missionary hymns, especially, tell us much about the Church's missionary enterprise. As the Cross followed the Union Jack into the nethermost corners of the Empire on which the sun was said never to set, the Church, if we are to believe its hymnody, was zealous in its efforts to "fling out the banner" and to "hasten the time appointed." It was bound and determined to "save from peril of perdition the souls for whom the Lord his life laid down." Chapter subtitles are taken from such hymns as a reminder that in many ways the Episcopal Church saw the black American population as ripe a mission field as "Afric's sunny fountains" or "India's coral strand" (although the proximity between the missionaries and the missionized in the United States proved to make domestic missionary endeavor a far greater challenge).[55]

But it is to Henry Hallan Tweedy's post-Victorian missionary hymn, "Eternal God whose power upholds,"[56] that we look to find something close to a theology of mission for black Episcopalians; and for this reason we have borrowed a line from it as the subtitle of this introduction. This hymn eschews the we-they, "Lady Bountiful" approach so prevalent in Victorian hymnody, and instead makes missionaries of *all* of God's children, not just those who believed their souls to be "lighted with wisdom from on high."[57] This hymn bespeaks an equality that blacks have ever striven to achieve in the Episcopal Church. They have wanted to be understood as an integral part of the Church, and not a group that must be specially treated:

Eternal God, whose power upholds
Both flower and flaming star,
In Whom there is no here nor there,
No time, no near nor far,
No alien race, no foreign shore,
No child unsought, unknown,
O send us forth, thy prophets true,
To make all lands thine own!

Last, to return to the Booker T. Washington quotation cited at the beginning of this chapter, we would suggest that wholesale acceptance of such a view has often resulted in the creation of a credibility gap, a great gulf fixed, as it were, between black Episcopalians and other black Christians (many of whom "view the Episcopal Church with antagonism, considering it the white people's church"),[58] as well as between black Episcopalians and white Episcopalians.[59] Perhaps more significantly, it has tended to negate the effect of the contributions of black Episcopalians on the history of the mission of African American Christians. As Bishop Burgess has observed, since "the vast majority of black people have decided that Richard Allen chose the wiser course," they have tended "to ignore or minimize the accomplishments of those black Christians who have chosen to stay with white church structures."[60] The fact that the first black Christians in America were Anglicans, and that it was the Episcopal Church that established the first black schools and trained the first black teachers, that Absalom Jones was the first black minister ordained in the United States in any major denomination, and that St. Thomas' Church, Philadelphia, was the first truly constituted black congregation are forgotten if they were ever known;[61] and such ignorance makes it possible for observers to believe that a quest for an enhanced social status is the only factor responsible for attracting blacks to the Episcopal Church. It is our hope that this study will, in a small way, serve to correct such misconceptions.

Part One

Receivers of the Gospel

Chapter 1

The Conditional Anglicanization of Negro Slaves

The race that long in darkness pined have seen a glorious light.

—J. Morrison (hymn text, c. 1770)

In 1978, a book entitled *The Power of Their Glory,* a tongue-in-cheek "exposé" of the Episcopal Church, appeared in print. Its subtitle, "America's Ruling Class: The Episcopalians," betrayed its not-too-hidden agenda, namely to suggest that the Protestant Episcopal Church, despite the fact that its members account for less than 3 percent of the population, "are by far the wealthiest, most eastern, best educated, and most highly placed professionally of any Christian denomination in the United States." The authors make at least two other comments that are particularly germane to this study. The first, significant because we are principally concerned with accounting for the presence and impact of a significant minority group within the Episcopal Church, is that "the church is heavily white, as might be expected, 94 percent to be exact." The second comment, not unrelated, gives us a clue as to the reason for the first, and also sheds some light on Episcopalians' historical understanding of evangelism: "Episcopalians' identification with the first American settlers [and] with the original growth of the corporate elite [account for] *a preference for family expansion rather than missionary activity as a means of growing as a religion.*"[1]

That the Episcopal Church traces its roots to the coming of the first English settlers is well documented. George Hodges recounts that in April of 1607 the storm-tossed English, having arrived at a place they named Jamestown ("thus connecting the King's name with English Christianity in America, as it was soon to be connected with the English Bible"), immediately prepared for Sunday worship: "seats they made of logs; a bar of wood between two trees served for a pulpit."[2] That was the Sunday after the Ascension. On the Third Sunday after Trinity, early in the summer of the same year, the Holy Eucharist according to the English Book of Common Prayer was celebrated for the first time in that colony, when "Robert Hunt, chaplain to the Virginia settlers, stood before a roughhewn table that served as the wilderness altar, while around him knelt the brave little band whose ships had brought them to Jamestown."[3]

The fact that Anglicanism was the religion of the slave-holding plantocracy might in and of itself be sufficient to account for the paucity of blacks in the Episcopal Church during most periods of American history. But other developments in the colonial Church militated against the likelihood that the Africans brought to the shores of America shackled in the holds of ships could enjoy a modicum of religious and social intercourse with the descendants of those ships' captains and passengers. For Virginia was not only the cradle of American colonialism and the font of American Anglicanism; it was also that place which, a scant dozen years after the founding of Jamestown, served as the first port of entry for African slaves. Ironically, it was in the same year, 1619, that "the Colonial Assembly made the Church of England the official religious settlement in the Virginia Colony, to be supported by everyone.... Clergy received grants of land, and a tax called the tithe was laid on the principal crops and collected for church expenses."[4] This served effectively to compromise the Church's position; being, as it were, Caesar's friend, "weakened the possibility that it could exercise leadership in the formation of overall colonial policy,"[5] particularly regarding the practice of slavery. As an institution, therefore, the Church, partly because its hands were tied, and partly growing out of a desire to protect its own interests, was silent when the colony took step after step to ensure that slavery would have a permanent footing. The Church said nothing, for instance, even when the General Assembly reversed English common law by making the legal status of a child born to a female slave and a male planter depend not on the father but on the mother.

In 1846, Bishop Wilberforce of Oxford described the Episcopal Church's complicity in the slave trade, as well as its apathy toward its victims, in no uncertain terms:

> What witness, then, has as yet been borne by the Church in these slave-states against this almost universal sin? How has she fulfilled her vocation? She raises no voice against the predominant evil; she palliates it in theory; and in practice she shares in it. The mildest and most conscientious of the bishops of the south are slave-holders themselves.... It is the first duty of the Church to reprove the sins of others, not to adopt them into her own practice; to set, and not to take the tone. The cruelty of their tender mercies should lead her to speak out more plainly; it should force her zealously to cleanse herself from their stain, and then

fearlessly leave the issue to her God. But she is silent here; and to her greater shame it must be added, that there are sects [e.g., the Quakers] which do maintain the witness she has feared to bear.[6]

It can be argued that blacks have never been regarded as an integral component of American Anglicanism. They have always been a special case, a class of people to be evangelized, missionized, worked among, or reached out to. At times, of course, blacks have also been patronized, marginalized, even ostracized. If an African presence in the Episcopal Church can be considered an anomaly, it must be remembered that this situation mirrored the lot of blacks in American society from the outset. During his visit to the United States in the 1830s, Alexis de Tocqueville observed:

> The whites and the blacks are placed in the situation of two foreign communities. These two races are fastened to each other without intermingling. . . . The Europeans chose their slaves from a race differing from their own, which many of them considered inferior to the other races of mankind. Nor is this all; they scarcely acknowledge the common features of humanity in this stranger whom slavery has brought among them. Although the law may abolish slavery God alone can obliterate the traces of its existence.[7]

Understandably, then, the Church of England in America treated the African slave with ambivalence. Even Morgan Godwyn, an Anglican priest in Virginia who in his 1680 tract, *The Negro's and Indians Advocate, Suing for their Admission to the Church,* attempted "to reclaim the church's role as a positive moral influence [believing that] the church was the one institution that could serve as an advocate for blacks and native Americans,"[8] did not go so far as to advocate for manumission. Godwyn's progressive thinking of the day was that slaves should come under the positive and moral influence of the Church, and indeed should be incorporated into the Body of Christ through the sacrament of baptism, a practice begun as early as 1623 when "Anthony and Isabel, black servants of Captain William Tucker, and their child, William, were baptized at Jamestown."[9] But such acts were not deemed to have any effect whatever on their civil status as men and women in bonds.

Some forty years later, Godwyn's views were considered somewhat less radical, and the baptism of slaves was more widely practiced. Such change in missionary strategy as evolved was due in large measure to the creation in 1701 of the Society for the Propagation of the Gospel in Foreign Parts (SPG). Its mission, which Hayden describes as "catholic, humanitarian and paternal," was twofold: "to provide a chaplaincy for Englishmen overseas, and to evangelize African slaves as well as indigenous people." This dual mission also created a potential for divided loyalties. In a spirit of compromise that many regard as the very genius of Anglicanism, the SPG, while it "accepted slavery as a vital factor in British prosperity" (a prosperity that helped to underwrite its activities), strove to represent the planters' interests by securing legislation that would ensure that slaves' civil status would not be altered by baptism; and represented the slaves' interests by insisting that they "were human beings equal to whites in every endowment and capable of salvation, education, and general uplift."[10] This view was echoed by the bishop of London, who urged that slaves should be considered "not merely as Slaves, and upon the same Level with Labouring Beasts, but as Men-Slaves and Women-Slaves, who have the same Frame and Faculties with yourselves, and have Souls capable of being made eternally happy, and Reason and Understanding to receive Instruction."[11]

Despite this theological legerdemain on the part of the SPG, there was renewed concern among Virginia's planters as to the status of baptized slaves. They appealed to the bishop of London for a clarification of the matter. The bishop's theological opinion exemplifies what one author describes as the "arrogance of faith" that characterized the accommodation of the religious establishment to the exigencies of the American racial climate.[12] The episcopal pronouncement was clearly designed to put to flight "the widely prevalent fear, based upon some provisions of medieval canon law, that any slave who became a Christian could claim his freedom."[13] More important, it gave theological sanction and respectability to colonial legislation that had been passed "denying that baptism altered the condition of a slave 'as to his bondage or freedom.'" Indeed, like many apologists for the evangelization of slaves, Bishop Gibson "felt obliged to prove that Christianity would actually make better slaves:"[14]

> Christianity, and the embracing of the Gospel, does not make the least alteration in civil property, or in any of the duties which belong to civil relations; but in all these respects, it continues persons just in the same state as it found them. The freedom which Christianity gives, is freedom from the bondage of sin and Satan, and from the dominion of men's lusts and passions and inordinate desires; but as to their outward condition, whatever that was before, whether bond or free, their being baptized, and becoming Christians, make no manner of change in it . . . and so far is Christianity from discharging men from the duties of the station and condition in which it found them, that it lays them under stronger obligation to perform those duties with the greatest diligence and fidelity.[15]

At least one SPG missionary, no doubt of the opinion that Bishop Gibson's letter would do little to assure the planters in his congregation that the slaves did not have ulterior motives, actually inserted a caveat in the order of service for baptism:

> You desire in the presence of God and before this congregation that you do not ask for Holy Baptism out of any design to free yourself from the Duty and Obedience you owe to your master while you live, but merely for the good of your Souls, and to partake of the graces and blessings promised to the members of the Church of Jesus Christ.[16]

From these and other writings of the period, it was quite clear, as Phyllis Barr points out, that "slavery was regarded as an acceptable and necessary fact of Colonial life, and educational efforts were focused on Christianizing slaves, not freeing them."[17] This was because in the Episcopal Church, as H. Richard Niebuhr observes,

> the relationship of masters and servants was of a patriarchal nature. Many a master was sincerely interested in the temporal and eternal welfare of his charges and took paternal pride in their religious progress. It was not the virtue of democracy, the practice of equality, but the virtue of aristocracy, *noblesse oblige,* which was exercised in this relationship.[18]

Despite colonial legislation, episcopal encouragement, and a brand of evangelism designed to benefit both slaveholder and slave, the conversion, religious education, and baptism of slaves did not proceed apace. George Freeman Bragg Jr., the distinguished black historiographer, attributes the "widespread indifference with respect to the religious training of the slave population" to the fact that "the white population in these colonies were not all the same class or quality; nor were the more numerous elements especially friendly to the Church of England and her method of presentation of the Gospel."[19] Also, many planters believed that the religious instruction of their slaves could be seen as an economic detriment, since catechetical instruction and worship took time that might be more profitably used in the field. As a distinguished historian of the Episcopal Church described it: "It is, obviously, a little difficult to take a benevolent interest in a man's future blessedness when you are energetically endeavoring to make him exist wholly for your benefit in this present life."[20] Others believed that Africans were too "brutish" to be instructed: "The gross bestiality and rudeness of their manners, the variety and strangeness of their languages, and the weakness and shallowness of their minds," observed the Virginia House of Burgesses, "render it in a manner impossible to make any progress in their conversion."[21]

The most serious objection, however, to the incorporation of African slaves into the fellowship of Christ's religion was a widely held perception that the slaves were *incapable* of instruction, "not only because of cultural differences but because of racial distinctions." The eminent philosopher Bishop George Berkeley suggested that such a view was born of the colonists' "irrational contempt for the Blacks, as creatures of another species, who had no right to be instructed or admitted to the sacraments."[22]

The official view that slaves were incapable of being instructed because of an inherent inferiority on their part was probably the most egregious impediment to mission. Planters might be convinced that, far from being an economic detriment, converted slaves "do better for their Masters profit than formerly, for they are taught to serve out of Christian Love and Duty";[23] and they might, when confronted with evidence of gentility among some slaves, be persuaded to disabuse themselves of a conviction that slaves were innately brutish. But an officially stated position purporting Africans' intrinsic baseness was contrived, it can be argued, as a means to justify the perpetuation of slavery. Their official classification as members of a virtual subhuman species creates an insuperable impediment to their evangelization. The failure of American Anglicanism to embrace the African can be charged to the prevalence of such an attitude, which, as will be shown, is by no means peculiar to the colonial era. Thomas Secker, archbishop of Canterbury from 1758 to 1768, in a sermon preached before the SPG, diagnosed the cause of such an attitude, and posited: "Some, it may be feared, have been averse to their slaves becoming Christians, because, after that, no Pretence will remain for not treating them like Men."[24] One is struck by the similarity between the archbishop's statement and that of a twentieth-century social scientist:

> Being "black" in America bears the mark of slavery. Even after emancipation, citizens who had been slaves still found themselves consigned to a subordinate status. Put most simply, the ideology that had provided the rationale for slavery by no means disappeared. Blacks continued to be seen as an inferior species, not only unsuited for equality but not even meriting a chance to show their worth.[25]

The efforts and exhortations of the Societies, learned bishops, devout clergymen, catechists black and white, pious gentlewomen, and even a few sympathetic planters notwithstanding, attempts on the part of the Anglican colonial establishment to bring the message of the Gospel to the "infidels in bonds," and, presumably, to share their faith with them, given the major impediments to such an enterprise cited above, was far short of an overwhelming success. Indeed, W. W. Manross comments that "it is probable that only a very small minority of them had been reached by [the Anglican Church] or any other denomination before the Revolution."[26] Even David Humphreys, SPG secretary, admitted, "It must be confessed what hath been done is as nothing with regard to what a true Christian would hope to see effected."[27] Bragg concurs. While allowing that "much practical good was realized," he concedes "there was no serious endeavor at Church extension among Negroes, nor could such have obtained in the presence of human bondage [under which system] the great body of the Church was wholly indifferent to the work of Negro evangelization."[28]

It could not have been otherwise. The quotations cited hint at but do not clearly identify the root cause of the attitude variously described as "patriarchal," "indifferent," and "paternal" — and that root cause is racism. Racism, which in recent years has been defined by the Episcopal Church as "the abuse of power by a racial group which uses power to its advantage to exclude, demean, damage or destroy a less powerful racial group,"[29] was the underpinning that provided slavery with a philosophical and ideological justification. The practice of religion, it must be noted, took place within the parameters of racism's premises. As Kortright Davis observes:

> The institution of slavery was heavily overlaid with racism, in that white Europeans brought black Africans from their homeland to be slaves on plantations, where they were treated as chattel and subhuman property. Plantation society thrived on a system that ensured to white propertied classes the permanence of a black laboring class; and every effort was made through the legal and social systems to guarantee that the structures of racism would remain in place.[30]

The Anglicanization — the Christianization — of slaves, therefore, during this period can only be seen as conditional, since evangelistic efforts were undertaken in order to help ensure the continuance of the institution of slavery, itself predicated on racism. Since emancipation, when it came, could change laws but not necessarily hearts, the descendants of slaves had to contend against the legacy of this institution. The struggle of subsequent generations of black Episcopalians for recognition in the life of the Church must be understood in light of this historical framework.

In that struggle, black Episcopalians benefited, more by default than by design, from what can be described as the last burst of pre-Revolutionary missionary zeal, namely the Great Awakening in American Anglicanism, brought about largely by the preaching missions of the Reverend George Whitfield, begun in 1739. His preaching style was distinctly un-Anglican in that he preached with both fervor and sentimentality, and he accomplished nothing short of rousing dyed-in-the-wool Anglicans from their lethargy. The major theological impact of the Awakening was that church members "began to pay greater attention to personal religious experience."[31] Adult conversions were the order of the day. But there was also at least a residual effect on missionary work among blacks.[32]

Owing to a rapid increase in the slave population, "the SPG purchased the slaves Harry and Andrew to serve as evangelists among blacks in South Carolina." Catechists were also appointed in Pennsylvania, Rhode Island, and New York. In addition to the SPG, another missionary society, Dr. Bray's Associates, whose sole function was to evangelize blacks, was formed. Hugh Neill, a priest in Delaware, reported that he had baptized 162 black persons in his congregation. In parishes where the Great Awakening had taken hold, the greatest advances in evangelism among blacks took place. According to Robert Prichard, this was no coincidence. He suggests that "Anglican clergy may have tested the simple message of personal reliance on Christ as a tool for evangelism for blacks before using the message with white parishioners."[33]

Robert Bennett, a black priest-historian, believes that there was an even more significant relationship between the Great Awakening and black evangelism. He suggests that "much of the emotionalism and unrestrained religious expression so often equated with the Black Church was a phenomenon originally associated with the Great Awakening." He observes, further, that "the first Black Episcopalians no doubt felt drawn to liturgical worship and Catholic theology as expressed in the ... Anglican tradition" much the same way as "Black men in the other Americas seem to have responded to Catholic liturgical worship [to a greater extent] than our forebears here heeded revivalism."[34] If, indeed, black Episcopalians were influenced in their religious formation by both these traditions, it can be argued that from the beginning they put their peculiar stamp on Anglican worship, effecting, as it were, a synthesis that characterizes black Episcopal worship even today.

In any event, the Great Awakening had the effect of increasing the number of black Anglicans, especially in the northern colonies (where many free blacks resided), thereby laying the foundations for the formation of the first independent black congregations, which came into being after the American Revolution.

Chapter 2

The Struggle for the Ordination of Black Priests and the Establishment of Black Congregations

How firm a foundation ye saints of the Lord.

—J. Rippon's *Selection of Hymns* (hymn text, 1787)

While the allegation that "white Episcopalians exhibited a racism that prompted them to treat their black brethren as step-children separated from the main body of the flock"[1] is an irrefutable one, many of the early black thinkers in the Episcopal Church believed that segregation, though an outward manifestation of racism, could be viewed as a blessing in disguise, as it provided an arena for self-determination and uplift. It is imperative, therefore, that we see the hopefulness on the part of blacks, brought about by the establishment of black congregations, through such a grid. Later, as black Episcopalians and their congregations became a force to be reckoned with, and attempts were made, for example, to establish racial ecclesiastical districts under white supervision, the same black thinkers saw such actions not only as overtly racist, but contrary to both the principle and the spirit of the Church's catholicity. In this connection, it should be noted that Bragg goes to great lengths to distinguish between legal (imposed) segregation and voluntary segregation:

> "Legal" segregation says that all the Colored People in a given diocese *shall* constitute a missionary jurisdiction of that diocese. There is no alternative. Such "segregation" is subject to the body creating it. Intelligent and thinking colored Churchmen simply can not accept such.... Colored persons have the right of becoming members of white parishes, but where there are enough of them they elect "voluntary" segregation, and constitute themselves into a parish of colored people. They are not forced by law to such a step. They take it of their own free will and accord.[2]

Although the establishment of black congregations and the ordination of blacks for the sole purpose of ministering to them were patently devised to ensure the separation of the races, both practices were regarded by many as *proof* of the Church's catholicity. These practices could be described as "catholic" because they demonstrated that Christ's religion was intended for all people, and that race, while a serious impediment to advancement in society, was no barrier to sacramental grace within the bosom of the church. Catholicity was also demonstrated by the belief, inherent in these practices, that the evangelization of blacks was not dependent upon the missionary activity of whites. Blacks could now be entrusted with the means of salvation, both spiritual and temporal, within their own communities. Thus, George Freeman Bragg could write:

> It is interesting to note that scarcely had the American Church been organized, following the close of the Revolutionary War, when it began immediately to interpret the Catholicity of the Church by creating Negro congregations, and ordaining black men to its Priesthood; when by the ordination of a Negro priest, and creation of a Negro parish, it declared racial organizations to be consistent with the Catholicity of the Church.[3]

What is more, Bragg maintains that the birth of such black congregations could not have taken place had the slave gallery not provided the necessary period of gestation. The slave gallery, as Bragg saw it, was "the native Negro Church, the great conservator of religious fervor and zeal," the incarnation of what had previously been an "invisible institution among the slaves."[4] He observes:

> The ordinary reader is apt to look upon the slave gallery... as a manifestation of prejudice, pure and simple.... But the slave gallery was a most convenient testing and proving ground. Here... provision was made for his acquirement of worldly knowledge and skill.... Out of the slave gallery came enlightenment, conversions, and *Negro churches.* Out of these came awakened powers and ambitions for group-leadership.[5]

Bragg's observations are both echoed and expanded in a statement by W. E. B. Du Bois, a prominent black educator and historian known for his studies of the "twoness" inherent in African Americans, in which he views the black church as the primary means for the conservation and preservation of the African half of the African American's identity:

> The rise of a church organization among Negroes was a curious phenomenon. The church really represented all that was left of African tribal life, and was the sole expression of the organized efforts of the slaves. It was natural that any movement among freedmen should center about their religious life, the sole remaining element of their formal tribal system.[6]

More recently, Kyle Haselden made a similar point:

> To be sure, under the circumstances nothing could have been more fortunate for the Negro than the establishing of the Negro church. The separated church became the center around which the Negro found his solidarity; it became the school in which Negro leadership was trained and developed; it became his refuge and shelter from the otherwise constant hammerings of an indifferent and hostile white society; it became the source of power, inspiring him toward the full expression of his humanity and undergirding his claims for a complete integration in American life with an inflexible conviction of divine approval. . . . The Negro church stands as the symbol of the white Christian's shame; yet it is a tribute to the power of the Gospel and to the faith of the Negro.[7]

Before considering the founding of St. Thomas' Church, Philadelphia, the first black congregation in the Episcopal Church, mention must be made of the Free African Society (hereinafter FAS), the first religious organization of freed blacks in the United States, out of which St. Thomas' grew. The FAS, in turn, grew out of the infamous incident in St. George's Methodist Church, Philadelphia.[8] It is commonly believed that those who had been ejected immediately formed two groups: the African Methodist Episcopal (AME) Church, led by Allen who reportedly took the majority of the people with him; and St. Thomas' African Church, founded by Jones, who led his somewhat smaller band of pilgrims into an affiliation with the Episcopal Church. In fact, *all* of the ejected black parishioners, Jones and Allen included, formed the Free African Society, as evidenced in the preamble of its Articles of Association:

> Whereas, Absalom Jones and Richard Allen, two men of the African race, who, for their religious life and conversation have obtained a good report among men, these persons, from a love to the people of their complexion whom they beheld with sorrow, because of their irreligious and uncivilized state . . . with these circumstances they labored for some time, till it was proposed, after a serious communication of sentiments that a society should be formed, without regard to religious tenets, provided that the persons lived an orderly and sober life, in order to support one another in sickness, and for the benefit of their widows and fatherless children.[9]

The FAS, it should be noted, "was not a church, but a benevolent and reform society like many others being formed at the time. [It] required of its members only that they be orderly and sober and pay one shilling a month toward provision for the poor."[10] One author described it as "a quasi-religious reform organization that included in its program for the 'free African's social redemption, the systematic building of the fund for mutual aid, burial assistance and the relief of widows and orphans.'"[11] It is clear, however, that the FAS was never intended to be an entirely secular organization. Its official nonsectarianism was, as it were, a "least common denominator," and grew out of a respect for the different religious beliefs of its members. As Gayraud Wilmore points out:

> One finds in the [FAS'] statement of purpose a certain ambivalence about religious and secular objects which has been a characteristic of Black religion in America. It was not [the founders'] original purpose to organize Blacks merely for community action and social welfare, as important as those concerns were to both men [i.e., Jones and Allen].[12]

Richard Allen, it should be noted, became disaffected with the direction in which the FAS was moving, and for a time was "accordingly disunited" from the Society "until he shall come to a sense of his conduct."[13] Lammers suggests that Allen's problems with the FAS stemmed in part from his objection to what he perceived to be an incipient influence of Quakerism. The FAS, which for the first four years of its existence had no religious services, adopted the practice of starting each meeting with fifteen minutes of silence. This practice "caused Allen's departure from the society.... Allen's resistance to Quaker worship and polity was consistent throughout, and seems to have been tied to his fervent attachment to Methodism."[14] His irrevocable severance from the FAS came when, in his own words, the "large majority voted in favor of [affiliating with] the Church of England."[15] Even then, Allen did not found the AME Church. It was sometime after the establishment of St. Thomas' African Church that Allen founded Bethel Church, and even then it was still affiliated with white Methodists. As Bragg points out:

> In such association continued Richard Allen and his fellows, vexed, harassed, and embarrassed, for more than a quarter of a century. Finally, in 1816, about 16 persons of the African race...got together and organized the A.M.E. denomination, electing Richard Allen as the first bishop of the new organization.[16]

"St. Thomas' African Episcopal Church of Philadelphia," in the words of its founding document, "to be governed by us and our successors for ever," became, in 1794, the first black congregation of the Episcopal Church, as well as the first black congregation of *any* denomination. It came into existence long before there was a black denomination. It is for these reasons that Bragg boasts that "the Episcopal Church welcomed the African race, received its church in full communion, with all the privileges of other Protestant Episcopal Churches."[17] The early history of the congregation merits particular mention, not simply because it was the first parish founded by and for black Episcopalians, but because the circumstances surrounding its founding and of the ordination of its pastor, Absalom Jones, the first black priest of the Episcopal Church, demonstrate the way in which the temporal exigencies of the ecclesiastical power structure and the catholic principles of the embryonic black church first clashed. Indeed, the scenario proves to be a prototype for a series of such conflicts that would be played out over the next two centuries.

The founders of the parish, like many blacks who "had believed deeply in the promises of the American Revolution, took steps to assert their right to self-determination in matters of religion."[18] Being "zealously concerned for the gathering together of our race into the sheepfold of the Shepherd and Bishop of our souls," they first petitioned the Diocese of Pennsylvania to recognize the FAS,[19] which had been previously founded by Jones and Richard Allen. They had good reason for doing so. "The Methodists had abused them, and continued to take a decidedly negative stand toward black people in their membership. The choice of a Methodist polity would have meant years of battling against the white Methodist church organization, as Richard Allen found out." They entered into affiliation with the Episcopal Church with great optimism. Although the Episcopal Church was not untainted by racism and also numbered among its communicants many significant slaveholders, they saw in the Episcopal Church a denomination that through the efforts of the SPG and the Bray Associates had done much for the education of blacks. They saw, too, in the Episcopal Church "a body whose authority, structure was somewhat fluid and whose philosophy, especially under Bishop White, favored the existence of an individual, self-governing congregation, while offering the necessary theological and liturgical structure and financial support."[20]

The "African Church," as it had become known, also asked, understandably, that they be "guaranteed local governance of their own affairs, and that one of their number be placed over them, and subsequently ordained."[21] The terms of the petition were accepted by the bishop and the standing committee of the diocese. Absalom Jones, a largely self-taught lay minister, who had been born into slavery in Delaware, was ordained deacon in 1795, at the age of 49, and advanced to the priesthood nine years later. At the time of his ordination to the diaconate, however, the diocese stipulated that because he had been dispensed from the examinations in Latin and Greek the bishop would proceed with the ordination only if the congregation would agree that it could "not be entitled to send a clergyman or deputies to the Convention or to interfere with the general government of the Episcopal

Church."[22] Although the provision was to be a temporary one, "being made in consideration of their peculiar circumstances *at present*,"[23] it was not until 1863 that the stipulation was rescinded, and St. Thomas' was admitted into union with the Diocese of Pennsylvania.[24]

Thus, the establishment of St. Thomas' came at a price. The diocese was happy to see the congregation flourish — and flourish it did, not only as a house of worship, but as a force for good in the community[25] — but it was the wish of the convention of the diocese that the congregation flourish apart from the mainstream of diocesan life, and that it would not enjoy the normal privileges accorded to white congregations. In a book about the founding of the African Methodist Episcopal Church, the black Methodist denomination begun by Jones's friend, Richard Allen, Carol George points out, correctly but for the wrong reasons, that this arrangement (which we might dub "separate but unequal") was part and parcel of the plan under which St. Thomas' was established:

> The Constitution of the Church [St. Thomas'] established its racial structure by limiting its members to Africans, although a similar restriction was not applied to the office of rector. St. Thomas', with its non-voting status... [was] assumed to be financially independent, but organizationally and doctrinally dependent, on the sponsoring denomination. As long as St. Thomas' respected the limits of their independence, they were free to conduct their own affairs without denominational interference.[26]

St. Thomas' was born of two concurrent movements affecting the development of the black church in the late eighteenth and early nineteenth centuries: an increased concern for personal freedom in the wake of the Revolutionary War, and the dramatic effect of the "Great Awakening" on American religious life.[27] The Awakening, also known as the "Great Revival," was the ecclesiastical counterpart to the Revolution, for it imbued hope in the minds of blacks that "society was on the verge of a major transformation that would hasten their liberation." One of the slogans of the movement was "'Christianity for All' implying that [it] comprehended members of different racial, ethnic and social groups." In light of such hopes, the reticence on the part of the diocese to grant full rights to the congregation must have dampened their spirits, and served to remind them of the second-class status to which they had been relegated, convincing them that "all was not well 'north of slavery.'"[28] George's explanation of this phenomenon is especially helpful:

> Segregated relationships . . . characterized life for the northern freedman in the new nation. More than a contradiction of Revolutionary promises, it suggested that interest in implementing claims for civil equality was practically nonexistent, and that the egalitarian mood of the war generation had changed into one that offered pity for black folks who could never make themselves white.[29]

It would appear that Jones was very much aware of these hard truths of postcolonial life in America, but was willing to make some concessions for the sake of the future of the black presence in the Episcopal Church. George comments:

> Jones had, of course, chosen to align himself with a religious body that regarded tradition as a major consideration, colonial developments notwithstanding, and he recognized that he must either respect those traditions or forego Episcopal affiliation. He apparently elected to abide by traditional practices, even if it meant some personal sacrifice, for the sake of psychological equanimity and denominational support.[30]

Several other congregations, all but one north of the Mason-Dixon Line, were founded in the decades following the coming into being of St. Thomas'. St. Philip's, New York City, was founded in 1818. Unlike St. Thomas', whose original members had been Methodists, St. Philip's people had been nurtured in the faith of the Episcopal Church at Trinity Parish in New York City. Peter Williams Jr., a lay reader, Absalom Jones's New York counterpart, was ordained immediately after the congregation's founding. In commenting on St. Philip's, Bishop Onderdonk reported to the convention of the diocese:

> A better ordered parish, the Diocese does not possess. Mr. Williams added to sincere and enlightened piety and a grade of talent of and theological requirements quite above mediocrity, great soundness of judgment, and prudence in actions and the just appreciation the sincere love and a consistent adoption of sound church principles.[31]

Nevertheless, Williams's prophetic leadership of his congregation caused the consternation of the bishop of New York and his brother bishops. Carter Woodson reports that when Williams took a firm stand in favor of abolition and against colonization, the bishops of the Church, "seeing . . . that this might bring the church to the point of having to declare itself on this important question . . . in keeping with the custom of that denomination, silenced Peter Williams with a decree that he should preach merely the Gospel *without interfering with the political affairs of the time.*"[32]

Too, St. Philip's, like its Philadelphia sister, was to spend a considerable period of time before the Church was fully enfranchised. It was not until thirty-four years after its founding that St. Philip's won a long battle to be admitted into union with the Diocese of New York. The vestry launched its seven-year campaign for admittance in 1845, and at the height of the battle one of the most vociferous opponents to St. Philip's recognition rose on the floor of convention and offered the following argument for not effecting any change in the parish's status:

> But this cannot prevent our seeing the fact that they are socially degraded, and are not regarded as proper associates for the class of persons who attend *our* convention. We object not to the color of their skin, but we question their possession of those qualities which would render their intercourse with members of a church convention useful, or agreeable, even to themselves.... It is impossible, in the nature of things, that such opposites should commingle with any pleasure to either.[33]

St. James', Baltimore, founded in 1827, is unique in its history in that it was established by William Leavington, a priest whom Bragg calls "our first great missionary hero of the black race," who was "the first of his kind to penetrate the land where slavery reigned, and successfully plant the cross of Jesus Christ."[34] Ordained three years earlier in St. Thomas', Philadelphia, he journeyed to Baltimore "and spent some little time investigating the possibilities of work in that city, but at that time the outlook was so discouraging that he returned to Philadelphia."[35] On a subsequent trip, however, he managed to secure the assistance of a few sympathetic blacks and whites, and the St. James First African Episcopal Church was born. Although the blessing and assistance of the bishop of Maryland were procured, impediments arose from an unexpected quarter, namely, some of the black founders themselves. For although Leavington fully intended that his newly founded congregation would be a place where, in the words of the bishop, "both bond and free might serve God and prepare for another world" (itself a telling statement, suggesting that blacks could not reasonably expect the benefit from the joys or temporalities of life on earth), it was also true, according to Bragg, that "a portion of the 'free colored people' were aggressively bent upon the exclusion of the slave population, and greatly aggravated the burdens of this black missionary by their persistent efforts in that direction."[36]

Just as a priest ordained in St. Thomas' became the incumbent of St. James', so did St. James', in turn, do its part by providing a priest for another prominent antebellum parish, St. Luke's, New Haven, founded in 1844. Eli Worthington Stokes, shortly after his ordination, settled in New Haven, where he found many black Episcopalians worshipping in Trinity Church on-the-Green. They organized under Stokes's leadership, and founded an association that they dubbed, appropriately enough, "the Colored Members of the Parish of Trinity Church," and occupied the basement of Trinity's Glebe Lecture Room until their own place of worship could be secured.[37] Trinity's rector, Dr. Harry Croswell, was instrumental in establishing St. Luke's, and indeed had all but singlehandedly ministered among the black population of New Haven prior to the arrival of the Reverend Mr. Stokes. Although staunchly opposed to the abolition of slavery[38] and a great advocate of the colonization movement, which sought to effect the "repatriation" of blacks to African soil, Dr. Croswell and his vestry gave their "consent and approbation" for the "formation of an Episcopal society in New Haven to be composed exclusively of colored persons," and in 1844 presented the Convention of the Episcopal Diocese of Connecticut, on behalf of the black parishioners, a petition requesting the admission of St. Luke's Parish into union with the Episcopal Church. The resolution read as follows:

> Whereas, it is deemed expedient to form an Episcopal Society in New Haven to be composed exclusively of colored persons, and the consent and approbation of the Rector and Vestry of Trinity Church having been obtained, Therefore Resolved: that a new parish be organized according to Law, to be under the name of St. Luke's Church . . . that the Revd H. Croswell be requested to make application to the next convention of the Protestant Episcopal Church in the State of Connecticut, for the admission of said parish into union with the Church.[39]

According to Edwards,

> there were 46 persons in the original congregation, amongst whom were the forebears of the famed Negro author William Burghardt [W. E. B.] Du Bois. The clerk [of the new vestry] was a Peter Vogelsang, who later during the [Civil] War, was to be the first Negro commissioned as an officer in the army for bravery on the field of battle. . . . An interesting note appears in the parish register—the last two Negroes sold as slaves on the New Haven Green in 1825 and immediately given their freedom papers by their purchasers, were listed as members of the new congregation.[40]

Stokes, still a deacon, had the pastoral charge of the congregation, and was advanced to the priesthood in 1846.[41] Despite his new status as priest and rector, however, he was not entitled to a seat in diocesan convention.[42]

St. Luke's fame, however, is more closely associated with its second rector, James Theodore Holly, an avid emigrationist who had been ordained to the diaconate in another antebellum black congregation, St. Matthew's, Detroit, founded in 1851, a parish closely allied with the abolitionist movement. In fact, the parish became a terminus of the Underground Railroad. Holly was ordained in St. Matthew's with the distinct expectation that he would work in the Haitian mission field. In the same year that he began his ministry at St. Luke's, he founded the Convocation of the Protestant Episcopal Society for Promoting the Extension of the Church among Colored People, an organization that was dedicated to promoting the Episcopal Church among the race as well as creating a strong black nationality in Haiti. In fulfillment of the latter goal, Holly left New Haven five years later, together with about forty recruits, and founded a colony at Drouillard, near Port-au-Prince.[43] Holly founded churches, schools, hospitals, and other institutions, and later became Haiti's first bishop in 1874. Today, Haiti is the largest missionary diocese in the Episcopal Church.

The lot of the antebellum black congregations[44] was not an easy one, despite the fact that most of them had been founded by free Northern blacks,[45] and were all, with the exception of St. James', located in the North. For the fact remains that Southern blacks were either members of churches dependent upon whites for pastoral and financial support, or, as was more often the case, denizens of the slave galleries of white congregations where they received separate instruction and often were accorded the privileges of divine worship at a different hour than white parishioners. They were, therefore, "under the paternalistic control of [their] bishops" while black Episcopalians in the North "suffered under the benign neglect of their bishops." As Bragg observes, "the work of the Episcopal Church among Negroes was founded by Negro clergymen through struggle with poverty and the indifference of the great body of the church." Moreover, "it was reserved for poor, and almost helpless, Negro priests, to become 'founders' and initiate the real constructive, self-respecting work of the Church in the great centers of the Negro population."[46] The first black Episcopalians, then, as Robert Bennett observes, "did not prosper, but neither did they die out. Their numbers spread in the coastal cities, first in the North and then into the South."[47]

Black Episcopalians in the North, as we have seen, although many still occupied slave galleries in white congregations, could often boast large independent parishes, not infrequently made up of the most prominent blacks in their respective communities, as well as black clerical leadership. In the antebellum South, however, with the exception of St. James', Baltimore, there were, understandably, no independent, that is, self-governing black congregations and no black clergy. Since it was the custom to establish separate black churches where numbers warranted such a practice (especially on plantations), several "separate congregations" were established.[48] Hayden points out that they had "a white minister who could appoint some of the black members to help him." Moreover, the property of the church was to be held by white trustees. Thus, there was no intention that a separate black congregation was to be free of white control and directed by its black members.[49]

So successful were these and other efforts to evangelize blacks that there was exponential growth among black Episcopalians in the South before the Civil War. Indeed, as late as 1860, nearly half of the 6,126 communicants in the Diocese of South Carolina were black,[50] in which diocese "there were 150 congregations of slaves in 45 different places of worship."[51] In many parishes that had not established separate congregations, it was not uncommon for black communicants to outnumber their white counterparts (not entirely surprising, since the slave population far outnumbered the white population). For example, Hayden informs us that three-quarters of the communicants at St. Paul's, Albany, Georgia, and more than half of the communicants at St. Andrew's, Darien, Georgia, were slaves.[52] Harris recounts that in 1824 the rector of Trinity Parish, Charles Country, Maryland, reported that "the black communicants present the most interesting appearance in their great devotion and regular attendance on Divine worship." In the same report, according to Harris, the rector reports "one white Baptism against twenty-six blacks who received the sacrament." Similarly, the rector of St. John's Parish, Lafayette Square, Washington, D.C., in his report to convention in the same year, indicated that "a class of colored people has been formed, amounting to about forty, who manifest an earnest desire to learn to read, and to unite in the forms of worship established by our venerable church."[53]

The existence of black Episcopalians in such numbers seems to have been the direct result of a virtually unbridled enthusiasm on the part of antebellum planters to bring blacks into the Episcopal fold. Indeed, in John Hope Franklin's chronicling of missionary activity among black slaves in the Diocese of North Carolina, for example, is documented the eagerness with which white planters went about the business of instructing, baptizing, catechizing, even marrying and burying black communicants. He cites the report of a diocesan committee on the state of the Church:

> They [the committee] trust that the members of the Convention will, in their several spheres, urge forward the Christian instruction of the colored class, *so entirely committed by Providence to the superintending care of the educated members of the church, and so dependent upon their benevolence and Christian love.*[54]

But these statistics must be seen in perspective. First, it must be iterated that Southern black Episcopalians were attached to white parish churches, but "too seldom did [such attachment] lead to their incorporation into the fellowship of the church."[55] Although catechized, baptized, and confirmed, slaves were often not inscribed as communicants in the parish register. Still others remained as catechumens. The marked dissimilarity between such arrangements and the situation that prevailed in the independent congregations in the North are factors that must be kept in mind when we examine postbellum demographics.

Moreover, while some blacks "had their own building... the usual practice... was to use the building of the white congregation when the white communicants were not using it." When, however, "the heavy schedule of the overworked rector or missionary, the indifference of the spiritual leader to the Negro, or the belief that the Negro required no special services for the interpretation of the Christian faith" existed, a special section of the church, typically a balcony or a section of pews in the rear of the church, was reserved for blacks.[56] Robert Strange wrote:

> In the Church we had no colored ministers; but the Negroes worshipped with us in separate parts of the same church building, and the white clergyman felt responsible for the black portion of his flock.... At the Holy Communion and at Confirmation, whites and blacks came together — the whites generally first.[57]

Most important, however, these data must be seen in light of the motivation of the evangelical effort on the part of the planters. It was, while perhaps not entirely devoid of some genuine religious impetus, a means of control. The planters realized, as Franklin explains, that "if the teachings of the Word were expounded from the point of view of the master, they might, indeed, have a most salutary effect upon the master-slave relationship."[58] As Hayden describes it, the evangelization of slaves was used as a tool for the "defense of the peculiar institution" of slavery.[59] Indeed, the pastoral letter promulgated by the bishops of the Protestant Episcopal Church in the Confederate States of America at their meeting in 1862 leaves no doubt as to the *raison d'être* for the evangelism of the slaves. In presenting an apologia for the necessity of bringing the Gospel to blacks, and citing, unabashedly, the fact that evangelization of slaves was especially incumbent upon Episcopalians because the Church contained "a very large proportion of the great slaveholders," the document stated: "Our national life is wrapped up in their welfare. With them we stand or fall and *God will not permit us to be separated in interest or in fortune.*"[60]

But there was a further, not unrelated motivation, and that was to remove the black slave from the sphere of influence of the black preacher, whom the plantocracy saw as a direct threat to their enterprise. Charles Cotesworth Pinckney, in an address delivered in Charleston in 1829, declared:

> We look upon the habit of Negro preaching as a wide-spreading evil not because a black man cannot be a good one, but . . . because they acquire an influence independent of the owner, and not subject to his control; when they have possessed this power, they have been known to make an improper use of it. Great efforts have been made to abolish this practice; but they have been attended with the usual effects of religious persecution, in secrecy and nocturnal meetings in old fields and plantations, where no white persons reside.[61]

On neither side of the Mason-Dixon Line, therefore, were blacks made to feel that they were an integral part of the Episcopal Church. Blacks had no pride of belonging in the South, owing to the paternalistic control of which Bennett writes, which, as we have pointed out, was a function of an economic system dependent upon the perpetuation of slavery. Since religious instruction was provided by the planter, it was seen as part and parcel of the oppressive system, and missionaries were regarded by the slaves as little more than their masters' ecclesiastical counterparts. Too, white Episcopalians in the South were often seen as possessing "a condescending manner and stiff formality [having] little attraction for slaves."[62] As John Henry Edwards observes:

> Negroes themselves often found it difficult to embrace the Christian religion and practice its tenets. For one thing, they were not free agents and consequently were dependent upon the good graces of their masters in performing Christian obligations such as church attendance. The marriage relationship was often destroyed because of the disruption of family life when one of the parties to the marriage was sold. The slave could also be compelled to do things which he felt were against his Christian profession. Then, too, the acceptance of Christianity could erect a barrier between the convert and his fellow slaves. The restrictions of religious life as taught at the time, with its puritanical emphasis on the abstaining from those amusements which were considered sinful, made the drab life of those in bondage even more dreary.[63]

Moreover, the Church's "identification with the planter, its austere service and its failure to explain the intricacies of its involved ritual"[64] further accounted for Anglicanism's limited appeal to blacks in those places where black men and women were in bonds. It is no wonder that W. E. B. Du Bois, himself an Episcopalian baptized in St. Luke's, New Haven, could later remark that the Episcopal Church had "probably done less for black people than any other aggregation of Christians."[65]

Although blacks may have held deeds to church buildings in the North, there was no inherent sense of belonging among them either. The "benign neglect" with which black Episcopalians were treated in the North meant simply that while black clergy and their flocks were often recognized for their genteel behavior, uplifting worship, or community outreach, their congregations were recognized as parallel entities at best, going through the motions, as it were, of the faith, but not really sharing in the governance of the whole Church. The early black clergy typically served in a series of black congregations or went to the overseas mission field, since other appointments were not open to them. Later, rectors of prominent black parishes tended to remain in their cures for the duration of their ministries, because deployment practices did not permit their serving outside of what had become, *de facto,* a separate black church within, or perhaps more accurately, tangential to, the larger Episcopal Church. This is surely what George Freeman Bragg had in mind when he wrote:

> Whenever the Episcopal Church gives a genuine interpretation with respect to the Negro, of the *spirit* of the words of St. Paul "There is neither Jew nor Greek, there is neither bond nor free... for ye are all ONE in Christ Jesus" and treats her Negro priests as men and not as children, then will she reap the harvest among the race destined by Almighty God. Until then she will continue to mark time.[66]

So even as the black Episcopal Church was being planted, there was, on their meager plot of earth, no dearth of encroaching weeds that threatened to choke the budding community of faith and prevent it from coming to flower. As we examine the period following the Civil War, we will see that the weeds had all but overrun the garden.

Chapter 3

The Defection of Black Episcopalians after Emancipation

We pray thee too for wand'rers from thy fold.
—William Harry Turton (hymn text, 1881)

In his sermon at the centennial celebration of St. Thomas', Philadelphia, held in 1892, the Right Reverend Henry Codman Potter, bishop of New York, declared to the congregation:

> I do not think it would have been very strange if the colored race, after it had been freed, should have refused to follow the white people's God. It shows a higher order of intelligence and an acute discernment in the African race to have distinguished the good from the evil, in a religion that taught all men were brothers, and practised the opposite.[1]

In this pithy remark is encapsulized the dilemma faced by black Episcopalians, as regards the issue of their future affiliation with the Episcopal Church following the Civil War and the Emancipation Proclamation. They had to decide whether to remain in the church of their baptism or to seek affiliation in some other religious body. The bishop of New York, it can be argued, was engaging in some homiletical flattery. The members of the oldest black congregation in the Episcopal Church must have felt rather pleased with themselves to have been commended for their good taste and good sense. But at a deeper level, the bishop recognized in the members of St. Thomas' what he perceived to be a certain theological acumen. He was telling them that they had been able, where others could not, to separate, as it were, the wheat from the chaff. The people of St. Thomas', spiritual sons and daughters of the first black priest in the Episcopal Church, were seen to have a real grasp of the intrinsic nature of the church and the Christian religion, the bishop suggested, although that same church was peopled with men and women who had "fallen short of the glory of God." Despite the fact that the behavior of Christians proved all too often to be inconsistent with the ideals of brotherhood and equality, which their religion taught, St. Thomas' parishioners, and by extension, all black Episcopalians, many of them members of independent congregations, North and South, which had sprung up after the war, discerned that the Episcopal Church, *in se,* stood for a higher standard. Bishop Potter was doing no less than commending those black Episcopalians who had been loyal to the Church for recognizing the fact that the Episcopal Church was, despite its "track record," a catholic institution. He was assuring them that the founders of the parish had not been misguided, and that their high expectations had not been displaced. He was applauding them for understanding that the former slave and the former slaveholder could now both find a spiritual home in the same branch of a transformed Christendom.

But the preacher was clearly speaking to a "faithful remnant." For the fact remains that after the Civil War black Episcopalians were few and far between indeed. While some black Episcopalians remained in the Church, both in white and black congregations, most black Episcopalians sought spiritual nurture and religious instruction elsewhere. The majority of the Episcopal Church's black membership, to use the bishop's own words, "refused to follow the white people's God." Indeed, George Freeman Bragg describes the period immediately following the Civil War as one in which the Episcopal Church experienced "a wholesale exodus of colored people."[2]

The phenomenon was rampant throughout the South. In the Diocese of South Carolina, where before the war nearly half of the communicants had been black, there were only 395 black members in 1868. The bishop of the diocese lamented to the delegates attending that year's convention: "You are aware how large a proportion of the colored population have been lost to our Church; we are not without hope that a more settled state of things, and a more mature judgement will bring many home again to the old fold."[3]

In Alabama, according to Hayden, only two black congregations remained after the war. "One of these, the congregation of the Chapel of the Good Shepherd in Mobile, gradually dwindled to nine communicants." In Virginia, only 64 black Episcopalians remained, a mere 1 percent of the membership of the diocese.[4] Even the great St. James', Baltimore, having been founded by free blacks, could not boast fifty members in 1867.[5] The dire situation was summed up in the report of the Board of Missions to the 1877 General Convention, which pointed out that while in 1860 South Carolina alone claimed more than 3,000 black souls, not even one-half of that number of blacks could be found in *all* the dioceses of the Church, North and South.[6]

As we are concerned with demonstrating why it was that black Episcopalians remained in the Episcopal Church, it would be instructive to explain why so many — indeed, a greater number — forsook it. First, it should be pointed out that "most... black Episcopalians joined the Baptist and the Methodist churches."[7] Bragg himself admits that former black Episcopalians played a major role in building up the latter, principally the African Methodist Episcopal Church, which had been founded by Richard Allen.[8] Although the majority of the faithful followed Absalom Jones to the Episcopal Church after the infamous incident in St. George's, Philadelphia, that secession proved for many to be little more than a temporary migration. One year after the Civil War, the AME Church claimed some 75,000 adherents, nearly four times as many members as they had had a decade before.[9] The swelling of the ranks of the black denominations was achieved in large measure because of the great number of rural blacks, many of whom had attended the slave chapels. Such numerical strength as there was among black Episcopalians, however, was to be found in urban centers, where there were free blacks and more "privileged" slaves.[10]

Explanations for the phenomenon were rife, but by and large they fell into two views, the white and the black. As Hayden points out: "White Southern churchmen were virtually unanimous in attributing this mass exodus to the antagonism of blacks to white tutelage, the predilection of blacks for a more emotional and less morally-demanding religion, and a preference for fellowship with other blacks."[11]

Whites were also given to lay the blame at the feet of carpetbaggers, black politicians, and others who had upset and undermined the irenic and harmonious relationships that allegedly existed between the races before the war. In an elegant turn of phrase, the bishop of Mississippi declared that the "tender ties" that had bound the blacks to the whites in "a filial relationship had been rudely broken" and that the blacks stood "in the cold, distant and unsympathetic relationship of hirelings stripped of those strong claims upon our regard which their late servile and dependent condition justly demanded at our hands."[12] Such comments tended to make the black defector into an ingrate. A like sentiment is reflected in an address of another Southern bishop, delivered at the General Convention of the Episcopal Church in 1871:

> The efforts in this diocese in the spiritual improvement of the colored race are not as promising of good results as are desired by the friends of the freedmen. While in some few cases they seem to appreciate the teachings and ministrations of the Church, in most cases they have separated themselves from the ministry of the Church, and *given themselves to the guidance of ignorant teachers of their own race, who are leading them into the wildest excesses of delusion and fanaticism.*[13]

Bishop J. P. Wilmer of Louisiana offered a similar lament:

> The defection from the Church is almost universal. In some parishes I have visited, which a few years ago numbered more than a hundred communicants, not one has come forward to kneel at the altar, and very few to enter the Church. The voice of remonstrance from their once honored pastors falls unheeded upon their ears, unscriptural revelations are substituted for the Word of God; the ancient forms of devotion are declared to quench the ministrations of the spirit, and the sober worship of sanctuary is exchanged for the midnight orgies of a frantic superstition.[14]

These last quotations bespeak an underlying factor that had a significant influence on the Church's missionary strategy, and that is fear — specifically, fear that white control would be relinquished once blacks formed their own religious institutions. As Niebuhr puts it:

> The white man's fear of Negro independence was as important a factor in the matter as the white man's concern for the Negro's soul. In many instances, the Negro was tolerated in the master's church merely because such toleration was the less of two evils. The desirable good was a prevention of all contact with the spiritual and cultural influences of Christianity. The greater evil was the segregation of slaves into individual and uncontrolled organizations. From the beginning of the missionary enterprise among Africans, many a master had been inimical to every effort at the conversion of his servants.[15]

The explanation that most black historians provide for the exodus tells a different story. Hayden states simply that blacks "flocked to churches where they would be free from white domination; black churches made possible black leadership."[16] Bragg maintains that blacks who left the Episcopal Church for black denominations saw them as "a great medium of service" to other black people and preferred membership in them to remaining "as mere 'hangers on' in the galleries of the white churches."[17] Alexander Crummell understood the exodus as "a drift to the black preacher." He comments: "When freedom came the emancipated class, by one common impulse rushed from the chapels provided by their masters, deserted in multitudes the ministry of white preachers, in search for a ministry of their own race."[18]

John Henry Edwards observes that "Methodists and Baptists were much more successful in their proselytizing efforts. For one reason, their ministers were not so educated as the Episcopalian clergy and consequently could reach the poor and illiterate with great appeal."[19] E. Franklin Frazier points out that "the emphasis which [Baptist and Methodist] preachers placed upon feeling as a sign of conversion found a ready response in the slaves who were repressed in so many ways."[20]

Even a cursory glance at assertions on both sides of the issue would cause us to more deeply appreciate the words of Bishop Potter cited at the beginning of this chapter. Perhaps it is remarkable that any blacks were left in the Episcopal Church at all. For it would take a real act of grace for the black Episcopalian to understand the Episcopal Church as a catholic entity in which all have an equal claim on its ministrations, in the light of the harsh reality that the planter's religion was used as a means for their continued subjugation.

Such an "opposite practice" is demonstrated, for example, in a sermon delivered by another bishop a half century before. Given its content, it is hardly surprising that blacks left the Episcopal Church in droves. Bishop Meade of Virginia exhorted a slave population in his diocese:

> Almighty God hath been pleased to make you slaves here, and to give you nothing but labor and poverty in this world, which you are obliged to submit to, as it is in His will that it should be so. If therefore, you would be God's freemen in Heaven, you must be good and strive to serve Him here on earth. I say that what faults you are guilty of towards your masters and mistresses are faults done against God himself, who hath set your masters and mistresses over you in His own stead, and expects you to do for them just as you would do for Him.[21]

It is axiomatic, then, that slaves, presented with religion under such conditions, would find it irreconcilable with their new status as freedmen. If, indeed, James Cone is right in stating that "the black church in America was founded on the belief that God condemned slavery and that Christian freedom meant political emancipation,"[22] belonging to the Episcopal Church, the majority of whose members in the South supported slavery, could be viewed as an incongruous act that threatened to sacrifice one's intellectual as well as moral integrity.

It must be stressed that while other church bodies condemned slavery, and indeed, as in the case of the Presbyterians and Methodists, actually split between North and South, the Episcopal Church fell short of such an action, out of deference to the large number of slaveholders. This meant that whereas Southern Negro congregations in other denominations could look to the North for support, and indeed were "adopted" by their sympathetic Northern cousins, black Episcopalians in the South remained "under white Southern bishops who might or might not be personally acceptable [and] who were regarded as part and parcel of white rule."[23] Indeed, one of these bishops, Leonidas Polk of Louisiana, an owner of 400 slaves, became a general in the Confederate Army and died in battle in the defense of the institution of slavery upon which the South's economy (and his personal fortune) depended.[24]

While it is true that the Episcopal Church did not split along regional lines as other denominations did, this was not because there was not in some quarters a desire to do so. The aforementioned Bishop Polk, and his counterpart in Georgia, Bishop Stephen Elliott, brought together representatives of the slave states in meetings shortly after the outbreak of the Civil War. By September of 1862, the Church in the Confederacy was duly organized, but remarkably, the Northern dioceses, wishing not to be involved in a "political issue" and because so many Northern churchmen were in sympathy with their Southern counterparts, refused to recognize that there was a secession. In commenting on the Episcopal Church's position (or lack thereof) on the question of slavery, Bishop Burgess queries "whether in the long run our unity was worth the price of moral indecision."[25]

When the House of Deputies of the Confederate Church met in General Council in 1862, its first resolution read that "this Church desires specially to recognize its obligation to provide for the spiritual wants of that class of our brethren, who in the providence of God, have been committed to our sympathy and care by the national institution of slavery." Similarly the Confederate House of Bishops' pastoral letter, reflecting a prevalent attitude among Southern Episcopalians that "to have attacked the institution of slavery... would have been treason to the Southern cause," urged "upon the masters of the country their obligation, as Christian men, so to arrange this institution as not to necessitate the violation of those sacred relations which God has created, and which man cannot, consistently with Christianity, annul."[26]

It is not surprising, then, that under such circumstances the Episcopal Church had less and less appeal to blacks. Nor is it surprising that at the end of the War between the States, they would have fled to Christian communities that appeared to be more hospitable. It should be pointed out, however, that while Southerners provided a theological justification predicated on their economic interests, a few Northerners, despite the lack of such interest, nevertheless defended the institution. And this phenomenon must bear some of the responsibility for the Church's failure to retain its black membership after the Civil War and its lack of success in claiming new black adherents. Two Northerners who passionately defended the institution of slavery are worthy of note. The first was Dr. Samuel Seabury, whose ancestor and namesake was the first bishop in the Episcopal Church. He published a book entitled *American Slavery Distinguished from the Slavery of English Theorists and Justified by the Law of Nature.* The other was Dr. John Henry

Hopkins, bishop of Vermont, who published in 1861 a pamphlet entitled "The Bible View of Slavery," which was followed by a two-volume work entitled *A Scriptural, Ecclesiastical and Historical View of Slavery.*

Perhaps the major point of divergence between white and black Episcopalians at the close of the Civil War centered around the two groups' understanding of the nature of the Church's catholicity. To the majority culture, it was a loosely understood tenet. If whites of the period believed that their "Father's house had many rooms," they clearly understood that to mean that those lodgings would differ according to the race and social class of their occupants. In other words, the Church's life would maintain the stratification inherent in the society of which it was a part. "The rich man," according to such a watered-down view of catholicity, would always be "in his castle, the poor man at his gate."[27] According to such a view, the Catechism required all "to do our duty in that state of life in which it shall please God to call us." Because in this version of catholicity there were no absolute, objective standards by which the Church would be judged and its behavior measured, the Episcopal Church could give *carte blanche* to their Southern counterparts to work out their own salvation as regards its view of slavery. Thus, one historian could comment that "the devotion of Episcopal churchmen to the catholic aspects of their religion had outweighed whatever concern there may have been for social and political issues which had disturbed and divided other churches."[28]

Black Episcopalians who opted to remain in the Church interpreted catholicity quite differently. They believed that the catholic religion, by definition (since the very word comes from the Greek *kath' olon,* "according to the whole"), embraced all of humankind. The rooms in which they would be accommodated in their Father's house would be equal in all respects to those of their white brethren. They believed that the Church, if truly catholic, must be guided by St. Paul's admonition to the Romans that it not conform itself to the pattern of the present world, but rather that it should be about the business of being an agent responsible for the transformation of the world (Rom. 12:2). Black Episcopalians were no less guided by the apostle's declaration elsewhere, that there be neither Jew nor Greek, nor bond nor free, but that all should be one in Christ Jesus (Gal. 3:28).

As the Conference of Church Workers among Colored People declared in 1906:

> It must be apparent that in the Church of God; in a society founded upon justice, liberty and brotherly kindness, the yearning of Christ's soul cannot be realized if all who are included in that society, are not accorded

the freedom, the justice, the equity, which He declares to be the right of all.[29]

The battle lines drawn between white and black Episcopalians, therefore, were not, strictly speaking, racial, but ideological and theological. An understanding of these distinct points of departure in the respective thought of the two groups is essential if we are to grasp the nature of the debate over entitlement, authority, and jurisdiction that was to be thrashed out on the floor of the General Convention for three-quarters of a century.

As we further examine these developments, another common thread emerges. Black Episcopalians, either believing in the catholic claims of Anglicanism, or seeking to find the principle elsewhere, place great importance on the presence and function of the black minister. If blacks viewed the church as little more than a spiritual filling station, if the priest was viewed as little more than a dispenser of the sacraments, then anyone duly ordained could function in this capacity. But the minister in the black community has historically been much more. That person has been a transmitter of the culture, an embodiment of aspirations, a person who shares the dreams of the people to whom he ministers, and who, most important, preaches a theology of liberation.

Strict sacramentalists might well reject such a view, since it runs counter to the *ex opere operato* doctrine, long considered a hallmark of catholicity.[30] But such a view bears little similarity to the existential realities of the Christian faith. As John Pobee points out:

> In the best Anglican tradition, tradition is seen not in static terms but rather as something representing the responses of particular churches to particular situations, challenges and problems. Tradition is a dynamic process which is also an aid to a sense of history and a guide to the present in its various components.[31]

It can be safely said that had there been black clergy in the Episcopal Church after the Civil War, there may have been some incentive for more blacks to have remained in the Episcopal Church. The black priest was seen by many as the *sine qua non,* a link that would have helped to legitimize the Church's claim of its catholicity. For we must not forget that it was the establishment of black congregations and the ordination of black clergy that were seen as signs of the Episcopal Church's catholicity—not the mere sacramental or canonical admission of blacks to the Church. The deeper significance of this development will be seen as we study subsequent periods in the Church's history.

Chapter 4

Efforts to Evangelize the Freedmen

Can we to men benighted the lamp of life deny?

—The Right Reverend Reginald Heber
(hymn text, 1819)

The Episcopal Church, as we have maintained, has consistently regarded blacks as something of an anomaly. The presence of blacks has at times been considered an embarrassment, an incongruity, a thorn in the Church's flesh, and still at other times a presence many wished would go away. The irony is that when many blacks, after the Civil War, did just that, the Church felt morally bound not only to minister to the faithful remnant, but to reach out to evangelize a new class of people, the freedmen. "All of the Church's efforts among the Negroes, previous to the War," as Bragg correctly observes, "was of a patronizing and charitable sort."[1] Black congregations in the North had often been treated by the Church hierarchy with what can be described as benign neglect. Those churches had been founded, as we have shown, almost exclusively by blacks who, by and large, had not received a warm welcome, or who had at best enjoyed second-class membership in established white parishes. Similarly, black congregations in the South had been established, by and large, by the plantocracy, who were assiduous in their efforts to take *fides anglicana* into the cottonfields as a means to control the slave population. In both North and South, therefore, black Episcopalians had been accorded an inferior status, *de facto* or *de jure,* in the life of the Church.

After the war, the Episcopal Church, it would seem, took to heart the words of James Russell Lowell's famous hymn, "New occasions teach new duties, time makes ancient good uncouth,"[2] and went about the business of changing its historical *modus operandi.* The Church devised a new missionary strategy that it deemed to be more in keeping with the times. The period after the War between the States, therefore, signaled the beginning of an era in which blacks were seen as a group to be "worked among." Those persons who at various times in

American history have been referred to as Africans, freedmen, coloreds, Negroes, Afro-Americans, blacks, and most recently (the nomenclature having come full circle) African Americans, have been seen not as part and parcel of the rank and file of church membership, but as a special case, a special group in need of special ministrations, special outreach, special programs designed to meet the peculiar exigencies of a group clearly understood, in every age, to be tangential at best to the status quo. As we shall see, those exigencies have been variously defined for 130 years, but the Church's basic understanding of blacks in its midst has not been appreciably altered.

The first agency established for work "among" blacks was the Freedman's Commission, which was made the responsibility of the extant Board of Missions. It came into being immediately after the Civil War, at the General Convention of 1865, which met in Philadelphia. "The Commission was instructed to act with the advice and consent of the diocesan bishops of the Church [and] an executive committee was formed which appointed a [white] Northern priest as its executive officer."[3] By the time the committee made its first report at the General Convention held in New York three years later, it had been renamed the Commission of Home Missions to Colored People in the hope that the new designation would show that "the work proposed was not altogether of a secular character."[4] It is noteworthy that the tenor of the commission's first report suggests that the Episcopal Church, which for two and a half centuries had done little to contribute to the uplift of blacks, and indeed in many places had used religion to further subjugate them, goes to great lengths to exculpate itself from any responsibility for the condition of blacks prior to their emancipation. Indeed, the committee, speaking on behalf of a church that had been conspicuous by its silence on the question of slavery out of deference to the vast numbers of its communicants who were slaveholders, seems to ignore this history and to seek instead the "higher ground" of a *noblesse oblige:*

> What has been done by us in this field must be regarded rather as an evidence of our good wishes toward these emancipated millions of the South than as a work commensurate with our responsibility or with the demands of the hour. We can claim no more than *we have tried to do something* to educate a race suddenly elevated to political power and equality in the midst of their ignorance and inexperience.[5]

Additionally, the committee, which seems to have been inspired by the words of the missionary hymn, "O Sion haste, thy mission high fulfilling,"[6] saw its role not simply as enabling former slaves to adjust to their new status, but as saving blacks from moral and doctrinal perdition:

> The crying want of this people is spiritual ministration. They are left emphatically "as sheep without a shepherd" after falling prey to irreligion and error, and sometimes, it is said, to the grossest forms of superstition.[7]

This, in turn, echoed the comment of Bishop Thomas Atkinson who opined that the freedmen had "separated themselves from the ministry of the Church, and given themselves to the guidance of ignorant teachers of their own race, who are leading them into the wildest excesses of delusion and fanaticism."[8]

Too, the language of the committee's report, in a statement suggestive of revisionist history, would imply that it saw these new efforts not as a compensatory gesture but as a continuation of a missionary endeavor of long-standing. In pleading for further funding, for example, it asked the convention: "Does it not become this Church, which formerly did so much for their spiritual care and nurture, to interpose [itself] between them and the gulf into which they are in danger of plunging?"[9]

Central to the work of the commission was the establishment of schools at which the freedmen could be educated and thus, presumably, prepared to take their rightful place in the new society. But the commission was clear in its resolve that the schools should be seen as an arm of its missionary outreach:

> Experience shows that the Negro will value the school only for the secular knowledge it imparts unless he be made to feel the Church working in and through the school as his spiritual guide as well as his temporal benefactor. The Church has no proper call to engage in the work of school teaching at all except she can make it subserve her dominant purpose, *viz.*, the gathering into her fold for religious instruction and discipline of those whom she teaches in her schools.... The true order of the work is the mission first and then the school, the one the chief, the other the auxiliary.[10]

Within three years of its founding, the prodigious sum of $100,000 had been raised, which enabled the commission to support 65 teachers and 5,000 students in thirty parochial and industrial schools.[11] Among the schools established by the Freedman's Commission, one of the most successful was St. Augustine's Normal School and Collegiate Institute founded in 1867 in Raleigh, North Carolina, for the purpose of training colored teachers, but later expanded to prepare men for ordination. (Now St. Augustine's College, it is the only institution founded by the Freedman's Commission still in existence.) The bishop of North Carolina, commenting on the new enterprise in 1868, remarked:

> The establishment of [the School] . . . for the education of colored scholars of both sexes, who are to bind themselves to become teachers for a certain number of years, of the ignorant of their own race, promises to be of incalculable benefit to that class of our population who so much need the influence of religious education to enable them rightly to understand and enjoy the privileges of freedom.[12]

Bishop Atkinson's statement reflects not only the commission's commitment to evangelism through education, but bespeaks a new commitment to the idea of a kind of racial self-determination, a concept that would have been alien to the mind of the antebellum Southern Episcopalian, and which would have proved counterproductive to the effective operation of economic institutions that were inextricably woven into the fabric of Southern life. This idea, in turn, is reflected in another of the recommendations of the Board of Missions, which was eventually adopted by the convention, namely "that every effort ought to be made at once to prepare colored men for the ministry, so that they may minister to their own people." This was perhaps the most radical suggestion, since before the end of the war there were no black Episcopal clergy in the South at all. The last of the recommendations to be adopted was that "one or more missionaries be appointed to visit the freedmen in the Southern Dioceses who were formerly communicants of the Church, to examine their condition and to ascertain what can be done to revive their former attachment and relation to the Church."[13]

No matter what its motivation, it must be said in its defense that the Freedman's Commission, in putting these recommendations forward, certainly demonstrated that its members were not entirely oblivious to the reasons for which the Church had experienced so dramatic a decline in the number of its black communicants in the South; and, moreover, that it was taking what it believed were the steps necessary to reverse the trend. By fostering the idea of admitting blacks to the ordained ministry, it recognized that this might well serve as a drawing card to those blacks who may have been desirous of affiliating or reaffiliating themselves with the Church. The Episcopal Church, in recognizing that the pastoral ministrations of black clergy would bode well for the evangelistic efforts among the freedmen, arrived at the same conclusion (if for different reasons) to which blacks had come some years before.[14] It might be said, then, that although the Church still believed the Gospel to be a treasure in earthen vessels, it was beginning to recognize the fact that the vessels need not all be fired in the same kiln.

Once fully cognizant of the fact that the prewar model of the black congregation (more often than not a plantation chapel) was, owing to the abolition of slavery, no longer a viable option, there seemed to be virtual unanimity among Southern churchmen on the desirability of raising up blacks for the ordained ministry. One churchman declared:

> The line of duty for the Church is as clear as a sunbeam. She must receive into her ministry duly prepared candidates of African descent, to minister to African people; and this reception cannot be postponed until a more convenient season, without peril or wrong.[15]

Another priest from a Southern diocese commented:

> I can see a decided tendency among our colored people to discard the instructions, counsels, etc., of everyone, it matters not whether it be North or South, unless the same comes through their own color. They demand a colored ministry, and if we would extend the church, we must comply with that demand.[16]

Despite this chorus, to which the voices of Alexander Crummell and other black clergy were added, very little was done. According to Hayden, between 1866 and 1877 only twenty blacks were ordained in the Episcopal Church, and of these, fourteen remained deacons and only six (of whom two had emigrated to the United States—one from the West Indies and the other from West Africa) were advanced to the priesthood.[17] Of the six, it should be noted, only two were ordained for Southern dioceses, where the need for black clergy was greater. The paucity of black ordinations and the fact that many languished in deacons' orders without being advanced to the priesthood was not due to a dearth of black aspirants, but to the unwillingness of dioceses to admit black men to holy orders. Since deployment was strictly along racial lines, and

> there were very few black churches in most dioceses, black men frequently had to locate a bishop with a vacant mission in order to be ordained.... In South Carolina [shortly after the Civil War], four black candidates, after waiting several years, withdrew from the [Episcopal] Church into the Reformed Episcopal Church. There was no black priest ordained in South Carolina until 1895.[18]

Nor was the reluctance to ordain blacks a phenomenon peculiar to Southern Episcopalians. Bragg points out that there was a certain sentiment maturing in the North as well as the South against the ordination of Negroes to the ministry:

> In the North, there was a certain priest by the name of the Rev. W. T. Webber, who in his paper, *The Standard*, argued earnestly and vigorously against the ordination of Negroes. In the South, there were not a few who maintained that such should not be permitted to go further than the diaconate.[19]

In some cases, bishops were in favor of ordaining blacks, but were prevented from doing so because of the canonical requirement that candidates for ordination be approved by the diocesan standing committee, made up of clergy and lay persons. Bragg documents such a case in the Diocese of North Carolina:

> Bishop Atkinson... battling in the face of a hard, bitter and unrelenting prejudice, organized colored parishes and had them admitted into union with his diocesan convention. And when the Standing Committee refused to pass the papers of a colored candidate for holy orders, invited two "Yankee" Negro priests from the North to come into his diocese, and admitted them into full privileges in his convention. Other Southern bishops labored earnestly to do the same thing, but could not.[20]

Indeed, the trickle of black ordinations gives us an insight into what may well be described, despite the establishment of several colored congregations and educational institutions by the Freedman's Commission, as the overall failure of the movement. Why was this the case? In the first instance, one can point to the fact that Southern bishops and parishes were less enthusiastic in their pecuniary support of the program than they were in their vocal support. The commission complained repeatedly of the "apathy of Church people in regard to the Christianization, elevation and salvation" of blacks.[21] At the 1874 General Convention in New York, less than a decade after the launching of the commission, the Church declared that there had never been "any sincere interest in this department of beneficence."[22] But the unwillingness on the part of members of a church to provide funding is normally symptomatic of a deeper malaise, and in the case of the late nineteenth-century Episcopal Church, the malaise was attitudinal. Although, as we have conceded, some of its instincts were correct, the problem is that the Church in its efforts to evangelize blacks was both misguided and naive, and the program, born of such nescience, was flawed *ab initio.*

The first flaw had to do with how the Church's racial perceptions caused blacks to be understood. As Dr. M. Moran Weston points out: "Racial attitudes, expressed in social patterns and customs of segregation, caused many churchmen, especially in the South, to view evangelization of Afro-Americans as a distant program of missions, comparable to those in China or in Liberia."[23] Like the unchurched in such distant climes, blacks within the borders of the United States "were seen as a group to be won for Christ and the Church."[24]

Such a view could predominate because it was virtually impossible for Episcopalians, especially in the South — a lost war and an Emancipation Proclamation notwithstanding — to recognize those formerly in bondage, indeed those whom they had previously owned, as equal citizens under the law. They were not part of society as society was understood, and to minister to them at all required them to be considered among those whom Bishop Heber described as coming "from many an ancient river, from many a palmy plain [who] call us to deliver their land from error's chain."[25] Since, however, the intended recipients of such evangelistic largess lived cheek-to-jowl with their benefactors, the Lady Bountiful approach, so endemic to Victorian missionary endeavor, was difficult, if not impossible, to carry off.

But Lady Bountiful, nevertheless, did leave her mark, which brings us to the second flaw in the strategy. The Church's patronizing attitude, under which it found it necessary to protect and provide for former slaves, resulted, as Bragg observes, "in an atmosphere which created a dependency on the part of blacks, whereby colored congregations were attached to white parishes or were placed entirely under the supervision and direction of the bishop," as separate congregations financially dependent upon the diocese, and without the status of parish.[26] Such actions stood in sharp contrast to the first black parishes, founded by blacks, all of which were self-supporting at the time of their inception.[27]

This missionary strategy, according to Bragg, had the effect of "discouraging and disheartening ... the aspiring self-respecting of our group,"[28] and proved to have a far-reaching and deleterious effect on the development of black congregations, North and South, as black Episcopalians, believing that a bishop or a diocese was morally bound to provide the church for them, readily accepted such largess even when they were able to provide for themselves. If indeed it is true that he who pays the piper names the tune, it can be seen that the move toward an authentic black self-determination was severely impeded by the Church's post–Civil War missionary endeavor. Indeed, Bragg's statistic underscores this point. In 1922, he could write:

> One way to realize the value of the seed planted by colored priests before the Civil War, is in tracing one-half of our present communicants in the entire country to their effort directly, or indirectly. And when we have given full value to the consecrated and loving services of white priests among our group, the significant fact remains, despite their prestige, and the financial resources at their backing, that in all our investigations we

> have not discovered *one* missionary effort initiated by them among colored people and brought to self-supporting efficiency.... The work of building up from within, into self-support and efficiency is peculiarly associated with the constructive leadership of members of the group whose self-expression is attempted.[29]

The third flaw was that since the Freedman's Commission was instituted as a national church program, there was a distinct expectation that the whole Church should underwrite the costs involved. However, there was resentment, chiefly on the part of Southerners, that the whole Church should determine local policy. As Weston observes, "The high disproportion of Southern members of the Convention, viewed in terms of membership and financial contribution to the Church, enabled them in matters on which there was regional agreement to maintain this point of view."[30]

The fourth flaw was the mistaken belief on the part of the Church that simply by providing vocational and religious training, simply by eradicating "ignorance," the problems of the black race in America could be solved. By making good citizens and Christians of them, the thinking went, they would be equipped to enter society, or in the words of Bishop Atkinson, "to understand and enjoy the privileges of freedom." This approach, the brainchild of Northern Episcopalians, betrayed a basic ignorance of race relations in the South, and as Weston rightly notes, "frankly ignored injustices in secular society."[31] In other words, the well-meaning architects of the Freedman's Commission confused the theoretical freedom that the former slaves had been accorded by the law with the existential reality of the situation in which the white power structure clearly demonstrated their unwillingness to facilitate blacks' transition from bond to free. Much less did whites concede to blacks the privileges granted by Lincoln's writ of plenary manumission known as the Emancipation Proclamation. Indeed, the very apologia for the establishment of the Freedman's Commission betrays its principal shortcoming, namely the belief that blacks now possessed a recently conferred "political power and equality." Thus, the president of the Pennsylvania branch of the Freedman's Commission, commenting on the act of arson that resulted in the destruction of St. Stephen's School in Petersburg, Virginia, could remark: "We had hoped that the day of burning Negro schools and houses had passed away, and that *the new political relations between the races* would protect them in a measure from this expression of antagonism, still so rife in Virginia."[32]

There was, of course, no such thing as "new political relations between the races." It would appear that the leaders of the Episcopal Church, in their zeal "to interest our colored people in religious teachings and thus in part at least pay back to them in spiritual gifts the debt which we owe to this long-oppressed and unhappy race,"[33] had not taken into account that "two hundred and fifty years of slavery were followed by one hundred years of official and unofficial segregation in the South and in the North."[34] Although Edwards could comment pridefully that "the early efforts of white clergymen to care for the educational needs of the Negro people bore abundant fruit,"[35] the fact remains that the black educational institutions founded by the commission were set up, as it were, as experimental cocoons, or greenhouses. Within these environments, blacks could thrive, but apart from that rarefied atmosphere they would be subject to the virulence of racial discrimination and prejudice as they existed in the very real world outside. Bragg put it this way:

> We have profited but little in direct church extension . . . under a system which failed to take note of the imperative requirements of the new trend of racial life. The colored people eagerly availed themselves of whatever educational opportunities that were presented. But with respect to their organized life as a body of Christians no organization could prevail among them which did not enter into their entire life, social, civil and intellectual.[36]

The Church's failure to understand adequately the new situation in which blacks found themselves stemmed from the fact that such understanding was not born of a desire on the Church's part to ameliorate the condition of former slaves in any concrete way. This was because, as Harry Rahming observes, evangelistic work among blacks "has never been scientifically organized, or has the responsibility for Negro conversion ever been determined. These causes alone lead logically to missionary failure since they are based more upon temporary racial conditions and attitudes than upon permanent situations."[37] Instead, the Church, apparently content to confer merely the outward and visible signs of improvement, was motivated in part by a desire to offer a kind of compensation, which was itself prompted by a desire on its part to assuage its guilt for its involvement, tacit or implicit, in the slave trade. Bishop Thomas Vail, for example, demonstrated such a view when, in challenging Episcopalians in Kansas to evangelize former slaves, declared that it was the Church's duty to "pay back in spiritual gifts the debt which we owe to this long-oppressed and unhappy race."[38]

The Episcopal Church, therefore, in attempting to redouble its efforts to bring the Gospel to blacks, was hoisted by its own petard. While sincere in its efforts to improve the lot of African Americans, it persisted in treating the group as separate but unequal, ministering to them as a special group and making no attempts whatever either to address the broader problem of racism in society, or to integrate blacks into the mainstream of the Church's life. Every act of the commission succeeded in further segregating the race, thereby creating a parallel—and inferior—ecclesiastical and social institution. Du Bois would later challenge the Church to confront such rank hypocrisy:

> Do not entice them [black Episcopalians] to ask for the separation which your unchristian conduct forces them to prefer. But simply confess in humility and self-abasement that you are not able to live up to your Christian vows: that you cannot treat these men as brothers and therefore you are going to set them aside and let them go their half-hearted way.[39]

While some blacks, therefore, as a result of the commission's "modest but useful contribution in physical relief and education,"[40] might have been a little better off at the end of the day, they were no more a part of society or an integral part of the Episcopal Church than they had been before. And what is more, the Episcopal Church never reclaimed the great numbers of black members whom it had lost, a goal that had been one of the chief motivations for the establishment of the Freedman's Commission.

This goal might have been achieved had the Church been willing to raise up black clergy in sufficient numbers to serve as pastors to the freedmen, since those whom the Episcopal Church had lost, believing that "none but their own leaders could guide them to the haven where they would be,"[41] had found their way to Baptist and Methodist churches with black ministers. Hayden points out that with the exception of the Church of the Good Shepherd, Mobile, Alabama, black congregations organized under white leadership did not survive, the membership choosing instead to defect to the black denominations.[42] When, however, the number of black ordinations had increased to such an extent that it became possible for them to head congregations, the picture changed radically. Black parishes were planted in such places as Key West, Florida (St. Peter's, 1866); Charleston (St. Mark's, 1866); Petersburg, Virginia (St. Stephen's, 1867); Richmond, Virginia (St. Philip's, 1872); Tarboro, North Carolina (St. Luke's, 1872); Washington, D.C. (St. Mary's, 1873); and Wilmington, North Carolina (St. Mark's, 1875).[43]

The circumstances under which these and other congregations in the South were established, however, is cause for less jubilation than it would seem. In case after case, the applications of these congregations to be admitted as self-supporting parishes with the rights and privileges of other parishes were summarily rejected because the same Southern Episcopalians who found it impossible to recognize those formerly in bondage as equal citizens under the law found it just as impossible to accord them equal privileges in the councils of the Church. During this "barren and rocky period," according to Thomas LaBar and Mary Wright,

> an effective majority of leading Episcopalians quashed any and all attempts by Negro Episcopalians to develop their own leadership. Negro parishes were generally excluded from diocesan conventions, Negro missionaries were barred from going overseas, and Negro delegates were refused admittance to General Convention.[44]

Bravid Harris, archdeacon for colored work in the Diocese of Southern Virginia, concurs with this assessment, and offers conclusive evidence that the Episcopal Church's halfhearted efforts to evangelize blacks, compared to the assiduous efforts of other denominations, has netted the Episcopal Church a minuscule number of black adherents:

> It is perfectly obvious, and we may as well admit it, that 54,520 communicants since 1794 shows inadequate growth. It does not compare favorably with the church as a whole, and is most unfavorable when compared with the denominations. The [black] Baptists began in 1793 at Savannah... and they have 3,196,623; the A.M.E. Church began officially in 1805 ... and they now have 545,814 members; the Methodist Episcopal Church, interracial as ours, has 456,913; and the Roman Catholics report 270,000, 147 churches and between 250 and 300 priests ministering exclusively to our people.[45]

In fact, Bragg sees this development as the turning point, if not the undoing, of the Episcopal Church's efforts to evangelize the freedmen:

> Just as the Church had cleared the way for real constructive effort, after so many years of hard and patient labor, in overcoming prejudices against the Church, a violent ecclesiastical storm broke forth, which arrested and sidetracked the harvest about to be reaped.... In South Carolina, after patiently waiting for ten years, St. Mark's Church, Charleston, made formal application to be received into union with the South Carolina diocesan convention. The convention was divided... and animated debates upon the "negro question" exercised a marvelous influence upon the colored race throughout the entire country. But it was injurious and hurtful to the interests of the Church and the negro.[46]

While it is true, then, that Southern churchmen wanted to build up the body of Christ among blacks, they clearly wanted the extension of the Kingdom to be on their terms. Although they were willing to concede certain outward and visible signs of self-determination, their unwillingness to accept black congregations on an equal footing, it would appear, was indicative of a desire on their part to exert as much control over the newly established black congregations as they had over the slave chapels on the plantations prior to Emancipation.

In 1877, the Freedman's Commission closed a chapter in the history of the Episcopal Church's work among blacks. At the General Convention of that year, meeting in Boston, the commission could make "no favorable report." It was decided that financial support be withdrawn from the schools it had established and that funds be used instead for missionary work. The report acknowledged that black Episcopalians had not returned to the fold in the numbers predicted; indeed, the commission, while reporting that the few black congregations in existence in the South in that year "consisted of those who had some education, some property and some social status," admitted that "the mass is untouched by our church."[47]

In commenting on the fact that those blacks who remained in the Episcopal Church were more socially prominent, more educated, and therefore economically better off than the majority of those who had sought affiliation in other denominations, Willard Gatewood writes:

> The relationship between social class and church affiliation among blacks in the late nineteenth and early twentieth centuries does not lend itself to easy generalization. In this era blacks generally perceived Episcopal, Presbyterian [and] Congregational... churches as those made up of "high-toned" people, who, undemonstrative during worship services, adhered to "book religion."[48]

C. Eric Lincoln cites a study on "church stratification and religious affiliation among blacks" that found that the black upper class "were attracted to predominantly white denominations such as the Episcopal, Congregational and Presbyterian churches," and points to another study that suggested that once blacks became upwardly mobile, they joined the Episcopal Church "to confirm their new status."[49]

We would like to suggest that these observations having to do with the correlation between blacks' social status and their affiliation with the Episcopal Church might also bear some relevance to our concern about the way in which blacks have historically understood the Episcopal Church's catholicity. Can it not be argued that those who, in the words of the commission's report, had some education and some social status were more likely to reason that the ministrations of the Episcopal Church should be as available to them as to anyone? Perhaps such persons were more likely to justify living with (and later challenging) the tension between the Church's repeated declaration that it was committed to racial inclusiveness on the one hand while often openly practicing, indeed institutionalizing, racial discrimination on the other. Perhaps those had enjoyed at least a *de facto* freedom before the war, and those who had been house slaves, accorded privileges and perquisites (which often included more benign treatment as well as educational opportunities), were more likely than less-privileged blacks to conclude that the limitations placed on their fellows "were based largely on regional, secular customs and the racial attitudes of individual church members rather than on the law of the church."[50]

Black Episcopalians who remained in the Episcopal Church knew well that it was the church of the plantocracy, and that the planters had interpreted and adapted its teachings so as to justify and perpetrate the institution of slavery. They knew well that "it became the custom of plantation owners to take their slaves to Church . . . because they thought religion would be a civilizing influence and thus make their property easier to handle."[51] Nevertheless, they also could understand that such uses to which the Church had been put were not intrinsic to the doctrine of the Episcopal Church, but instead were aberrations of it. Black Episcopalians remained in the Church to recapture that intrinsic nature; they remained in the Church not because they were social climbers, as Gatewood, Lincoln, and others might suggest, but out of a sense of entitlement. Black Episcopalians rejected an arguably racist view that they had no place in the Church that had missionized them now that slavery had been abolished. Like W. E. B. Du Bois, who declared in 1907, "I refuse to be read out of the church which is mine by inheritance and service of my fathers,"[52] black Episcopalians remained in the Church because they believed that its historical identification with the white ruling class did not by virtue of that fact render it unsuitable as a locus for black religious expression. As Taylor points out:

> Black people have found an attraction to the Anglican expression of Christianity in spite of the fact that it is the church of a large number of those who upheld the enslavement of Blacks. It has been among the churches which by word and deed has consistently negated the worth of Black people and yet it is the church which can rightly boast of a noble line of Black clergy and lay persons whose devotion and piety, together with sound scholarship and unwavering loyalty, have enriched immeasurably the fabric of life in the Episcopal Church.[53]

The utterances of black Episcopalians bear consistent witness to this unswerving belief. Alexander Crummell, in an address delivered at the laying of the cornerstone of St. Thomas' Church, Philadelphia, in

1890, exhorted his black brothers and sisters, appealing to what could be called a *"noblesse oblige noire"*:

> In an age when liberty is not seldom taken to mean license, we are able to take the yoke of Jesus upon ourselves as a token of our *loyalty* to truth and order; ... In our ancestors and their history we were taught, unwillingly and crushingly, the Discipline of Slavery and Caste. It is our privilege now, with the franchises of the state, *and with the high teachings of God's church,* to learn for ourselves and our children the noble Discipline of freedom.[54]

Edward Thomas Demby, fully aware that racism was alive and well, even in the bosom of the Church, believed that such imperfections were due not to the nature of the Church, but to the imperfections of those who are, despite their shortcomings, the stewards of its mysteries. Thus he could write in *The Colored Churchman:* "Despite the pronounced color-line exhibited against us everywhere in America, in every walk of life, including the church, yet we must be faithful children of the church until it speaks."[55]

Even while challenging the Church, the great orator George Frazier Miller made it clear that blacks' commitment to the faith as the Episcopal Church had received it was not to be questioned:

> Imperfect though we are, still are we servants of God whose every work must bear the stamp of faith, the faith deeprooted and unswerving. While claiming the liberty of unreserved expression on men and measures, we protest our loyalty to the Church of the living God, loyalty to the worship and discipline of the Book of Common Prayer, loyalty to the constitution and canons of the Church of our ordination.[56]

Such loyalty was echoed in the writings of George Alexander McGuire, who in a letter to the *Church Advocate,* which he wrote while archdeacon for colored work in the Diocese of Arkansas, made it very clear that despite the abuses heaped upon blacks by prejudiced whites, "we who are now in the Church love our Mother, and dare not become schismatics."[57]

A committee of the Conference of Church Workers among Colored People (CCWACP), in a statement on the racial episcopate, made it very clear that their espousal of such a plan did not alter in the least blacks' loyalty to the Church:

> Stimulated by what God has wrought among us, encouraged by the assurance that God will neither leave nor forsake us, we appeal to our people [black Episcopalians] all over the land to be steadfast in the faith, and humbly pray that God's grace may enable them, under all circumstances, relying upon his protection and care, to stand openly and

> privately, for righteousness, goodness, and truth; to be loyal and true to the great gospel, and faithful to its supreme command.[58]

It is instructive to note that nearly a century later black leaders in the Episcopal Church echo the convictions of their esteemed forebears in the faith. In a sermon on Absalom Jones Day, 1971, Bishop Burgess, in presenting an apologia for the existence of the Union of Black Episcopalians, made it clear that he and his fellows stand on the shoulders of the Church's black pioneers, and made it abundantly clear, as Miller and others had done, that there was never a question of the black people's loyalty to the Church:

> We love the Church — its doctrines, its liturgy, its way of life, its fellowship. And it is because of this love for the Church that we want it to be truly the Church. Absalom Jones gathered his people together to develop their own potential, their own resources, for he was tired of being thwarted because of his color, insulted, managed by people who had no interest in the black community but to keep it under their control. *But he did not sever St. Thomas's from the main body.* The parish waited several generations before it was taken into the convention, as a witness to the true character of the Body of Christ.[59]

Black Episcopalians, then, could join and remain in the Episcopal Church because they saw it as their particular mission to help it make its practice conform to its catholic ideal, or to use Gray's phrase, because they understood that "the Gospel carries implications which transcend the understanding of those who proclaim it."[60] As we chronicle the momentum that gathered among blacks in the century following the demise of the Freedman's Commission, we shall see, in various guises, the black struggle for a truly catholic church manifest itself time and again. And as the Church founded new agencies, commissions, and bureaus to facilitate its work "among" blacks, blacks themselves began to form organizations and caucuses both for their own uplift as well as for providing a platform from which they could best remind the Church that its institutional racism was not only inconsistent with its character, but an impediment to its mission.

Part Two

Sowers of the Gospel

Chapter 5

The Question of a Racial Episcopate in a Catholic Church

Give of thy sons to bear the message glorious.

—Mary Ann Thompson (hymn text, 1870)

The Episcopal Church on the Horns of a Dilemma

As the number of blacks in the Episcopal Church grew, as more black parishes were founded, and as the number of black men in holy orders increased, it was inevitable that the question of the consecration of black bishops would be raised. This should not be surprising, for even without the issue being "raised," thoughts, words, and deeds pertaining to the "office and work of a bishop in the church of God" are ever-present in a church whose very name declares to all and sundry that its identity, validity, and authenticity are predicated on some kind of belief in the centrality of the role of the bishop. The Episcopal Church, like the thirty other autonomous churches that find a spiritual home in Canterbury, believes the episcopacy to be, to use John Pobee's term, "a non-negotiable of the Anglican ethos."[1] Too, the episcopacy is seen as essential to the Church's continuance, since only at the bishop's hands can candidates be ordained to the three orders of the Church's ministry; and only at those hands can laypersons, through the sacrament of Confirmation, be commissioned to carry out their apostolate in the world.

But the bishop is considered to be essential to the continuance of the church in other ways, which, although not (strictly speaking) sacramental, are nonetheless seen to be inherent in the office. The Episcopal Church fully subscribes to the Cyprianic view that the bishop is the symbol of the Church's unity,[2] who is expected, in the words of the ordinal, to be "an example to the flock of Christ" and to encourage "quietness, love and peace." Moreover, the particular functions of the office are seen to include maintaining the purity of doctrine, correcting and punishing the disobedient, and caring for the needy.[3] But as we consider the nature of the office vis-à-vis the concerns of the post–Civil War Episcopal Church, as it struggled with the problems inherent in electing blacks to it, it must be remembered that the bishop is looked upon, first and foremost, as one in authority. Indeed, Anglicanism has not moved far from the view espoused by Richard Hooker (1553–1600), who wrote that the bishop has "a further power to ordain Ecclesiastical persons, and a power of Chiefty in Government over Presbyters as well as Lay men, a power to be by way of jurisdiction a Pastor even to Pastors themselves."[4]

The Episcopal Church, especially in the South, where there continued to be for several decades after the war a *stated* desire to bring more persons of African descent into the fold, found itself on the horns of a dilemma. It believed, in principle, that a black bishop could do much to evangelize people of his own race, but despaired that "under existing church law individual dioceses elected bishops to supervise church work in their regions, which would mean that a Negro bishop would have jurisdiction over both Negro and white churches," a concept that was not appealing even to the more liberal Northern dioceses.[5] Understandably, then, blacks were desirous of the episcopate for the very reasons that the largely white Church would have barred their access. For white and black Episcopalians fully grasped that bishops are not only successors to the apostles, chief pastors, and spiritual governors, but also powerful, significant personages in church and society. Because of their "spiritual authority, prestige and lifelong tenure, and often considerable political, economic and social clout in the overall society, they shape and guide the life of the church to a greater degree than clergy or laity."[6] The consecration of black bishops, therefore, was to the black consciousness absolutely essential. Without it, they realized, it would be impossible in a church that defined itself by the episcopal office to maintain even a semblance of equality. If both *potestas* and *auctoritas,* those attributes peculiar to the episcopal office, were denied them, they could not be taken seriously.[7]

One solution was the proposal for suffragan bishoprics for colored work. Under such a system, the question of power and jurisdiction would be resolved, since such a bishop would supervise only clergy and people of his own race, and would, in turn, serve at the pleasure of a white diocesan bishop. Accordingly, a proposal was put forward by the Diocese of Texas at the 1874 General Convention, "when it asked the Convention to appoint a suffragan bishop for supervision of the freedmen." This was not an altogether novel proposal, since the Freedman's

Commission, in its eighth annual report a year earlier, had drawn attention to the idea of "a bishop for the freedmen," which had been put forward by the bishop of South Carolina at his diocesan convention, an idea that reputedly had the endorsement of the bishops of Kentucky, Tennessee, and Georgia.[8] The Board of Missions, to which the Freedman's Commission reported, had appointed a committee that found that "a bishop, to whom shall be committed the ecclesiastical jurisdiction of Freedmen, scattered throughout the several Southern Dioceses, is not desirable, either for the interests of the Colored people, or for the welfare of the several Dioceses within which Freedmen are found." Another solution was proposed at the 1874 General Convention by the bishop of Maryland, who suggested the creation of special missionary districts for different races, which would have the same rights and privileges as other missionary districts, headed by bishops of the particular race.[9]

To address these issues, a committee of the House of Bishops, charged with preparing a report on the "episcopal supervision of freedmen," was appointed. When it made its report at the next General Convention three years later, it declared that it was "inexpedient to take any actions in regard to providing Bishops exclusively for persons of different races and tongues," but voted in favor of the creation of suffragan bishoprics as the need arose.[10] This was but the first round of a heated debate over how best to missionize former slaves — through a black suffraganate or a separate racial district. The topic would be discussed at General Conventions for the next six decades. Dr. M. Moran Weston refers to it as the "hardy perennial."[11]

Black Missionary Districts under White Bishops

The most dramatic moment of the controversy came in 1883 at Sewanee, Tennessee, when a group of Southern church leaders met at the University of the South for the purpose of putting the matter to rest. They succeeded, however, in accomplishing quite the opposite; the decisions they reached resulted in a bifurcation in the life of the Episcopal Church, from which, it can be argued, the Church has never fully recovered. In April of that year, the senior bishop in the South, the Right Reverend W. M. Green of Mississippi, wrote to his brother bishops:

> Among the many subjects that may justly claim the consideration of our approaching General Convention will, doubtless, be that of the relations of our Church to the late slave population of our States, and the best means that can be adopted for their religious benefit. As this

> subject seems to be awakening the serious attention of both the patriot and the Christian, North as well as South, it has been suggested to me, by several of our Bishops, that it would be well if all the Bishops of the late Slave States would meet in council, and after due consultation, agree upon some plan to be laid before our General Convention for the accomplishment of that purpose.[12]

The letter also urged the bishops to bring with them "some one of your Clergy who, either from much experience in instructing the negro, or from a becoming interest in his behalf, may be qualified to aid us by his counsel." A subsequent letter extended the invitation to prominent laypersons as well.[13]

In its report, this all-white, unofficial, but certainly influential body of Christian gentlemen, after due deliberation, acknowledged the "difficulties surrounding this subject of the work of the Church among the coloured people of the South," and the "grave embarrassments attending each and all of the proposed methods for the accomplishment of the work which is undoubtedly imposed by the commandment of the Lord." The committee dismissed as "inexpedient" the idea of "establishing any separate, independent ecclesiastical organization for the colored people dwelling within the territory of our constituted jurisdictions," but opined that

> because of the peculiarity of the relations of the two races, one to the other, in our country, because of their history in the past and the hopes of the future, there is needed special legislation, appointing special agency and method for the ingathering of those wandering sheep into the fold of Christ.[14]

To this end, that specially convened congress made a recommendation that was subsequently proposed to be enacted as canon law at the General Convention a few months later: "In any Diocese containing a large number of persons of colour, it shall be lawful for the Bishop and Convention of the same to constitute such population into a special Missionary Organization under the charge of the Bishop."[15]

Perceiving that the enactment of this proposed canon would result in the total disenfranchisement of black Episcopalians, and would remove any vestige of hope that a black man could be elected bishop, a group of black churchmen met in New York immediately following the Sewanee gathering. They reviewed the white churchmen's proposal, and decided to send a delegation to the convention for the purpose of protesting the approval of the proposed canon. The wishes of the black churchmen won the day, and the General Convention rejected the "Sewanee canon," as it had become known, on the grounds that it drew "lines of classification and distinction between the followers of our common Lord."[16]

But this action of General Convention proved, at best, to be a pyrrhic victory for blacks in the Episcopal Church. As if in retaliation against the convention's rejection of their plan,[17] the Southern dioceses began what could only be described as a systematic disenfranchisement of blacks, reflective of the Jim Crow laws being enacted in the secular arena. Separate "colored convocations" were organized in the South, as parallel and subordinate to the diocesan conventions. Those convocations, however, "lacked the important rights of electing their own bishops, making their own rules, and sending delegates to the General Convention."[18] It is interesting to note, however, that in establishing such convocations, Southern bishops often went to pains to explain that the actions were not based on race or color per se, but on an alleged deficiency inherent in blacks, which prevented them, intellectually and morally, from participating in the governance of the Church. The utterance of the bishop of Virginia is representative of the Southern dioceses' approach to the situation, in that it is a reflection of what we would dub a theological schizophrenia on the part of white Episcopalians, which Hayden describes as "benevolent paternalism." Bishop Alfred M. Randolph, like many of his contemporaries, "viewed blacks as fellow human beings altogether inferior to whites in intellect, culture and morality, but capable of considerable improvement through judicious and high-minded white guidance." More important, the white churchmen were concerned with maintaining the *appearance* of catholicity and were "unwilling to see racial distinctions written into canon law but... actively supported racist practices as a desirable, or at least necessary, conformity to segregation."[19]

> The government of a church by the people is the highest mission of this world to which the people can be called. The determination of the doctrine, discipline and worship of a church by the people involves a strain upon intelligence, upon moral principle and upon all the elements of character which results from the highest discipline of Christian civilization.... Is it justice to the doctrine, discipline and worship of that grand church which we have inherited to entrust its purity, its stability and its mighty mission under God to a people who have had no such training, no such discipline of ages of self-control and of moral and intellectual progress. *The question, with reference to the Negro as a legislator in the Episcopal Church, is not a question of race, a question of color, but it is a question of faculty, of ability. It is a question of capacity of character.*[20]

The situation among black Episcopalians in the South was exacerbated, moreover, as they found that they could depend less and less on the championship of Northern liberal sympathizers. *The Churchman,* a church publication in New York, declared, for example, that "the wisdom of the action" of the Diocese of South Carolina to exclude blacks from its diocesan convention "must after all be decided by their own knowledge."[21] In short, although the Sewanee canon failed to be enacted as a matter of national Church policy, its spirit prevailed in the South, where diocesan conventions accomplished that which the General Convention did not. Indeed, as Hayden points out, "Southern whites [pressed] for ecclesiastical segregation to match the disenfranchisement, segregation, and economical peonage being structured in the South as a replacement for slavery."[22]

It should be noted that the Episcopal Church's successful attempts to severely limit the power of its black members were not unique. In commenting on the policy of the Presbyterian Church, Gayraud Wilmore remarks: "No church was more high sounding and profound in its Biblical and theological analysis of slavery and did less about it." He further explains that although the Presbyterian Church split over slavery, the church was guilty of "rank hypocrisy" on this matter.[23] After the war, the Southern branch of the Presbyterian Church rejected a proposal to reunite with the Northern branch, stating that although the institution of human bondage may have been wrong (a conclusion at which they arrived two years after insisting on its divine justification), the respective positions of master and servant were "correct and unassailable."[24]

The Methodist experience was similar. After the Civil War Methodists "continued to exhibit a split personality toward the race question." Although they had originally made overtures to welcome blacks into fellowship in white congregations, by the 1880s they had adopted a policy of "racially pure Denominationalism" resulting in the fact that by 1895 all of the Methodist conferences in the South were segregated.[25] This seemed to be motivated by a fear of a black takeover. A *Northern* Methodist minister, convinced that total separation of the races was absolutely necessary, predicted that in seventy years the black population, if unchecked, would number 50 million, and being "illiterate, licentious, and intemperate" would overwhelm the white population![26]

While neither postbellum Presbyterianism or Methodism spawned a separate black denomination, the Baptist Church did. The National Baptist Convention was formed in 1895 in reaction to an escalating and particularly virulent form of racism among Baptists, who "were among the leaders of what quickly became 'the dogma of Negro inferiority.'" The editor of the Baptist *Religious Herald* advocated complete separation of the races, beginning with the churches themselves.[27]

To return to the situation in the Episcopal Church, it should be observed that despite the flowery language of Bishop Green's letter, and the elevated theological tone of the committee's report in which its writers purport to uphold "the apostolic character of the Episcopal office because of the Ecclesiastical unity thereby maintained and exhibited,"[28] it is clear from reports of the deliberation that the decisions of the body were motivated by at least two basic factors. The first was a belief that the Church did not have any business changing the "natural" social order, and indeed should preserve the status quo. According to *The Churchman,* Bishop Hugh M. Thompson, Green's coadjutor in Mississippi, commented that

> the Church had nothing to do with the question of social equality. He had knelt by the bedside of dying negroes in the most wretched hovels, had officiated in their cabins and at their graves, but this had nothing to do with the question whom he should invite to his table or visit socially.[29]

The other, not unrelated factor was clearly a fear that enfranchising blacks would, in their minds, adversely affect the balance of power, that is, would deprive whites of what they perceived as their inalienable right to exercise authority in all things spiritual and temporal. Accordingly, Colonel Miles, attorney general of South Carolina, one of the lay delegates to the Sewanee meeting,

> spoke against admitting colored ministers to the diocesan lists on the same basis as the white clergy, since it was possible, with the great majority of negroes in South Carolina, that they might come into the Church in such numbers as to be able to outvote the white clergy, and the Church would be practically in their hands.[30]

The Churchman commented that Miles was so eloquent in describing the political situation in South Carolina that he "did much to determine the final action of the conference."[31] It should be noted that Miles's views represented a not-insignificant proportion of white Episcopalians of the day who simply did not approve of membership being extended to former slaves. As Hayden points out:

> Most white Episcopalians were indifferent to the mission to blacks. They frankly did not want blacks in their churches, schools, seminaries, charitable institutions, or legislative conventions. They felt that... the Episcopal Church was "so closely identified with the Anglo-Saxon character" that it was unsuitable for blacks.... The "apathy" of most churchmen and the "failure" of the Church at large to support the Church's schools and churches among blacks was the constant lament of everyone actively involved in southern missionary work, whether black or white, north or south.[32]

Black Missionary Districts under Black Bishops

The Conference of Church Workers among Colored People (CCWACP), which had come into existence in the crucible of the debate on the Sewanee canon, had rigorously objected to that proposed legislation, and to any other plan smacking of segregation or differentiation based upon race. They took a hard look at the situation, however, and came to the conclusion that it would be virtually impossible to elect a black bishop in the climate that prevailed at the end of the nineteenth century. Moreover, the Southern bishops' 1891 decision to reject their appeal for black bishops, recommending instead the use of archdeacons for colored work, further suggested to the black churchmen that such a compromise was as far as the Church hierarchy was willing to go.[33] The black churchmen, therefore, dropped their opposition to the segregation of dioceses in the South, which Reimers calls "a strategic retreat."[34] Realizing that they were powerless to elect a black bishop through the colored convocation process, and knowing that no black bishop could be elected who would have any jurisdiction whatsoever over whites, black churchmen began to endorse the creation of separate Negro dioceses or missionary districts. The difference between such missionary districts and those proposed at Sewanee was that they would be under the authority of black bishops, not white. Hoskins explains how the system would work:

> Advocates of the proposal suggested that Southern bishops and dioceses should cede jurisdiction over all congregations of colored people within their territory to the General Convention. These congregations then were to be formed into a missionary district. The colored bishop of this missionary district and the members thereby would have full representation in both Houses of General Convention.[35]

The CCWACP's change in strategy was due in part to the fact that black bishops were essential to the real growth and development of the Church among blacks. Bragg, for example, believed that

> white Episcopalians . . . thwarted the [blacks'] potential growth because they feared the influence of blacks in church governance. Whites tolerated black priests because they ministered only to other blacks. Bragg also maintained that *black bishops would be tolerated if their episcopacy could be limited to other blacks.*[36]

Moreover, the black churchmen insisted that such missionary districts would have equal rights with all other missionary districts.[37] Bragg explained the proposal succinctly in an editorial in *The Church Advocate:*

> By the missionary plan there would be representatives of both the colored clergy and laity of the church. And this point is absolutely vital. ... We seek not quantity, but simply recognition of a fundamental principle, to-wit: representation in our national body of the colored race, in the episcopal order, clerical ranks and the laity.[38]

Clearly, in this "strategic retreat" black churchmen were taking a risk, but it was a calculated one. History has shown that they made the right decision. They sought equality of recognition in the office of bishop, which they saw as essential to their future in the Episcopal Church. Original objections to an episcopate described in racial terms stemmed from a fear that it could be seen as second-class. But they reassessed this line of reasoning, believing that it was easier, as it were, to achieve access to the first-class carriage of the train from the second-class compartment than to attempt a leap from the side of the tracks.

The most eloquent apologia for the black missionary district plan was put forward by George Frazier Miller, rector of St. Augustine's Church, Brooklyn, New York, in a sermon delivered before a meeting of the CCWACP held in St. Luke's Church, New Haven, in 1903. Father Miller, believing that the situation had become untenable, in which "colored churchmen must choose between existing without any fixed status as an appendage to the white church, or, have an independent being apart from the local white church, with union in the General Convention,"[39] describes the plan as a matter of justice and expediency, grounded withal in the context of a sound and defensible theological framework. Noting that "the question of color was interjected into the councils of the church by others, not by ourselves," he declared:

> The Missionary Episcopate of colored people to colored people has been, with us, a crying demand for a considerable number of years. If you exclude us from diocesan conventions with all the rights and privileges inherent in their membership, then give us jurisdictions of our own wherein we may exercise the function of legislation and not be limited to spheres of petition.... That we should acquiesce in disfranchisement, and resign ourselves to the estate of pariahs and serfs in the Commonwealth of God, or in the civil privileges of our national life, we say *never,* so long as the Omnipotent One shall imbue our souls with the spirit of understanding, and enlarge our mouths with the power of protest.[40]

After the meeting at which Miller's sermon was delivered, the CCWACP sent a delegation to Washington, D.C., to meet with a group of Southern bishops to promote the cause of the racial episcopate, proposing a canon under which it would be lawful "to constitute into a missionary jurisdiction their territory, as pertaining to the colored race." They further stated:

> As at present constituted, it would seem utterly impossible for the colored clergy and laity to receive equal and impartial treatment and consideration in the several diocesan conventions.... We are led to ask of you your good offices in securing such additional canonical legislation as will remove us from the humiliation and undignified position in which we find ourselves in the Church. The Historical Episcopate does not touch us as closely and as helpfully as the needs of the great body of our people demand. Diocesan convocations for colored people, subject to the control of diocesan conventions, as established in several dioceses, do not meet the requirement of the situation and have not been fruitful of satisfactory results.... The persecution [i.e., the carrying out] of our work in the Southern States, among the colored people, should be placed more directly under the general Church. We believe that there should be missionary jurisdictions extending through two or more dioceses, with a Bishop at the head of each, drawn from the same race represented by the clergy and people among whom he is to labor.[41]

The matter was considered at the Boston General Convention of 1904 and referred to the next triennial gathering held in Richmond in 1907, where two special bodies were established: the Joint Commission on the Memorial of the Church Workers among Colored People, and the Joint Committee on Suffragan Bishops. Despite a valiant fight, the proposed canon was defeated in deference to a plan to have suffragan bishops for colored work, for which procedure the canonical groundwork was laid at the Cincinnati General Convention in 1910. Still believing that the racial missionary district plan was superior, and citing the fact that in six years since the enabling legislation for suffragan bishoprics no black bishop had been consecrated, the conference made a last-ditch effort at the St. Louis convention in 1916. Their eloquent plea for the establishment of a racial missionary district plan appealed to certain anthropological truths:

> We respectfully but boldly urge the consideration that in presenting their memorial for the establishment of racial district, the Negro race has... consistently interpreted not only the necessary conclusion from God's creation, but the natural result of our ecclesiastical training. Viewed from their viewpoint their request is a natural one. Viewed from the vantage of Church practice, it is a natural outcome of her consistent procedure. Viewed from the vantage of the law of racial life, it is natural that the Church should thus conform herself to God's law, which she can not change, rather than to ecclesiastical law, which may be changed and modified when conformity to that which is higher is desired.[42]

The framers of the majority report, it should be observed, believed themselves to be holding up the highest of moral ideals; indeed, they saw the establishment of racial districts as a stop-gap measure, until such time as the Church militant on earth could truly be reflective of God's greater purposes:

> When we have helped the Negro to the achievement of racial self-sufficiency, which is born of accomplishment, to self-mastery, which follows moral victory, and to pride of race, which is only possible when these victories have been gained, we shall have fixed within him the passion for social integrity, which is as justly natural as is that for racial reproduction. Separation of races is greatly misinterpreted, if it is not recognized to be the first necessary step towards the achievement of those ends.[43]

But as blacks were not united on this issue, the foregoing was only the majority report. It was the minority report that held sway at St. Louis:

> The plan of a separate racial jurisdiction for Negroes in the South, if once put into operation, will in our opinion make it exceedingly difficult, if not impossible, to try the plan of a Suffragan Bishop as provided by the General Convention if it shall be found expedient and possible in the future to do so. No race prefers to occupy a subordinate position, however necessary and beneficial such subordination may be considered under certain conditions. But when race development is once appealed to, and race ambition once excited, the Negro will quite certainly aspire to equality with the white man in every particular. Many of them will, therefore, prefer a bishop of their own race, with an independent jurisdiction separate from the white man, rather than a suffragan bishop, who however well qualified for the episcopate, would still be under the jurisdiction of the white bishop. For this reason, the plan of a separate racial district will make impracticable and futile any attempt on the part of a southern bishop or diocese to try any other plan.[44]

Bragg maintains that the minority report, to which both those opposed to any color line as well as those who believed blacks should be restricted in their rights, subscribed, actually supported the majority's position, and argued from the same premises while drawing different conclusions. It is another example of the belief in the inherent prerogative of whites to be superior to blacks in matters both spiritual and temporal. Such a view was espoused by the Right Reverend William Montgomery Brown, bishop of Arkansas, who in an address to the House of Bishops in 1907 stated, "A God-implanted race prejudice makes it impossible that Afro-Americans and Anglo-Americans should ever occupy the same footing in a dual racial church." He also believed that the separation of the races in the Church along racial lines was "a question of expediency, pure and simple."[45] The suffragan bishop plan, then, was preferred clearly because it would keep blacks in a subservient and dependent condition, even though the dignity of the episcopate had been conferred upon them. Bragg underscores, nevertheless, that black churchmen, in a demonstration of characteristic filial loyalty to the Church, would work within whatever system ultimately becomes operative:

> Since white churchmen are the ones who . . . demand a white convention with a white bishop, they should be willing to concede to their black brethren the same liberty and independence which they claim for themselves. But whether they concede it or not, we can not deny our own manhood by failing to contend for all the rights of man. . . . The attitude of colored churchmen found expression in the words of Abraham to Lot: "Let there be no strife between us, for we are brethren." And this attitude took definite shape in a memorial to the General Convention, for an alternative plan, Missionary Districts. So that by its employment the occasion for any future unpleasantness would be avoided. On this effort of peace and goodwill, as well as the preservation of our own manhood and self-respect, we are willing to go down to posterity.[46]

But in order to fully grasp the position embraced by Bragg and the members of the CCWACP, we must again return to the inability of the two groups to see eye-to-eye on the matter of what it means to be a catholic church. Bragg maintains that

> in so strenuously striving to preserve the real catholicity of the church, those in authority have not been able to clearly see that the necessary adjustment can be made without the least injury to catholic principle. Sooner or later such adjustment will be made. The present plan of diocesan unity, and oneness will not be altered or changed. . . . But an honest way will be found to fully recognize that postulate of racial life which has come to stay, at least for a long while. It is possible for such an extraordinary, but permissive plan to obtain which will recommend itself in certain contiguous territory, not only to the bishops, but as heartily to both races.[47]

Suffragan Bishops for Colored Work

After the 1907 General Convention approved the provision made for suffragan bishops (it being understood that such provision would allow the election of a Negro bishop),[48] many black leaders voiced opposition to the plan. Bragg labeled the suffragan bishop a "suffering bishop." Another writer, a communicant of St. Mark's, Charleston, predicted that suffragans would become "puppet bishops," mitred versions, as it were, of traditional black servility.[49] George Frazier Miller, for his part, denounced the idea of suffragans for colored work in no uncertain terms:

> Now the bishop suffragan is as worthy of esteem as deference as a diocesan bishop, though lacking in jurisdiction. But the suffraganate, at best, affords only the opportunity of petition and recommendation, precluding absolutely the power of initiative and decision inherent in the diocesan and missionary episcopate. The estate of a suffragan as per the scheme outlined in South Carolina would be an abomination and a reproach; and it is beyond the comprehension of some of us, if not all of us, how any man could so far be oblivious of his personal dignity and the exaltedness of the apostolic office as to kneel for consecration on such ignominious terms.[50]

There were several reasons for such skepticism on the part of black churchmen. First, they believed that the suffragan bishop plan would not end the disenfranchisement of the Negro in the South, whereas separate but equal districts could at least enable them to send delegates to General Convention. Separate but equal rights were seen as better than no rights at all. Moreover, suffragan bishops were to have no vote in the House of Bishops, thereby rendering them second-class bishops.[51] David Reimers observes that the suffragan bishop plan smacked of paternalism, not equality,[52] and expresses some incredulousness that it passed nevertheless.

But the suffragan bishop plan passed precisely because of its paternalistic nature. Indeed, when the debate over black suffragans reached fever pitch in 1907, no less a personage than the archbishop of Canterbury

> confidentially advised the American authorities to withhold a decision until the matter could be considered by the Lambeth Conference of 1908. The General Convention commission studying the proposal, clearly desirous of keeping in line with the imperialistic and racist practices which were gaining sway throughout Anglicanism, corresponded with Anglican dioceses overseas and found that *the most satisfactory pattern was supervision by white bishops with natives as assistant bishops.*[53]

Thus, the suffragan plan would enable the Episcopal Church to effect a classical Anglican compromise. It "would prevent *formally* dividing the Church on racial grounds but would also deprive the Negro bishops of any vote in the General Convention."[54]

The Episcopal Church's strategy pertaining to the consecration of black bishops conforms with what we have observed relative to its understanding of sacramental grace. Be it through the baptism of slaves, the ordination of blacks to the priesthood, or the consecration of black bishops, it was seen to be dispensed conditionally. That is, although no one would question the status, from a canonical or sacramental point of view, of such persons, they were nevertheless accorded second-class citizenship in the Church's life. Likewise, when it came to the issue of church governance, the slave chapel, the separate congregation, the colored convocation were the order of the day. The Church's actions as it ministered to blacks, on behalf of blacks, or among blacks, made it abundantly clear that it was never its intention to incorporate blacks fully into the fellowship of the Church, but to keep them, as it were, on the outside looking in. It is not surprising, therefore, that when legislation was passed to allow the elevation of blacks to the episcopate, many saw it as a new way to keep Negroes under white supervision.[55] As the Reverend Edward Rodman observes:

> The office of Suffragan Bishop grew out of the controversy of how to deal with "colored work." For in fact, there were those who believed that black suffragans under the authority of white diocesans would be a more effective missionary strategy for managing the growing number of small and primarily rural congregations that were developing in the south after the end of slavery.[56]

Two black priests were consecrated to the episcopate under the black suffragan plan, and their experience would suggest that Bragg and others were prophetic. Edward Thomas Demby, archdeacon for colored work in the Diocese of Tennessee, and Henry Beard Delany, archdeacon for colored work in the Diocese of North Carolina, who had spent most of his ministry at St. Augustine's College in Raleigh, were elected to the suffragan bishoprics of Arkansas and North Carolina, respectively. They were consecrated in 1918, and it should be noted here that the black suffragan scheme began and ended with them. "Without real authority, they were revered by black Episcopalians as symbols of achievement, but castigated unfairly as 'the deaf and dumb bishops.'"[57] Delany died ten years after his consecration, having made little impact on the life of the Church beyond North Carolina. He had received his entire education at St. Augustine's, where he was a teacher and later vice-principal, and where Mrs. Delany was employed as matron of the girls' residence. He was 60 years old at the time of his consecration, and his new duties took a heavy toll on his physical strength. The circumstances under which he had to work, not surprisingly, sapped his emotional and spiritual strength. Two of his ten children, Bessie and Sadie Delany, in a recent book report that at Bishop Delany's first Confirmation service, his family was forced to sit in the Church's balcony.[58]

Demby, on the other hand, served in his post until 1939, and remained active in his retirement until his death in 1957. His impact on the life of the Church was considerable, not only because of his long life and ministry, but because he had charge over colored work not only in Arkansas, but in the province of the Southwest, which included Kansas, Oklahoma, Texas, Missouri, and New Mexico as well.

Demby was not the choice of the "Negro establishment." The Reverend Harry Rahming observes that "Demby was practically unknown by the colored congregations outside of the Diocese of Tennessee."[59] Michael Beary points out that Demby rarely attended the annual meeting of the Conference of Church Workers, and was labeled as suspect since he had been elected bishop by an all-white convention without any input whatsoever from black churchmen. Demby also had the misfortune, in the eyes of the conference, of having been a convert.[60]

But the principal source of skepticism on the part of black clergy was that they "felt that those who had been appointed would not be outspoken and would submit to a position of inferiority."[61] Similarly, according to Harry Rahming, "Delany was not liked or trusted by most of the colored clergy, as to them, he presented the voice of Southern bishops and their dioceses, and not the voice of the colored clergy and their congregations. In short, to the colored clergy, Delany was an Uncle Tom."[62]

But it was for these very reasons that Demby and Delany were found acceptable to the white establishment. For unlike men like Bragg (a candidate for the post to which Demby was eventually elected), who consistently challenged the Church and reminded it of its racist practices, and Crummell, who had founded the CCWACP in the wake of the Sewanee canon controversy, Demby and Delany were by comparison "safe" candidates, who had quietly gone about their work among their own people. They had, in the eyes of the white church, "remained in their place." Bragg, in an oblique reference to the elections of Demby and Delany, remarks that a black bishop "must be chosen with respect to his real ability, and not chiefly because he is 'a good and safe Negro.'"[63]

If, as we have maintained, it was the Church's intention to pay lip-service to the idea of the extension of the Kingdom among its black constituents; if, indeed, the Church was desirous of maintaining temporal as well as spiritual control over blacks; if, indeed, the suffragan bishop scheme was seen as preferable to the missionary district scheme precisely because it would help to ensure that blacks would have little control over their own destiny; then it would follow that a black priest with a reputation for "rocking the boat" would have scant chance of election.[64]

Demby's lot was truly to be that of a "suffering bishop." The recipient of a meager stipend from the national Church, and dependent upon the capricious largess of white churchmen, he found himself in the position of being called upon to make bricks without straw. He suffered, too, from the strain of traveling over his vast geographical area and from the not-infrequent calumnies of racial injustice. In a letter, dated December 23, 1933, addressed to his friend and champion Bishop James Winchester, he wrote:

> I am now passing through deep waters and the waves are rough; at times they almost cover me—with the "cuts," "recuts" and still cutting by the National Council with my same expenses, cost of living, it is most trying and difficult, so much so that I am only existing, not living, but I take my lot patiently, saying all the while, it is as our Lord would have it. The mission of the Church of my people, especially in the Southwest, is not being supported.[65]

What is remarkable is that despite his trials and tribulations, Demby throughout his ministry remained unfeignedly loyal to the Church. In his first address to the diocesan convention in Arkansas he declared:

> The church has evidenced her belief in her catholicity as well as her practical conception of the great fundamentals of Christianity and American democracy in the election, ordination and consecration of two colored American priests as bishops in the Church of God—to do work among their people in this country. This makes it more and more clear that the Church is the church for all Americans. This is a new era in the history of the American Church. She has done the one great, big, right and needed thing.[66]

In his last address before the diocesan convention, immediately prior to his retirement, he was no less devoted:

> Notwithstanding the fact that the twenty years of service in the interest of the extension of the church among my people were years of personal sacrifices, handicaps, discouragements and misunderstanding, accompanied with doubts and fears within and without, I never took my eyes off the Cross of Christ, nor lost faith in Him who promised to be with the bishops and priests of the church until the end of the world.[67]

It is worthy of note that despite his heroic efforts, Demby, late in his ministry, argued persuasively that the missionary district plan, which had been proposed yet again shortly after his retirement, be abandoned:

> For twenty-two years I have been sitting in this House of Bishops, and this is the first time I have spoken; the problems brought before you have not been concerned, for the most part, with Negroes, but this matter does. If the request of the Fourth Province [the dioceses in the South] for a missionary district for Negroes is passed, it will be the greatest setback to our Negro work that it has ever had. We want Negro bishops, but as Suffragans working as assistants of the Diocesans, helpers of the Diocesans.[68]

Demby got his wish and more. For with the abandonment of the missionary district plan the idea of a suffragan for colored work disappeared as well. There was never again to be a "suffragan bishop for colored work." The next black bishop elected for wòrk in the United States was John Melville Burgess, as suffragan of Massachusetts, in 1962. Formerly archdeacon of the diocese, he became, as Demby had envisioned, suffragan bishop for *all* members of the diocese, black and white, and was later elected (as Demby perhaps could not have envisioned) diocesan bishop, the first black man to occupy such a position in the history of the Episcopal Church in the continental United States.[69] Perhaps even more significant is that there was not to be another election of a black priest to the episcopate in the South until 1993, when the Reverend Canon Antoine Lamont Campbell of the Diocese of South Carolina was elected suffragan bishop of Virginia.[70]

Parallels in Anglican Missionary Strategy

It would be instructive at this juncture to point out that the dilemma in which the Episcopal Church found itself was not unique in the Anglican Communion. Indeed, the idea of a racial episcopate and the convoluted theological reasoning that questioned the fitness of black men to exercise authority over white clergy and laypeople were factors that were present in the controversy surrounding the ministry of Anglicanism's first black bishop, Samuel Ajayi Crowther, consecrated in 1864 in Canterbury Cathedral to head the Diocese of the Niger. As Preston Hannibal observes, "He was forced to experience a subtle and often not so subtle racism that continually called into question the legitimacy of his episcopal orders."[71]

The African counterpart of the American black suffragan plan and the racial missionary district plan was the West African Native Pastorate Scheme, whose chief architect was Henry Venn, Honorary Secretary of the Church Missionary Society (CMS) from 1841 to 1872. The plan differed ostensibly in many respects from the American schemes for a racial episcopate, as one would expect. Whereas in Nigeria it was clearly Venn's intention to prepare indigenous clergy to assume, eventually, the pastoral oversight of the Church, virtually all of whose members were African, the American plan was born of a realization that mitred black men might assist in attracting or retaining black Episcopalians, a group always seen as a distinct minority in a predominantly white Church. The election of black bishops in the Episcopal Church, however their ministries were defined, was basically a concession, as we have seen, to the pressure of blacks who were desirous of recognition within the Church's hierarchy, or of whites who saw a limited episcopacy for blacks as a further means for their control.

A native, indigenous episcopate, therefore, as embodied in Crowther, was the principle upon which the entire movement depended. Venn saw Crowther's appointment as a means to the Church's complete organization and self-extension, much in the same way that proponents of a racial episcopate in the United States saw it as a means for the furtherance of the Kingdom among blacks. Venn's missionaries labored assiduously to bring to fruition his high ideals, which in turn had been endorsed by the CMS, but a new and rising race consciousness proved to thwart such progress.

David Hinderer, an English missionary in West Africa, was one of the first to register an objection:

> Not that I should have the slightest objection to Bishop Crowther being over myself and the congregation which God may give me. On the contrary, I can only respect and love him . . . but . . . *because God gives us influence as Europeans among them,* . . . if they hear that a black man is our master, they will question our respectability.[72]

This echoed an objection raised earlier, when Crowther had been proposed as bishop of Sierra Leone. Another CMS missionary, Henry Townsend, cautioned Venn: "Crowther will not be acceptable to us as such, and whatsoever opinion one may form of his personal worth, it will not do to make him a bishop."[73]

As a result of such reservations, the boundaries of Crowther's jurisdiction, as set forth in the royal license, were described as "the countries of Western Africa beyond the limits of the Queen's domains," namely "West Africa from the Equator to Senegal, with the exception of the British colonies of Lagos [Nigeria]; the Gold Coast [later Ghana] and Sierra Leone." As Hannibal observes: "This, in reality, meant that his see was to be set in an African region that had no established European colonies, which as we have seen, was a stipulation of his acceptance of the appointment."[74]

Venn, therefore, was frustrated in his efforts by the "conservatism of contemporary missionaries" whose increasing cultural imperialism brought the plan to ruins.[75] His grandiose plan was virtually dismantled by what Hayden calls "the triumph of racism and imperialism in the Western world... reflected by a rejection of black leadership throughout the Anglican Communion.... Bishop Crowther was gradually deprived of his authority and then humiliated by the CMS."[76] He was succeeded by a European diocesan bishop, and as a compromise two African priests were consecrated to serve as suffragans.

It is worthy to note that some 2,000 miles to the west, in the fledgling Diocese of Liberia, a remarkably similar pattern developed, although the object of the mistreatment was not a bishop. Alexander Crummell, who had been refused admission to General Theological Seminary in New York and had obtained his theological degree at Queens College, Cambridge, arrived as a missionary in Liberia only two years after the appointment of John Payne, a white missionary bishop from Virginia. The bishop feared that this articulate young black priest might have been sent to replace him, an idea that he thought would gain wide acceptance on the part of the indigenous clergy. Given the independence of Liberia, it was reasonable to expect them to gravitate to black leadership. Bishop Payne therefore urged his clergy to establish a *separate church organization* in Liberia, which would be under foreign control for forty years! This plan, similar in its intent to the Sewanee canon that would be proposed to Southern bishops three decades later, was rejected outright. This development set the stage for an ongoing conflict between Crummell and Payne, which resulted ultimately in Crummell's resignation from his post.[77]

The parallelism between the missionary strategies on both sides of the Atlantic is striking. Although, owing to contextual, political, and historical differences, the strategies played themselves out in different ways, they both could be seen as evolving from a school of thought dominated by a missionary strategy, according to which "people are best ministered to by ministers who share their language and culture; and that mission churches should become self-supporting, and in turn, evangelize other areas." What is more, such a strategy could be implemented because of the existence of "paternalistic, liberal and influential whites who believed that blacks were capable of providing episcopal leadership and that the time had come to attempt the experiment."[78]

The irony is that the motivations for such a strategy were well founded, for each virtually redefined the concept of the office of the bishop, especially as regards his jurisdiction and authority,[79] in order to accommodate the prevailing racial attitudes of the day. But it is essential to note that the change in heart on the part of the white power structures in both cases came about not because the movements failed, but because they showed signs of *succeeding*. Such success was seen by whites as an indication that their sense of inherent superiority was threatened or, at the very least, that they were no longer needed by those whom they had long deemed to be their inferiors, both morally and intellectually. When such threats became apparent, the very persons who had conceived of and implemented various schemes for a racial episcopate attempted (in some cases successfully) to stop such movements dead in their tracks. The maltreatment suffered by Bishop Crowther, resulting in large measure from the dismantling of the infrastructure that had supported his episcopate, is all too similar to the trials and tribulations later to be borne by his American cousin, Edward Thomas Demby.

But there is a further extraordinary parallel, which in many ways brings our discussion of the racial episcopate as understood by the Anglican Church full circle. The Episcopal Church consecrated two black bishops prior to the elevation of Demby and Delany in 1918. They were James Theodore Holly, consecrated in 1874 as missionary bishop of Haiti, and Samuel David Ferguson, consecrated in 1885 as missionary bishop of Liberia. Although both, like Crowther, suffered calumny at the hands of the mother church, and although both, victims of the racism and imperialism of the day, were succeeded by white bishops, their exemplary ministries helped to plant in the minds of black Episcopalians the idea that black bishops could and should be consecrated for the domestic church. Specifically, the seed was planted by the Reverend Paulus S. Moort, M.D., a West Indian ordained in the United States but who was working in Liberia at the time under Bishop Ferguson, who called for the election of black bishops in four or five American dioceses.[80] It was largely because Moort held up the examples of the black missionary bishops that the Conference of Church Workers among Colored People, beginning in 1889, eschewed their previously held objection to a racial episcopate. Formerly of the opinion that a request for a racial episcopate "would fall into the hands of those southern whites pressing for ecclesiastical segregation to match disfranchisement, segregation and economical peonage being structured in the South as a replacement for slavery,"[81] "they conducted a strong campaign to convince the Episcopal Church that the mission work among blacks would not develop until a black bishop was at its head."[82]

The Episcopal Church, therefore, it is reasonable to argue, as a result of its experiences with Holly and Ferguson (and the English experience with Crowther) might well have abandoned any further attempts at ordaining black men to the office of bishop. But the valiant efforts of those very men provided an impetus and incentive to black Episcopalians to replicate the missionary experiment at home. They believed that the experiment was necessary because "educated, self-respecting middle-class blacks to whom the Episcopal Church had a special appeal would not be drawn to a church which limited black achievement."[83]

It can be asserted, then, that while the Church tried to paint the pioneer black bishops as failures and did everything in its power to thwart their enterprise, black church leaders saw in them strong role models, who having succeeded in making bricks without straw had exhibited extraordinary grace under pressure. If black American bishops abroad could accomplish all this despite oppressive tropical heat and severe lack of resources, the conference reasoned, they should be no less successful on their native soil.

Chapter 6

West Indian Anglicans: Missionaries to Black Episcopalians?

Isles of the southern seas, deep in your coral caves.

—CHARLES E. OAKLEY (HYMN TEXT, C. 1860)

Were it not for the influence of West Indian Anglicans, the history of blacks in the Episcopal Church would have taken an entirely different course. It is clear that the black presence in the Episcopal Church, accounting for approximately 5 percent of its communicant strength,[1] would be, but for the West Indian influence, appreciably smaller than it is. Indeed, Bishop Quintin Primo, whose father was a priest from British Guiana, commented that if it were not for West Indians, there would be no black Episcopal Church to speak of![2] Even a cursory look at the major factors accounting for the West Indian presence among blacks in the Episcopal Church supports such a view. The first is that in the decades following the end of the Civil War, scores of West Indian students came to the United States at the invitation of American bishops, studied for the priesthood, and were ordained to serve black parishes both in the South and in the North. Second, there has been a steady influx of West Indians into the United States since the turn of the century.[3] Indeed, "by the 1920s, one fourth of Harlem's population was West Indian."[4] Since a substantial percentage of West Indian immigrants have been Anglicans, their coming to the United States has resulted in a swelling of the ranks among black Episcopalians,[5] and more particularly in a shift in the concentration of the black Episcopal population from the South to the North.[6] Last, West Indian clergy came to the United States in great numbers in the 1960s, 1970s, and 1980s. Most of them sought to fill vacancies in black congregations, of which there has historically been a plethora, owing to a dearth of African American vocations;[7] others came in response to specific calls to Episcopal parishes made up primarily of West Indian immigrants.[8] Today more than one-third of the active black Episcopal clergy were born in the Caribbean, the majority graduates of Codrington College, Barbados.[9]

But we would argue that the West Indian influence on the black Episcopal Church has been far more than numerical. Caribbean Afro-Anglicans came to the United States already steeped in Anglican faith and tradition. In 1910, the archdeacon of South Florida, commenting on "colored work" in his diocese, remarked, "Large numbers affiliated with the church's mission are from the West Indies where they have had most excellent church training; they desire the same here and especially for their children."[10] More recently, John Burgess observed that "the knowledge of the Church and loyalty of [West Indians] are unsurpassed. Centuries of Anglican tradition have produced a devout, intelligent and enthusiastic churchman that has no equal in the Anglican world."[11] West Indian immigrants were not dependent, therefore, upon the often halfhearted efforts of the Episcopal Church, described by a distinguished West Indian cleric as "lethargic, penurious and lacking in enthusiastic and united action,"[12] which as we have seen have characterized the evangelism of blacks. Moreover, to West Indians, who came from a church almost all of whose members were black, the idea that the Anglican Church was "a white man's church" was an alien concept.[13] These newly arrived Anglicans, constituting "for the first time . . . a body of aggressive, articulate, and concentrated Negro Episcopalians in Eastern cities,"[14] either sought out or, in many cases, founded Episcopal parishes. It can be argued that West Indians brought to their American cousins an understanding of Anglicanism that did much to shape the self-image, influence the strategy, and determine the destiny of black Episcopalians, which in turn has laid the groundwork for a long-term impact on the life of the Episcopal Church. As John Henry Edwards observes:

> A large segment in most all of the Negro congregations has consisted of people from the West Indies. Several of the early men were from the West Indian islands and through the succeeding years many of the leading preachers and church builders among Negro Episcopalians have been from this region. The West Indian laity have been well trained by the Church of England, and they possess a strong sense of the Anglican ethos, without the inhibitions of the American Negro.[15]

Not insignificantly, the West Indians' "Anglican ethos" has also been exhibited in the mode of worship of black Episcopalians. The fact that the worship style of most black congregations has been "high church" or Anglo-Catholic is directly attributable to the importation of such ritual and ceremonial from the West Indies, where, with the exception of Jamaica, such practices are *de rigueur.*[16] The leadership style of West Indian clergy was, perhaps, another aspect of that ethos: According to Canon Thomas Logan, a senior priest in the Diocese of Philadelphia, "West Indian priests didn't mingle with their people. This enabled them to be disciplinarians who challenged their congregations to uphold strict standards."[17]

It is not unreasonable to claim, therefore, that West Indian Anglican clergy perceived themselves as a unique grouping of missionaries—with all the negative as well as positive connotations of that term—to black Episcopalians. Describing West Indian Anglicans as missionaries is not to suggest that they were bringing the Gospel to those who had not previously been exposed to it. West Indians did not bring the Anglican *faith* to American blacks; rather, they brought a particular *understanding* of it, born of a significantly different cultural experience, as to how that faith should be lived out. In this connection, John Burgess observed that black Anglicans from the Caribbean, where they number some one million strong, have brought "to our fairly puny church life a wealth of experience, devotion and race consciousness, a basic strength and power, that not only will benefit our American church life but be a determining factor in the councils of the worldwide Anglican Communion." In a similar vein, Robert Bennett identified the increase in numerical strength of black Episcopalians caused by the immigration of black Anglicans from the West Indies as one of the developments that inspired hope, and encouraged solidarity among black Episcopalians, and emboldened them to fight for equality during the civil rights movement.[18]

We shall see this influence exhibited as we examine the nature of the West Indian/African American dynamic, and how this dynamic manifests itself in the relationships between the two groups. This issue is especially important since, although the cultural differences and resultant tensions between the two groups are facts of life with which blacks in American society in general and the Episcopal Church in particular are painfully aware, its significance is, by and large, lost on the majority of whites. As one historian observed: "For the bulk of white-skinned Episcopalians, any dark-skinned person was a Negro, and that was that."[19]

The strategy implemented by American bishops after the Civil War bore much fruit. Hayden presents us with the startling statistic that of the 203 black men ordained or received into the Episcopal Church between 1865 and 1918, 92 were born overseas, all but five of them in the Caribbean, principally the British West Indies. All told, West Indian clergy accounted for 45 percent of all black clergy during the period between the end of the Civil War and the outbreak of World War I.[20] Indeed, the first black man ordained in the United States after the Civil War was Joseph Sandiford Atwell of Barbados, priested by the bishop of Virginia in 1867, who became the first rector of St. Stephen's, Petersburg, the first black rector of St. Stephen's, Savannah, and later rector of St. Philip's, New York City.

Seen from the vantage point of supply and demand, the postbellum Episcopal Church, especially in the South, was at a distinct disadvantage. Only twenty-five black clergy had been ordained prior to 1865, sixteen of whom served as missionaries to West Africa, especially Liberia (the other nine, for the most part, were rectors of Northern parishes).[21] Partly as a result of the work of the Freedman's Commission, and partly as a result of efforts on the part of blacks to establish an independence within the life of the Church, several new black congregations had come into being (see chapter 2). The founders of these congregations, as we have shown, expressed strong preference for black leadership, which they saw as essential to their quest for self-determination. But there were simply not enough black priests available to staff black congregations.[22] Bishops, especially in the South, had previously done little to encourage black vocations, and indeed had often deemed blacks to be unworthy of the sacerdotal office, not infrequently keeping candidates in deacons' orders for inordinately long periods.[23] Indeed, "in that period it was not uncommon for Negro clergy to remain deacons throughout their ministry."[24] Now, given a sudden need for black clergy, American bishops found themselves inadvertent victims of their own racism. Faced with this dilemma, they looked for assistance to their English counterparts who headed dioceses in the West Indies.

But to explain the actions of white Southern bishops solely in these terms would be to give a facile explanation of a complex and fascinating chapter in the history of Anglican mission. For the invitations that American bishops extended to black West Indian students to come to the United States to prepare for the priesthood must be seen in broader perspective. While it is true, as Hayden points out, that the West Indies was a generation ahead of the United States in terms of emancipation,[25] this by no means meant that Caribbean blacks enjoyed the same rights and privileges as the English in the Caribbean. Although the British placed great emphasis on the education of former slaves, it was not their intent to equip blacks for positions of authority and governance in the colonial system; rather, they were concerned, at best, with enabling blacks to improve the lot of their own people. It must be remembered that although the freeing of West Indian slaves preceded

American emancipation by a little more than two decades, American independence preceded the independence of the former British colonies in the Caribbean by nearly two centuries. West Indian blacks, while free from slavery, were not free from colonial rule, and it was abundantly clear that the colonial powers were there to stay. The Church, established by the Crown, lest we forget, was no exception:

> The Anglican Church, which was favored by the establishment, saw their task as a *slow* process of civilizing black people. It adopted a cautious approach of giving any responsibility to black people . . . who were allowed to rise to the humbler positions of lay readers, catechists and of course, school masters.[26]

Such a policy, therefore, meant that there were virtually no vocational opportunities for black West Indians. Students at Codrington College in the last decades of the nineteenth century eagerly accepted the American bishops' invitations because they had little if any hope of ordination and appointment to cures in the West Indies. In commenting on the ministry of the Reverend George Plaskett, a West Indian priest who served as rector of Epiphany Church, East Orange, N.J., Bishop Burgess remarked:

> Although many of his West Indian brethren disparaged the American Church in comparison to their own churches, . . . they had to admit that at the turn of the century, when so many came to the States, the white West Indian bishops had refused to ordain their native men because they "were not ready." It was the American bishops who welcomed them and ordained them.[27]

In this connection, it is interesting to note that the reluctance of the West Indian church to admit blacks to the priesthood was exceedingly slow in changing. E. Don Taylor reports that as late as 1956 black West Indian vocations to the priesthood were discouraged. In that year,

> a Black Barbadian young man who expressed to his English rector the desire to enter the priesthood was told that he should remove the idea from his head because as far as he (the rector) could see into the future, there would always be an adequate supply of English priests for Barbados and so there would be no room for him.[28]

But it must be kept in mind that the American bishops were successful in attracting West Indian blacks because the ecclesiastical establishment in the West Indies, especially in Barbados, was involved at the time in an effort to send blacks to the African mission field, where it was hoped that they could help "civilize" and Christianize the African masses. The United States, then, provided another field of missionary endeavor to which Codrington-trained clergy could be sent. The Church in the West Indies, where, as Kortright Davis reminds us, "white churchmen held West Indians in general in low esteem," was eager to join the British effort to evangelize the "heathen" in Africa, believing that "the West Indies owed a debt to Africa on account of the Slave Trade." English clergy and prominent laypersons in the West Indies, therefore, seized the opportunity to deploy their own black missionaries to assist in the effort, because they believed "that the mission of West Africa would be peculiarly suitable to the church in the West Indies where the population consists so largely of persons deriving their origins from that part of the continent."[29]

The movement was described as both "an act of charity" and "an act of reparation."[30] Nevertheless, as was the case with a similar effort launched in the United States (see chapter 7), the West Indian attempt to evangelize Africa was initially launched "in connection with the colonization scheme, which proposed to repatriate to Africa a certain number of the released slaves." Alexander Crummell reports that to further the cause of the Christianization of Africa, Barbados was heavily involved in this movement. He writes that by the 1860s, many Barbadians, most of them Anglicans, responded to an invitation from the president of Liberia to join blacks from the United States who had settled in the colony.[31]

In 1851, three missionary societies were established in Barbados for the purpose of sending missionaries to Africa. The Barbados Church Society declared in its charter that "it would especially become Barbados to be forward in this great and good work." The African Mission prayed that the "Lord of the harvest would send forth laborers disposing also the members of the West Indian Church to unite in the work of others in England to assist it." And the West Indian Church Society came into being for the "furtherance of the Gospel in Western Africa in connection with Codrington College." Credit for bringing the plans to fruition goes to the principal of that venerable institution, the Reverend Richard Rawle, who had also been instrumental in supplying black ministerial candidates for the Episcopal Church. But Africa was his first love. So committed was he to the idea of African mission that he later instructed that he be buried on the top of Society Hill on the Codrington estate in St. John's Parish, Barbados, so that in death he could, as it were, look across the Atlantic to Africa. He said of the movement: "We look from our windows towards that dark land, and she seems to stretch out her hands to us today and say, 'Come over and help us.'" Rawle, who had been a pioneer in the movement to educate freed slaves, provided, at the request of William Hart Coleridge,

Barbados's first bishop, "the requisite accommodation on the grounds of Codrington College for the reception of missionary students to be trained for missionary work," thus giving form and substance to the Rio Pongas mission.[32]

The first candidates for the mission were white West Indian natives. But in 1842, Archdeacon William Parry of Barbados, who was later to succeed Coleridge as bishop, suggested "that Exhibitions be provided at the College for candidates for Holy Orders — men of colour who would go to the Coast of Africa."[33] This provision was soon thereafter implemented when it was decided, following the deaths of several white priests, that only black clergy would be sent to the Rio Pongas.[34] The dispatching of black missionaries marked the beginning of the mission's most successful period. Eventually, it boasted fourteen black clergy, seven mission stations, and no fewer than 1,000 natives who had embraced Christianity. Black West Indian missionaries, through whose "agency many souls have been translated from the kingdom of darkness into the kingdom of light," also succeeded in translating the New Testament and the Book of Common Prayer into the Susu language.[35] It should also be pointed out that the Rio Pongas mission became, by default,

> the only white-controlled mission in Africa to be manned by an all-black staff. The consequent developments in this mission were quite different from the patterns established in its predecessors. In the absence of local European leaders, European-West Indian conflicts which had been found in the earlier experiments were non-existent.[36]

The early migration of West Indians to the American church, therefore, must be seen in light of this broader development. In the eyes of all parties concerned — both the West Indians themselves and the whites who recruited them — the West Indians were seen as missionaries. Although the church establishment in the West Indies saw their own former slaves as well as those in the former colonies to the north as just one step removed from the lot of the "uncivilized" masses on the Western coast of Africa, they would clearly have rated West Indian blacks a notch higher.[37] The American church establishment, for its part, perceived West Indian blacks as superior in education, intellect, and refinement in comparison to the prospective ministerial candidates in their dioceses, especially in the South. As Hayden observes: "These West Indians were generally very much applauded, and were much sought after by [American] bishops because they were well-instructed, strong, zealous Anglicans."[38] The West Indians themselves, flattered perhaps by the opinions of both English and American bishops, believed themselves to be missionaries particularly suited to minister to their "less fortunate" American cousins, but for an entirely different set of reasons. If they regarded themselves as better equipped than American blacks, it was not because they felt that they were innately or biologically superior. Rather, they believed that their superiority stemmed from their Englishness. Having been immersed in an educational system predicated on the concept of the British *imperium,* which stressed the inherent superiority of the English over the rest of the world,[39] black West Indians could embrace such a view not only in relation to American blacks but to all Americans, regardless of color. "Without the inhibitions of the American Negro," according to Edwards, "they have spoken and acted boldly for recognition in the Church's life."[40] It has been suggested that this is due to the fact that "the Afro-West Indian has somewhat misguidedly, always felt that he was a free man in the West Indies. Today, in the United States, he has numbed himself into believing that he is as free as any white American."[41]

In this connection, Taylor's comment is instructive:

> Each succeeding West Indian generation became further removed from its background.... They were taught to eschew those things that were African and to adhere to those things which were British. They were brainwashed by a religious and educational system which was totally English, they fell prey to an almost total eradication of their own background. West Indians emerged as a new breed of Black people with a strong love for, and indeed, a mastery of the English way of life which has caused many an Englishman to marvel.[42]

The attitudes of such West Indians, then, was in many respects virtually identical to white Englishmen's views of American culture. Indeed, the West Indian has been likened to "a black Englishman who either is ignorant of or just finds it more convenient to ignore his own African roots [who] negates his blackness and stands aloof from the American black." Such a West Indian, Taylor further argues, is an understandable result of the fact that

> the West Indian Church developed in a geographical area of small island communities cut off from the colonial center of action by thousands of miles of sea. This provided a favorable unit for complete indoctrination. ...The result was that all the decadent practices of nineteenth century English life were transplanted to the West Indian colonies with increasing success.... The people of the West Indies, who were ninety percent Black, were reared for generations on a colonial system which carefully patterned every aspect of life on that of the English, and packaged it

> in so skillful a manner that everything worthwhile had to be English or white, and everything contrary was just bad.[43]

There is virtual unanimity among writers — Afro-American, Afro-Caribbean, and white — that out of the Caribbean historical and cultural crucible have emerged black West Indians who had certain assumptions about their place in American society. Specifically, according to Raphael, "ambition, education and pride are three words dear to [the West Indian's] heart; and since he is hung up on these three words, he sometimes accuses Afro-Americans of having no ambition, wishing no education, and possessing no pride."[44] Such attitudes inevitably created a situation in which tensions developed between Caribbean and the American blacks with whom they lived cheek-to-jowl in the United States. Clarence Coleridge, the first of two Caribbean-born bishops in the American Episcopal Church, shared the following reflection at a gathering of Afro-Caribbean clergy in the United States:

> I was trained, and in most West Indian families, I know it was the same, to be upwardly mobile. One knew that one could make it. One perhaps knew that one had to go abroad to get, as they said, your papers — higher education, but one had the confidence that one could succeed. And I suppose that is responsible for the sense of arrogance which many West Indians are accused of. You always *knew* you could make it.[45]

Although West Indian colonialism was no less racist a system than its North American version, the inculcation of Britishness, accepted uncritically by black West Indians, made it possible for them to believe that class was a more important determining factor than race. West Indians "were accustomed to class rather than colour consciousness, and were particularly insulted by the American colour bar; Negro Americans had long been forced to accept it."[46]

West Indians found it difficult to comprehend, therefore, the virulent and overt forms of racism that they encountered in the United States. Henderson Brome, a native of Barbados who is the rector of an Episcopal parish in Boston, observes:

> The native Black held an inferior status in American society and therefore [for the West Indian] to assimilate within the black community would inevitably mean acceptance of a lower status. Secondly, the unfavorable reception which the West Indian immigrant received from the black community impaired any possible relationship with these two groups to the point where interaction between them became virtually non-existent.[47]

It is not surprising, therefore, that West Indian immigrants, believing there to be a cultural divide between them and black Americans, have often tended to segregate themselves into their own ethnic groupings, maintain West Indian churches, societies, cricket clubs, and other groups, and "not least of all, strived to retain their British accents."[48] Such behavior may well have been reflective of the historical fact that "African cultural survivals were much more common in the West Indies, where new Africans continually reinforced their homeland cultures,"[49] resulting in a distinct cultural difference between West Indians and American blacks.

Understandably, then, West Indians have been accused of importing their culture — lock, stock, and barrel — to American shores without due regard for the fact that they have joined the ranks of an already extant culture of blacks who have a peculiar history — a history from which West Indians have historically distanced themselves. As Taylor describes it:

> Not least of all the problems is the apparent failure of the West Indian to appreciate and respect the agonies and injustices which white people have for so long perpetrated against black people of this country, which have rightly created an angry people who have a strong sense of urgency about recovering their God-given rights at all levels in American society.[50]

Such a phenomenon prompted Lennox Raphael to suggest that "there is obviously a need on the part of the West Indian who comes to the U.S. to put himself in the place of the African American; share the burdens and lend his shoulders to the pressing struggle for equality for all, and understand the minority status of Afro-Americans."[51] In a similar vein, Haynes further suggests that each group has characteristics from which the other can benefit: "The West Indian needs the resourcefulness, stamina, skill and sense of humor of the Afro-American. The Afro-American needs the daring, the independence, the pioneering spirit of the West Indian."[52]

Another source of tension between West Indians and American blacks has been that the economic success that has characterized the experience of the West Indian immigrant "has not always been accompanied by a readiness to establish fertile and mutually constructive linkages with their brothers and sisters who are native to the U.S."[53] The fact remains that one of the principal reasons for Caribbean migration to the United States for the last 150 years has been economic.[54] As Davis observes:

> Hundreds of thousands of Caribbean people have migrated to North America to seek their fortune and to provide sustenance for their relatives in the home region. Most of them have managed to thrive well in the United States. As with other immigrant groups, Caribbean people

in the United States have generally acquitted themselves industriously and have tended to make full use of their educational and economic opportunities.[55]

These data bear especial relevance to the early West Indian clergy who like other immigrants came to the United States to improve their lot. While they were not averse to the idea of being perceived as missionaries by those who dispatched them or those who received them, they came primarily to seek a self-advancement afforded by the black presence in the Episcopal Church and opportunities in the broader society. Such possibilities for advancement were, as we have shown, totally absent in the West Indies.

A further source of tension between the two groups has been ignorance of and often reluctance to learn about each other's common struggles. "Each group has been occupied with its own problems, oblivious to the fact that many of these are mutual problems which stand a better chance of being solved if the two groups could get together and work towards a common good."[56] Historically, both groups have failed to recognize that they share a common heritage in slavery, and that the solution to the problems arising out of the historical tensions are found in recognizing that basic similarity.

But the recognition of that similarity has been, for West Indians, elusive, because the commonalities have not always been readily apparent. While racial oppression and the injustices of slavery were no less in evidence in the West Indies, West Indian slaves, it can be argued, experienced a psychological advantage over their North American counterparts. The fact that they constituted an overwhelming majority of the population afforded them the luxury of believing that the island that they inhabited was *their* island, on which the slaveholder was an interloper. By extension, the Anglican Church was *their* church, even though administered by whites. While righteous indignation on the part of African Americans was by no means nonexistent, it was an indignation predicated on the perception of being *denied access to the power of the white majority,* whereas West Indians' indignation was predicated on the belief that their *birthright had been taken away.* Thus, when in the 1960s independence came to the Caribbean islands, and West Indians assumed control of the Church's affairs,[57] there was a sense in which they believed they were coming into their rightful inheritance, not merely assimilating into, or being accepted by the majority culture.

It would be unreasonable to expect that such tensions, epitomized perhaps by the "bitter, personal and regrettable controversy between

...Marcus Garvey (a Jamaican) and Dr. W. E. B. Du Bois (an African American) over the merits and de-merits of the rival programs of the UNIA and the NAACP,"[58] should be absent in the Episcopal Church, in which those steeped in a West Indian brand of Anglicanism and those whose Episcopal faith grew out of the peculiar racial and social realities of the United States found themselves worshipping at the same altar. Not surprisingly, then, West Indians in the Episcopal Church have often been seen as having "a blind fanaticism for the Anglican Church, her rituals, hierarchy... while ignoring how these things apply in everyday American life."[59] Indeed, the Episcopal Church, for black West Indian immigrants, "provided a central meeting place for old friends.... Religion and the church are the last bulwark of the Negro immigrants' traditional system;... the churches keep alive the traditions of the homeland."[60]

Perhaps it was this high visibility of West Indian Anglicans in the United States which led E. Don Taylor to postulate that for the past 150 years there has existed a stark dichotomy in the black population of the Episcopal Church.[61] He comments: "A black person who finds a spiritual home in the Episcopal Church today falls roughly into one of two categories. We either have our Judaeo-Christian roots in the West Indian Anglican Church, or we are converts from one of the Black American churches."[62]

Taylor's contention is grossly incorrect. All black Americans who are Episcopalians are not converts from a black denomination. There are, in fact, many black Episcopalians whose families have been members of the Episcopal Church for generations. Hayden cites the existence of several families — both in the North and in the South — who were "cradle Episcopalians" and who had been in the Church for generations. The Braggs themselves were prime examples. The grandmother of George Freeman Bragg Jr. was Caroline Bragg, who had been a house slave to Episcopal clergy, and who at her death was hailed in the press as the "mother of the colored church in Petersburg, Virginia." Bragg, whose life and ministry was greatly influenced by his grandmother, wrote in 1899 that he "never knew the time when I was not a member of Christ and a child of God."[63]

Other such families include the Russells — James Solomon who founded St. Paul's College, Lawrenceville, Virginia, and his descendants; and the Bishops, Hutchens Chew and his son, Shelton Hale, whose combined rectorships at St. Philip's, Harlem, comprised sixty years. The Logans of Philadelphia boast three generations of clergy spanning a period from the late nineteenth century until the present, as do the Middletons of Mississippi.

These examples are important because they demonstrate that black Episcopalians do not constitute a new phenomenon. Booker T. Washington's comment notwithstanding, there are many African American families who have never known a church other than the Episcopal Church, and whose religion, therefore, has never been "tampered with." Taylor's comment, then, in its inaccuracy, betrays a belief on the part of West Indians that they are Anglicans by birth, even by right, whereas black Americans are Anglicans by "adoption and grace." This attitude has doubtless contributed to the historic tensions between those two groups in the life of the Church, tensions that are to be found between the same groups in American society at large.

Most West Indian clergy in the United States moved within a world that amounted to a transplanted culture, learned to live within the American racial system, and indeed prospered within it. They built up power bases centered on strong black congregations. Henry Laird Phillips, "an energetic, patriarchal Jamaican," who was archdeacon for colored work in the Diocese of Pennsylvania and rector of the Church of the Crucifixion in Philadelphia, is a prime example. W. E. B. Du Bois refers to the Church of the Crucifixion as the religious institution as "the most effective church organization in the city for benevolent and rescue work" and attributes its success entirely to Phillips.[64]

When Phillips began his ministry in Philadelphia in 1875, there were only two "colored" congregations, historic St. Thomas', and Crucifixion. He oversaw the transformation of Crucifixion from a moribund mission to a thriving parish that sponsored several outreach programs including a savings bank, a center for the homeless, and Philadelphia's first gymnasium for blacks, which later grew into the Christian Street YMCA. Crucifixion became the center of black cultural life in Philadelphia, and was the home of the American Negro Historical Society, of which Dr. Phillips was a founding trustee and treasurer. After founding two other black congregations in Philadelphia — St. Simon the Cyrenian and St. Augustine's — he accepted, at the age of 65, an appointment as archdeacon for colored work for the diocese in which position he prospered for eighteen years. Upon his retirement, there were eighteen black congregations in Philadelphia. Phillips died in May 1947, two months after his 100th birthday.[65]

Another example was Edmund Harrison Oxley Sr., who served as rector of St. Andrew's Church, Cincinnati, from 1912 to 1958.[66] Born in Trinidad in 1881, he emigrated to the United States, where, like so many of his fellow West Indians, he sought to obtain the best education available. He was graduated from Howard University with B.A.

and B.D. degrees, where he earned prizes in Hebrew and debating; and from Harvard University with an S.T.B., where he won the Billings Prize in Elocution and Pulpit Delivery. Under Oxley's leadership, St. Andrew's made the transition from mission to parish status, and moved into a new church building. Striving to provide opportunities for empowerment and uplift in the black community, Oxley initiated cultural, educational, health, and social activities at St. Andrew's in addition to providing a spiritual home for blacks. The St. Andrew's Settlement School of Music, the first black Boy Scout troop, and St. Andrew's Day Nursery were among those programs. In the wider Cincinnati community, Oxley was a member of the boards of the Juvenile Protective Association, the Negro Civic Welfare Association, and a trustee of the Evangeline Home for Colored Girls.[67]

Oxley's influence, however, was by no means confined to Cincinnati. In June of 1934, he submitted a seven-point program for the Church's work among Negroes, which called for the appointment of a joint commission of the General Convention to advise the National Council on Negro Work. It asked for the appointment of a Negro priest as executive secretary. The seven-point program was presented at the sixth Triennial Conference of Church Workers in October 1937. The General Convention of that year adopted the program, virtually in its entirety. This led ultimately to the appointment of Archdeacon Bravid Harris as secretary for Negro work.

To this list could be added such men as J. DaCosta Harewood from Barbados who served parishes in Florida and Pennsylvania; Edgar C. Young, a Jamaican, who distinguished himself as a professor of Old Testament at the Philadelphia Divinity School; E. Sydnor Thomas, from the Virgin Islands, who was rector of St. Barnabas' Church, Germantown, Philadelphia, for 50 years, and Kenneth dePoullain Hughes, a native of Grenada, distinguished rector of St. Bartholomew's, Cambridge, Massachusetts, a strong advocate for civil rights, and a founder of the Union of Black Clergy and Laity.

It should be pointed out, however, that many West Indian Anglican clergy who could not make an adjustment to the new American paradigms of race and class found the Episcopal Church untenable. It was a source of great disappointment for them not to be accorded the prestige and respect they thought was their due as Anglican priests. They quickly discovered that their race, and not their class, intellect, or professional status, determined their deployment and preferment. It soon became apparent that the black parish, which many had seen as "a foot in the door," became, in effect, a "stained-glass ceiling," the only arena in which they were permitted to exercise their ministry.

Taking these factors into consideration, and believing that there was no possibility for uplift and self-esteem for blacks within the Episcopal Church system, many became missionaries in the West Indies, Africa, England, or South America, joined other denominations, or entered other professions, often exercising bivocational ministries. Nathaniel Joseph Durant from Barbados, after serving parishes in Pennsylvania, became dean of the theological college in Haiti. John Love, a Bahamian, earned a medical degree and migrated to Haiti as its first medical missionary. Paulus Moort, from the Virgin Islands, also became a physician, and migrated to Liberia, where he practiced medicine while rector of Holy Trinity, Monrovia. Another Barbadian, D. Augustus Straker, escaped the racism of the Episcopal Church and affiliated with the AME Church. He earned a law degree at Howard University and became Michigan's first black judge.[68]

Perhaps one of the most striking examples of this group is a Trinidadian, Arnold Hamilton Maloney.[69] Upon graduation from General Seminary in 1910, he served St. Philip's, Annapolis, Maryland, and St. Philip's, Indianapolis. He clashed with parishioners in both places who regarded "religion as a plaything and the church as a playhouse," and gradually became disenchanted with the Episcopal Church. Various experiences with his parishioners and his bishops led him to believe that he had little future in the Episcopal Church. Maloney, therefore, made a radical vocational transition and was graduated from the University of Indiana Medical School and obtained a Ph.D. in pharmacology from the University of Wisconsin. He later became a professor at the School of Pharmacy at Howard University.

George Alexander McGuire and the African Orthodox Church

Others built upon the self-determining theology as articulated in the black missionary episcopate plan, and defected to the African Orthodox Church (AOC). The AOC was founded by George Alexander McGuire, a distinguished West Indian priest who migrated to the United States in the late nineteenth century. While strictly speaking McGuire and his cohorts became schismatics, we would suggest that their actions were different more in degree than in kind from those of the catholic-minded black clergy who advocated for a black missionary district, and for this reason McGuire's odyssey provides us with an example through hyperbole, as it were, of the West Indian's experience in the Episcopal Church. Indeed, as White observes, the AOC "moved out of the Episcopal Church though it always remained within the Anglican ethos."[70]

Both the advocates of the missionary district plan and the founders of the AOC sought a catholic church in which color would not be a barrier to advancement in the Church; a church in which blacks would not be second-class citizens; a church that would be an ally to blacks who sought self-empowerment. Black clergy who stayed in the Episcopal Church during this period never really achieved parity with their white brethren; they could not exercise their ministries among whites; and they could not reasonably expect to be elevated to the episcopate. The colored convocation system, by then institutionalized in Southern dioceses, severely limited their orbit, effectively cutting them off from the decision-making bodies of the Church. The catholicity achieved was no greater than that which was heralded by Bragg and Demby[71] — that is, the conferral of the dignity of the priesthood (and, by 1918, in the two instances of suffragan bishoprics for colored work, the episcopate) on colored men, and a recognition of their orders. But that sacramental recognition did not carry with it a sharing of power in the governance of the Episcopal Church.

Whereas other denominations split prior to the Civil War over the race issue, effecting a *fission,* the Episcopal Church split internally following the Civil War, causing a *bifurcation.* Black Episcopalians constituted a church within a church, or to use McGuire's term, *"ecclesiola in ecclesia."*[72] McGuire and those who defected to the AOC founded instead an *altera ecclesia,* with all the benefits of the catholicity enjoyed by the faithful remnant in the Episcopal Church, with the important added advantage of also being self-determining. The AOC, described in one of its liturgies as "the portion [of the Church] which thou hast graciously planted among our race," would, according to its constitution, be controlled by Negro members though open to all races, a characteristic, it will be noted, that parallels the founding principles of St. Thomas', Philadelphia.[73] McGuire, who had sought in vain for *auctoritas* as well as *potestas* within the structure of the Episcopal Church, at long last got his wish "to dwell under his own vine and fig tree."[74] His departure was presaged in his comment in 1907:

> What the distant future may accomplish in the way of obliterating racial lines in State, in Church, or in Society, is no very grave concern of ours. The fact cannot be denied that at present there must be total cleavage — complete separation — all along these lines, if we desire peace, success, and full development of all parties.[75]

Even a cursory study of the life of George Alexander McGuire provides us with significant insights,[76] not only into the nature of the AOC but, more particularly, into the West Indian Anglican's quest for catholicity. A native of Antigua, McGuire was baptized in the Church of England (to which his father had belonged) but became an adherent of his mother's Moravian faith, attending that church's theological seminary on St. Thomas, in the then–Dutch Virgin Islands. After serving as a Moravian pastor on neighboring St. Croix, he returned to Anglicanism in stages, first serving as an AME minister in the Virgin Islands. After emigrating to the United States in 1894 at the age of 28, he was confirmed in St. Matthew's, Wilmington, Delaware, and was ordained deacon in 1896 and priest a year later by the bishop of Southern Ohio. Partly due to the mentorship of Henry Laird Phillips (see chapter 5), his rise through the ranks of the Episcopal Church was almost Ambrosian.[77] After ordination, he served the rectorships of St. Andrew's, Cincinnati; St. Philip's, Richmond; and St. Thomas', Philadelphia, the historic parish founded by Absalom Jones. In 1905, he accepted a call to the Diocese of Arkansas as archdeacon for colored work.

The experience in Arkansas proved to be pivotal in McGuire's development, but he was ambivalent about accepting the post. On the credit side of the ledger, he was anxious to demonstrate that blacks in the Episcopal Church could excel under black leadership; on the debit side, however, as Burkett observes, "he would be subjecting himself to the racial mores of the deep South at a time when relations between the races were growing steadily worse. Moreover, he would be forced to work under the eccentric Bishop William Montgomery Brown," who took pride in a particularly virulent form of racism, and who was later deposed for his espousal of Darwinism and Marxism.[78] McGuire was successful in Arkansas; he founded ten missions for black Episcopalians and brought several hundred blacks into the fold; but the circumstances under which he was forced to work proved to be insufferable. Matters came to a head in 1908 when he was forbidden to make his report in person to the diocesan convention. McGuire saw this as an outward and visible sign that his color would be a barrier to full participation in the life of the Church. As White observes:

> McGuire had learned two things from his Arkansas experience. First, that Negro suffragan bishops or archdeacons could never have full authority if the white diocesan bishops wished that authority to be limited. Second, that [Bishop Brown] who had seemed most sympathetic to Negro aspirations was actually moved by strange and erroneous doctrines of race.[79]

McGuire, having until then defended the suffragan bishop plan as a means of working within the system, "converted" to the missionary district plan, likening the resultant relationship between blacks and whites as "two rails of the track, parallel [to] each other throughout the journey, supporting the same train, without meeting at any point."[80] He further avowed: "Unless the Church shall provide race bishops for work among their people, she will never reach nor influence more than a few hundred Negroes in each Southern State."[81] In a statement reminiscent of an observation made by an early West Indian immigrant that "the outstanding contribution of West Indians to American Negro life is the insistent assertion of their manhood in an environment that demands too much servility and unprotesting acquiescence from men of African blood,"[82] McGuire believed the racial attitudes and social conventions of the day would render it impossible for a white bishop to be anything but patronizing:

> My manly dignity, my self-respect, my whole nature, intellectual, social and spiritual yearns for a bishop of my own race who, besides giving me godly admonitions, will enter into my life as he alone can, and who is not prohibited from intermingling in every way, with me and the congregations committed to our charge.[83]

Although disheartened, McGuire did not leave the Episcopal Church when he left his position in the Diocese of Arkansas. He doubtless attributed part of his problem to the fact that as an archdeacon responsible to a white bishop he would be forever frustrated in his efforts to empower black Episcopalians. He sought, therefore, to return to the parish, where he believed he could exercise some autonomy. Accordingly, in 1909, he accepted a call to St. Bartholomew's, Cambridge, Massachusetts. McGuire's coming to St. Bartholomew's followed an interesting, and somewhat amusing turn of events. Its membership had been drawn from St. Peter's, Cambridge, where blacks comprised a significant minority. When their numbers increased, and they desired that their children receive religious education, the white rector established separate Sunday school classes for blacks and whites. According to Edwards, "one of the Negro laymen, Mr. John S. Brown, protested to the rector about the matter and stated that unless segregation was abandoned, 'we would be compelled to seek a church home of our own,' to which the rector replied, 'For which, let us pray.'"[84]

The black communicants asked the bishop for permission to form a parish; they were denied that privilege, but were encouraged to worship at St. Bartholomew's, a moribund congregation with only a handful of white parishioners, which had originally been established for poor immigrants from the Canadian Maritimes.[85] Once outnumbered, the whites left, and turned over the parish to the black newcomers. The new blacks rejected a plea from the incumbent rector that he continue as their pastor, insisting on black leadership.[86] Enter George Alexander McGuire.

Upon arrival at St. Bartholomew's, McGuire went about his work with characteristic assiduity, increasing the membership more than tenfold after only a few months in his new position. Despite its numbers, and the fact that the congregation was able to support itself, the Diocese of Massachusetts turned down St. Bartholomew's petition for full-fledged parish status.[87] McGuire looked upon this development as the proverbial last straw, and left the congregation two years later. After a two-year stint at the Episcopal Church's New York headquarters as field secretary for the American Church Institute for Negroes, he returned to the West Indies.[88]

It was at the time of this final sojourn to the Caribbean (during which he pastored an Anglican parish in his native Antigua) that McGuire became aware of the Universal Negro Improvement and Conservation Association (later the Universal Negro Improvement Association and African Communities League or UNIA) founded by Marcus Garvey, a Jamaican journalist, orator, and social reformer committed to the uplift of the black race. "The largest mass-based protest movement in black American history... [the UNIA] rejected the racist assumptions of much of white American Christianity, namely that God had created the black man inferior and that He had intended Negroes to be a servant class, 'hewers of wood and drawers of water.'"[89] The embracing of the ideals of that organization, in which McGuire served as chaplain-general, was to signal the beginning of the last chapter of McGuire's spiritual journey. Upon his return to the United States, he almost immediately affiliated himself with the Reformed Episcopal Church, and established, under its aegis, a black congregation, the Church of the Good Shepherd in New York City. Inspired by Garvey's vision, McGuire later led his congregants into the Independent Episcopal Church, intended to be a black branch of the Episcopal Church, analogous to the AME relationship to Methodism. This was to be only a transient status, however, for by 1921 McGuire, taking Garvey's inspiration to what could be called the next logical step, had established the African Orthodox Church. After appealing to the offices of Old Catholic bishops to ensure a valid apostolic succession, he became bishop, and later Patriarch (Alexander I) of the new church.[90]

McGuire's quest was complete. His restlessness, if we can call it that, was one shared by his colleagues and namesakes George Freeman Bragg and George Frazier Miller. All three Georges were troubled by the incongruity between the Episcopal Church's claim that it was catholic and its practices, which belied that claim. But while Bragg and Miller and many African American clergy strove to challenge the Episcopal Church to live up to its ideals,[91] the same nagging inconsistencies drove only McGuire to found his own church. Why was this the case?

In the first instance, the West Indian Anglican population, some of whom were disaffected with the United States in general and the Episcopal Church in particular, provided for McGuire a ready-made constituency for the nationalistic, self-government gospel that he espoused. The fact that the AOC's primary appeal was to West Indians in the Episcopal Church is significant, for it points first to a basic difference in ethos between the West Indian and the African American. For West Indian immigrants, unlike African Americans, assimilation was an alien concept. A central West Indian coping mechanism, developed in response to a largely hostile, unaccepting, and distrustful environment in the United States, was always to identify, even after raising children and grandchildren, with the island from which they came. Like those in exile in Babylon, they found it difficult or, at least, less than beneficial to sing their song in a strange land. That is, West Indians may well have discovered that vis-à-vis the white community, they had much to gain by differentiating themselves from black Americans, much in the same way that members of the black elite sought to differentiate themselves from less-educated, less-sophisticated migrants from the rural South. The AOC, then, provided for West Indians a living reminder of their spiritual as well as cultural roots. In contrast to African Americans, West Indians had *chosen* to come to North America to make a better life, and they therefore retained the psychological and physical possibility of leaving those shores, if and when that proved desirable. Affiliation with the AOC assisted them immeasurably in this process. That church became one of those precious intangibles to which they, unlike their African American brothers and sisters, could lay claim: "West Indians in Harlem always seem to have precious things that others around them wanted but usually didn't have — most important, a faraway 'home' to retreat to when America balked on its promise."[92]

It is interesting to note in this connection that the AOC "spread to the West Indies, where it never had much success, and to Cuba, where it had a little more, and from the start, had a parish in Nova Scotia."[93] Since the AOC was predicated in part on reinforcing the cultural roots of a group in exile, it would follow that it would not flourish in the West Indies itself, where it would be considered an ecclesiastical as well as societal redundancy. It also follows that it would be somewhat successful in Cuba (where many West Indians had migrated to work on sugar plantations). Although the largest island in the West Indies, it was a Spanish-speaking (and largely Roman Catholic) country where immigrants from the British (and largely Anglican) islands would find a need to provide for themselves both the spiritual and cultural reinforcements afforded by the AOC. It should be noted, too, in light of recent historical developments, that the AOC had a major impact in South Africa, where its message of self-determination had wide appeal.

Signs of Rapprochement between West Indians and African Americans

Moreover, the fact that the AOC had attracted West Indians almost exclusively suggests major differences between the ecclesiologies of the two groups.[94] As White observes: "West Indian militants had always looked to independence with their own social structures run by themselves; Negro Americans looked more to acceptance in a common American way of life." Apparently, this difference in temperament would hold equally true in the Church, which has historically exerted more influence on blacks, both Afro-Americans and Afro-Caribbeans, than any other single institution. Thus, "it can be understood that when McGuire began his new church the West Indians, or some of them, pulled out of the Episcopal Church while the native-born stayed put."[95] But among those West Indians, who like native-born African Americans stayed put and did not follow McGuire, most used the Episcopal Church as a vehicle to preserve their unique cultural characteristics.[96] If the black Church, then, as McGuire suggested, was an *ecclesiola in ecclesia,* we would suggest that the West Indian church was, and to a certain extent still is, an *ecclesiola in ecclesiola in ecclesia;* and this phenomenon has contributed considerably to the tensions between African American and West Indian Episcopalians to which we have alluded:

> Ethnicism has its difficulties.... Love for national origins and culture can mark a withdrawal from the real world of here and now; aloofness above the currents that sweep through our neighborhoods; a refusal to be part of the local scene and its troubles. The love for Prayer Book offices, plus reminiscing about Church life in Barbados or Jamaica, are not always conducive to committed involvement in the American community.[97]

Clarence Coleridge, in no uncertain terms, warns his fellow West Indian clergy who are in the employ of the Episcopal Church against this all-too-prevalent tendency to isolate themselves from the problems of the African American community:

> You can't enjoy the sweetness, the salary, the advantages of living in America while at the same time standing aloof and superior from the

> problems of the people you face, whether the problems are in the parish or in the neighborhood or the problems of Black people here or the problems of a sociological, political, or economic nature in this country. It's all God's world. He's concerned. You're God's priests. You've got to be concerned. You can't keep saying, "Well, this is not home for me." If you are earning a living here, well it is home while you are here. And if you really understand the socio-economic positions of the world in a more than just a superficial manner, you'll understand that everywhere is home.[98]

White is quick to point out, however, that the alleged aloofness of West Indians is not the only factor that has contributed to the existence of a "great gulf fixed" between the groups. Equally culpable have been African Americans who have exhibited hostilities born of xenophobic resentment:

> The West Indian has been accused of being a black Englishman who negates his blackness and often stands aloof from the American black. ... To many black Americans, the West Indian comes across as arrogant, selfish, class-oriented, and at times hypocritical in that he is quick to speak about his glorious Anglican heritage, but too often his pocket is slow to respond with corresponding enthusiasm.[99]

Such enmity has often manifested itself in a kind of internecine warfare:

> There were Negro Episcopal parishes where West Indian immigrants were as unwelcome as European immigrants would have been in certain white Episcopal parishes. In the year that McGuire formed his church there was one particularly notable row, "Wealthiest Negro Church [St. Philip's, Harlem] in Throes of Dissatisfaction,"[100]

in which a Jamaican curate was threatened with dismissal by his African American rector, allegedly because the former had been, as it were, too successful in evangelizing Harlem's West Indian community, thereby threatening St. Philip's American-Caribbean "balance." The parallels between that development and the concern by white Southern Episcopalians after the Civil War that admitting blacks to the Church would effect an undesirable shift in power are as instructive as they are painful.[101]

Some successful attempts have been made in recent years to ameliorate the relationships between the two groups. The Afro-Anglican movement has done for black Anglicanism what the Pan-African movement has done for blacks in general — that is, to stress commonality of purpose among Anglicans throughout the diaspora. Davis, commenting on the first Conference on Afro-Anglicanism, proffered the following:

> [Afro-Anglicanism] proclaims a level of solidarity that was based on common experiences and expectations quite unique and unprecedented in the history of Anglicanism.... Afro-Anglicanism constitutes a radical affirmation of an underlying awareness which has been hitherto assaulted by that overpowering tradition of the British ethos. Anglicanism has traditionally encouraged its adherents to emphasize who they were not, theologically and liturgically. It has not actually encouraged much affirmation of who they were culturally. It is with the emergence of... statements about their theological, existential and intercultural solidarity, that Afro-Anglicans have broken new ground in forging a new form of consciousness and identity.[102]

The Reverend Enrique Brown, a native of Panama of West Indian parentage, dared to suggest that blacks together must "re-invent the church... to re-think what it means to be God's people in this time and place." He further accuses his fellow West Indian clergy of an unwillingness to do so, "because we have had the whole thing handed to us in a mold by missionaries."[103]

Resolutions passed at the Caribbean Anglican Consultation held in Arlington, Virginia, in 1990 put forward some correctives to those sources of tensions that have strained West Indian–American relationships. Among the strategies adopted by Caribbean clergy were the following:

- to take the initiative and bear the burden of understanding our Black American brothers;
- to uphold the Union of Black Episcopalians and use that instrument to build bridges and to be the forum for our mutual concerns and goals;
- to empower the American clergy with the insights which have been the commonplace experience of Caribbean clergy who have had a people-focused ministry;
- to keep open the lines of communication, keep up the dialogue, however complex that may be.[104]

In such suggestions, the perception of West Indian Anglicans as missionaries to black Episcopalians has been transcended. While acknowledging the unique gifts that West Indians bring, the sense of superiority and aloofness, now recognized as counterproductive to the common struggle, are being replaced with full acknowledgment of the unique gifts of African Americans in a common enterprise. Seeds have been planted in the hopes that a heightened cooperation between Afro-Caribbeans and Afro-Americans might come into flower.

Chapter 7

Black Episcopalians as Missionaries to Africa

Where Afric's sunny fountains roll down their golden sand

—Reginald Heber (hymn text, 1819)

The American bishops (and their predecessors in office) who invited West Indians to come to the United States to serve black congregations had also encouraged those few black clergy ordained prior to the Civil War to serve in the mission field in West Africa. Indeed, as we have noted, sixteen of the first twenty-five black priests ordained in the United States were thus deployed, principally to Liberia.[1] The African Mission School (AMS), based in Hartford, Connecticut, was established for that very purpose,[2] and was preparing black Episcopal clergy and laypersons for the African mission field during roughly the same period that Codrington College was dispatching West Indian missionaries to the Rio Pongas mission. The AMS is worthy of note because it is representative of an important period in missionary endeavor. The story of both its founding and its premature demise tells us much about how the Episcopal Church viewed its sense of missionary obligation in the early nineteenth century.

The African Mission School Society, as it was officially known, was founded "to establish and support a school for education of free persons of color, who have attained the age of 18, and who can read the English language with facility and can write, and have acquired knowledge of the rules of common arithmetic,"[3] with a view to their becoming missionaries, catechists, and schoolmasters in Africa.[4] It was not its intention to undertake missionary activity per se, or to determine the Church's missionary policy. Its founders were content to leave those responsibilities to the Domestic and Foreign Missionary Society (DFMS),[5] "in whose wisdom and zeal the most entire confidence is reposed."[6] The AMS's connection to what we would dub "the circular missionary route" is seen in the fact that the society was founded not at the behest of the DFMS but in response to an urgent plea from the Church Missionary Society (CMS). The CMS, committed to African

…, but mindful of the fact that so many of England's own
…n victim to tropical disease, articulated a need for black
…which was based, to put it more charitably, on a theology
…diency. Edward Bickersteth, secretary of the CMS, wrote
to Bishop …illiam White of Pennsylvania on October 25, 1826, asking his assistance in procuring "persons of colour . . . who would be willing to devote themselves wholly to labour in Africa to diffuse the Gospel."[7]

The document containing the record of the proceedings of the African Mission School Society, recognizing receipt of Bickersteth's correspondence, read in part:

> Letters have been received from the CMS in London, declaring that they anxiously looked to this country for a supply of pious, intelligent and active men of colour for the service of Africa, to a number of whom they are prepared to give immediate and ample support. They have been convinced . . . that the constitution of the white man cannot long endure in the climate of that country. . . . There is a loud call then, throughout the world for African missionaries. How is this deficiency so universally and deeply felt to be supplied? The question admits of but one reply. Pious and intelligent young men must be selected from our numerous African population, and trained up for service in a mission school.[8]

Jonathan Mayhew Wainwright, rector of Grace Church, New York City,[9] and vice-president of the society, suggests in another document that another "universally and deeply felt" desire to send African Americans to the mission field was born not only of a wish to provide "suitable" missionaries, but of a desire to remove free blacks from a society that had no place in its polity or economy for blacks who were no longer in shackles. Moreover, he seems to have been concerned with the preservation of the white race, which many believed to be in danger of decimation in the event that freed blacks became too numerous.

> Emancipation is the cry. But it is the language of ignorance. Emancipation at the present day is an impossibility. . . . Suppose them [Southern planters] all willing at any moment to give up their slaves. What is to be done with them? Where are they to be sent? They would be the immediate destruction of the white population and the first intelligence we should have be an earnest summons *to go and save our brethren, of our bone and flesh, from the horrors of universal menace?* . . . A beginning has been made; and we have full reason to hope that the country from which the parents were cruelly torn may receive the children into its bosom. The colonizing of Africa is our only hope. *It is the only means by which a drain is to be made to carry off our surplus coloured population.*[10]

The AMS, then, while founded in response to an appeal from the CMS to provide personnel for its mission in Sierra Leone, quickly shifted its focus to Liberia, in order to be of greater service to the Episcopal Church. As Liberia had also become the principal focus of activities of the American Colonization Society (ACS), the AMS's concentration on Liberia meant that it would be furthering the ACS's goals as well: "When we observe how judiciously [Liberia's] foundations have been laid under the able and persevering direction of the agent of the Colonization Society, whose disinterested and successful experts are worthy of all praises we cannot esteem our anticipation in any degree extravagant."[11]

The AMS was, as Burkett described it, "a short-lived effort."[12] It was also a particularly ill-fated one. In its 1830 report the board of directors stated that its attempt to "select from our numerous African population, pious and intelligent young men" had yielded in a two-year period only six students.[13] That same year, two of the school's students, Gustavus V. Caesar and Edward Jones, a graduate of Amherst College, were ordained by Bishop Thomas C. Brownell of Connecticut. Caesar went with his wife to Liberia, but died three years later; Jones relocated to England, but later became a CMS teacher and missionary to Sierra Leone from 1831 until 1864. Another student, William Johnson, went to Liberia as a catechist and schoolteacher, and died within weeks of his arrival.

Jacob Oson, also an alumnus of the AMS, was ordained deacon by Bishop Brownell of Connecticut on February 16, 1828, and priest the following day. He was slated to go to Liberia as a missionary but died in Connecticut shortly after his ordination, immediately before he was to set sail for Africa. Bishop Brownell, addressing the convention of the Diocese of Connecticut in 1829, remarked:

> In my last address, I stated to you that the Rev. Jacob Oson, a man of colour, had been admitted to holy orders, with a view to missionary services in the colony of Liberia, on the coast of Africa. The ardent hopes of usefulness which he had cherished were frustrated by his death as he was about to embark for the scene of his labours. By this disposition of divine providence the first efforts in our church in the cause of foreign missions has been defeated. May it operate as a salutary trial of our faith and patience and stimulate in us renewed exertion in so holy a cause.[14]

It should be pointed out, however, that several missionaries who had been duly trained and prepared by the AMS were found unworthy for missionary work. The screening committee of the DFMS "voted to revoke its connection with Jones, the Caesars, and the Johnsons," so that when they did go to Africa "they no longer had the imprimatur of the Domestic and Foreign Missionary Society."[15] Such actions on the part of the Episcopal Church would suggest that the Church did much to thwart the very project it had inaugurated. Reasons given for the disqualification of prospective candidates for the mission field would suggest that the Church seemed entirely unwilling to make allowances either for the rudimentary education with which many of the candidates were equipped, on the one hand, or their enthusiasm and willingness to serve, on the other. Thus Caesar was deemed, despite certification of the AMS, to be "not sufficiently well-prepared for the profitable exercise of ministry," and Johnson was found to be "utterly destitute of those qualifications." Mrs. Johnson was found unsuitable because of a "want of attachment on [her] part to the mode of worship of the Protestant Episcopal Church."[16] But there might well have been another, deeper motivation for such actions on the part of the screening committee. Although there had been much fanfare about sending blacks "back" to Africa because they were uniquely suited to ministry to Africans, there was still a desire for whites to exercise control, and therefore "there was hesitancy within the Foreign Committee about initiating the work through the agency of a nonwhite Episcopalian."[17]

The failure of the school, which its founders often claimed was due to the fact that blacks were unaware of its existence,[18] has been more accurately attributed to Negroes' prejudice against emigrating to Africa, especially under the auspices of the ACS, with which the Episcopal Church identified, and to masters' unwillingness to allow their slaves to be educated.[19] On this latter point, it is true enough that the AMS's demise was hastened by the fact that in 1831 a Convention of Free Blacks, held in Philadelphia, demanded the establishment of a Negro college in New Haven. White residents of Connecticut were angered at such a prospect, which "led to a call for a prohibition against the instruction of free Negroes in the State."[20] This action was indicative of the attitudes of many whites of the period, including the founders and administrators of the AMS, who were pleased to support efforts to underwrite the studies of blacks for service abroad, but not for service at home.

Indeed, Wainwright's comments in a sermon delivered before the DFMS on the subject of missions in general, and the AMS in particular, are particularly instructive. Although he cites the ills of slavery he eschews emancipation as a corrective and suggests instead that its remedy lay in taking the Gospel to Africa:

> As loving brethren, as faithful citizens, as true and benevolent Christians, we should unite, heart and hand, wealth and wisdom, enterprise and prayer, to avert the evils, to redress the injuries, to remove the disgrace consequent upon the introduction of Slavery into this western world. To talk of any general or immediate emancipation to the injured sons of

> Africa, except the freedom which Christ can give, is to talk language, the origin of which is ignorance, the consequences of which are cruel suffering to our brethren and friends. The freedom of Christ, then, let us proclaim to Africa, and let it be our determination that her sons shall enjoy it. And let her sons too be its heralds. Africa must be civilized and Christianized by Africans; but in America must the work be prepared.[21]

Most free blacks of the period, however, were loath to enroll in such schools because completion of the course "meant immediate emigration to Africa."[22] This was seen as undesirable since the overwhelming majority of former slaves wanted to taste the fruits of their newfound freedom in the United States, and were not anxious to cast their lot with Africans in a land with which, their roots notwithstanding, they were totally unfamiliar. As one African American historian commented, blacks were wary "of giving up the known quantity for the unknown."[23] Moreover, while some blacks felt that true equality in the United States was an elusive goal, and were willing to emigrate, most felt an obligation to labor in the United States on behalf of their brothers and sisters still in bonds. Meeting in Philadelphia in January 1818, only one month after the founding of the ACS, blacks "denounced the goals of the Society and stated that they would not abandon their brethren to slavery."[24]

It must be understood that the Church's efforts to send blacks to Africa as missionaries was the ecclesiastical version of the colonization movement, which had been gaining momentum since the early nineteenth century. And it would appear that the willingness to accept the tenets of the ACS was a criterion that weighed heavily in the DFMS's screening process. Edward Jones, one of the few priests who was an alumnus of the AMS, was prevented from serving in the mission field because of a question of his "loyalty to the cause of Liberia *and to the Colonization Society with which the mission school was so intimately associated*,"[25] that is to say, because of his antislavery opinions. The colonization movement was motivated by an unwillingness of the part of whites to live as equals with blacks as well as a fear on the part of whites that "a steady increase in the Negro population would result in a reversal of the roles of master and slave."[26]

Indeed, Benjamin Silliman, an apologist for the colonization movement, in an address entitled "Some Causes for National Anxiety," opined that the greatest danger to American society from the existence of slavery was not miscegenation, but the likelihood of insurrection by the slaves, aided and abetted by the large free black population. The best solution, therefore, according to the prevalent view of the period, was a wholesale removal of free blacks to their "native climate" of Africa, where they could carry out Christian teachings to that continent's "rude race of men."[27] Even President Lincoln would later see it as "a viable solution to mass emancipation." The ACS, whose founders, board members, and other prime movers were disproportionately Episcopalian, was formed to execute this plan, believing that "this course would atone for the evil of the African slave trade, help put an end to slavery, restore the Africans to their divinely ordained homes, and to help civilize Africa."[28]

The plan came under attack, it should be noted, by radical abolitionists, notably William Lloyd Garrison, who argued that far from putting an end to slavery, that pernicious institution was made even more secure by the ACS's attempts to remove free blacks from the United States. Moreover, the plan allowed for masters to free slaves with the proviso that they be sent to Liberia, effectively removing the potential for any influence they might have had on the free black population on American soil.[29] William Watkins, a free black from Baltimore, who has been credited with influencing Garrison on this matter, was eloquent in his objection to this enterprise:

> It appears very strange to me that those benevolent men should feel so much for the condition of the free coloured people, and, at the same time, cannot sympathize in the least degree, with those whose conditions appeal so much louder to their humanity and benevolence. Nor, is this all: we are apprised that some of the most distinguished of that society, are themselves, Slaveholders! Now, how those men can desire so ardently, and labour so abundantly, for the exaltation of the free people, thousands of whom they have never seen, and feel so little concern for those who are held in bondage by themselves; whose degraded condition is directly under their observation, and immediately within the sphere of their benevolence to ameliorate, is a philanthropy, I confess, unaccountable to me. Indeed, I have thought that a philanthropic slaveholder is as great a solecism as a sober drunkard.[30]

It can be asserted, then, that the Church's missionary enterprise was more than a version of the secular movement toward colonization. It was seen as its necessary complement. Thus Wainwright could assert:

> To make colonization effectual, it is not sufficient that the arts of civilized society be carried to the new country. The Gospel is essential. ... Civilization, without Christianity, is valueless.... Now where is Africa, dark, degraded, ignorant Africa? Where is it to obtain this blessed gift? How shall they hear without a preacher, and how shall they preach except they be sent? How shall they be sent except by our exertions?[31]

The churches' exertions toward this end were legion. Regardless of doctrinal or denominational allegiances, religious bodies were bound and determined to "introduce the Gospel to Africa... with civilized and Christianized free black Americans, who would not only carry the word but would also serve as role models for the natives."[32] Such a well-developed theology of compensation was common to virtually all missionary movements in the nineteenth century. It was complemented by a theory of expiation, which in many ways was a theological justification for the expulsion of blacks from the United States and their "return" to the so-called dark continent, much as an earlier, equally suspect theology was invented to justify blacks' forced removal *from* Africa in the first place. It is instructive to compare the two sides of this specious theological coin. James Habersham, a seventeenth-century Virginia planter, could justify slavery by theorizing:

> I once thought it was unlawful to keep Negro slaves, but I am now induced to think that *the Gospel may have a higher end in permitting them to be brought to this Christian country....* Many of the poor slaves in America have already been made freemen of the heavenly Jerusalem and possibly a time may come when many thousands may embrace the Gospel and thereby be brought into the glorious liberty of the children of God. These and other considerations appear to plead strongly for the limited use of Negroes.[33]

Two centuries later, in an impassioned defense of the colonization/ missionary movement, which was seen as both a favor to the black missionaries and as a means to atone for the cruelties of slavery, Wainwright denounces his forebears for their rape of the African continent, pleading all the while a Christian responsibility to "return" black slaves to their so-called native soil:

> I can almost feel reconciled to the thought, that our forefathers unjustly and cruelly tore these hapless people from their homes and brought them to our shores. *If we can send them back with the Gospel of Christ, and thus give them, as a reward for their extorted labours and long continual sufferings, the pearl of great price, our guilt will be lessened, and our condemnation will be taken away.*[34]

It would appear that the determining factor in each case was the locus of the Gospel. The importation, sale, and exploitation of slaves in the United States were justified because it was in America that the Gospel, Christianity, and civilization were presumably to be found. Slaves' exportation to Africa was justified because it was alleged that having been Christianized and civilized they should share these gifts with those still in Africa, whither the Gospel needed to be sent.

Supporters of the AMS went to pains to show that the organization was motivated by only the purest of Christian ideals, which were "not shackled with the *political* chimera of removing three millions of people from their country and their home." Their motivation, instead, was to be seen as fulfilling the Dominical injunction to preach the Gospel to all nations:

> We owe this continent heavy debt for the injuries which have been inflicted upon it by our forefathers; and how can we better repay it, than by sending blessings of civilization? The graves and tears and blood of millions of her children have been wrung from that unhappy land, by the rapacious cruelty of the white man, and of the white man bearing the name of Christian, but disgracing its character as a religion and violating its principles. *Let those, therefore, who have been brought to a better state of mind, be earnest in the work of repatriation.*[35]

It is clear upon examination of the data that the ACS's repatriation scheme and the churches' enthusiasm in dispatching black missionaries to Africa shared the same goal, namely the prevention of blacks from any possibility of effective participation in church and society. The powers-that-be believed that it was as chattel that blacks had served their usefulness to society. "Free black," therefore, became to many in the white majority a contradiction in terms. Similarly, the Church had evangelized the same slaves conditionally; had made it clear on more than one occasion that the freedom that baptism bestowed bore no resemblance to freedom within the broader society; and had used religion as a means of control of the slave population. Therefore, it was entirely consistent that the Church saw fit to assist American society in further limiting the influence of blacks in the American religious arena by removing them to a church and country of their own, separated from white religion and society by 4,000 miles of ocean. Such thoughts were uppermost in the minds of church leaders in the United States, England, and the West Indies, who undertook the monumental task of dispatching freed blacks to "Afric's sunny fountains" under the pretense that they were best equipped to "deliver their land from error's chain."[36]

In this connection, it is interesting to note that the Episcopal Church, whose policies often mirrored those of the political establishment, in 1831 was the first denomination to send freed American blacks to the African mission field. Indeed, the Church was cited at the end of the century for having "done more than any other denomination in lifting the heathen into civilization and Christianity."[37] One of the first African Americans to have a long and successful ministry in Liberia was not a priest but a laywoman, Elizabeth Mars Johnson Thomson, whom we have already discussed in reference to the difficulties she encountered as she sought to become a missionary. She and her husband, William Johnson, sailed to Liberia in 1833. After William's death, Elizabeth married another emigré, James Madison Thomson (a native of British Guiana who had studied in England and lived in New York), who had come to Liberia during the previous year at the behest of Peter Williams Jr., rector of St. Philip's Church. The Thomsons operated a mission school for boys and girls in Cape Palmas. Of their work, the Department of Missions commented:

> God has signally blessed our Mission in raising up such servants. In their self-denying labors, he sends over a voice to the church at home, for the prayer of faith, for persevering effort, for great self-denial and greater consecration of money, body and soul to the great work of Africa's redemption.[38]

Such unbridled praise notwithstanding, William Johnson, who in 1834 had been appointed colonial secretary, was removed both from the mission and from the roll of candidates for holy orders in the Diocese of Connecticut owing to an accusation, never substantiated, that he had seduced both colonial and African girls. Dunn suggest that the charges had racial overtones, having been "made in the socio-political context of white missionaries' disputing colonial authority—leadership having been transferred from the white governor to the first black governor."[39] Upon Thomson's death in 1838, Elizabeth, satisfied that her husband's deathbed reconciliation with the Church had helped to clear his name, resumed service to the mission. She was later dismissed, however, for reasons not entirely clear, by the Missions Board. But after an urgent plea in which she said that the committee's decision "has thrown me into deep anxiety and regret" and that "I have not felt that I could conscientiously engage anywhere else,"[40] she was reinstated. Upon her return to Africa, Elizabeth Thomson took up a position at the Mount Vaughan Mission High School in Cape Palmas, where she served until her death in 1864. After her funeral, she was eulogized in *Spirit of Missions* as "a consistent Christian, a faithful Christian teacher, and a constant friend ... to all friendless persons, ... particularly ... orphans and little children."[41] All told, Elizabeth Thomson served in the African mission field for thirty-three years, a period of service matched by only one other American missionary to Africa.[42]

The Thomson affair, both in the vilification of James and the humiliation of Elizabeth, underscores the tensions that existed between white and black Episcopalians in the Liberian mission field, which mirrored black-white relationships in the Church in the United States. It is extremely ironic that the Liberian mission should have been plagued by such problems, since both the colony and the Church's mission had been founded, in theory, to provide an arena in which black Americans could experience autonomy, both spiritual and temporal, among members of their own race. But it would appear that the same persons who were motivated to send forth and empower the African American missionaries could not resist the opportunity to follow them to the field in order to continue to exercise control. Three white clergymen — Thomas Savage, who was also a physician; John Payne; and Launcelot Minor — were recruited from the Virginia Theological Seminary in 1836 and sent to Liberia. In his commission Savage was challenged:

> The great aim of your mission is toward the native African. You are sent to establish a mission which seeks nothing less than the Christianizing of Africa.... There is, we believe, something of awakened supplication throughout the church in favor of Africa and her benighted children.[43]

Dean Arthur Holt observes that this document is fraught with assumptions typical of nineteenth-century missionary enterprises. The four characteristics that he enumerates are the cultural ("white man's burden"); religious (Christianity's uniqueness not being shared by Africans); role assumption (America having a moral debt to Africa because of slavery); and most important, racial (that administrative control of the mission should be in white hands).[44] It is this last characteristic we wish to emphasize, as it was to have a less-than-salubrious effect on the service of African American missionaries. John Payne, the only member of the original trio to have a protracted ministry in Liberia,[45] and who served as bishop from 1851 to 1871, believed that the mission of the Church, *"under the direction of white men,"* was to "elevate the colonists and natives together, and prepare them for the enjoyment and civilization and Christianity in the community."[46] Payne clashed with Eli Worthington Stokes, first sent to be his assistant in 1841. He called Stokes "insubordinate and utterly lacking in judgment and efficiency." As a result of those difficulties, he fired Stokes and reported that he had strengthened his conviction "as to the suitability of getting any qualified colored agency directly from the United States."[47] In an attempt to reverse the very policy under which black missionaries were sent, Payne then advocated for indigenous Liberian clergy, a group without the "arrogance" of American blacks, over whom he felt he could exercise more control.

The most famous Episcopal missionary of the period was Alexander Crummell. After having been rejected for admission to the General Theological Seminary, he sought and received the support of Bishop Alexander Griswold of Massachusetts. He served congregations in Rhode Island and Pennsylvania. He started a mission in Pennsylvania but resigned in protest of the fact that he was excluded from the diocesan convention. He went to England where he was well received and given a curacy. He was graduated from Queens College, Cambridge, in 1853, and left shortly thereafter for Liberia. Crummell, as has been previously noted, was an exemplar of the tenets of the ACS.[48] Lukson E. Ejofodomi, in describing the mindset of this most prominent black Episcopalian missionary, comments:

> Because of the intensity of his belief in the uniqueness of Christianity and the universal application of Christian values, Crummell felt that the thrust of missionary concern went beyond the spreading of the truth. The main thrust of missionary work "in every heathen land" according to Crummell, "is reconstruction of society." The task of reconstructing society meant that the bodies and souls of the Africans were to be redeemed. But the altruism of the missionary concern of the rebuilding of society was tinged with a spirit of condescension. This spirit of condescension was rooted in the nineteenth century Protestant missionary movement. Crummell inherited this spirit, or more accurately was a product of the missionary tradition.[49]

Crummell, to whom civilization and Christianization were virtually synonymous, believed that civilization "never springs up, spontaneously in any new land. It must be planted."[50] Moreover, Crummell, whom Hayden describes as a "cultural nationalist,"[51] believed in the special adaptability — physical and temperamental — of the black American. Evangelization, to Crummell, was dependent upon "men of like sentiments, feelings, blood and ancestry." For the propagation of the faith, he held, "the main lever and agency must be indigenous." Crummell brought two other strongly held beliefs to his work. First was his theory of Providential Design, which "saw African-Americans as an elect race who had been exposed to Christian civilization, tested by the 'sorrow, pain and deepest anguish of slavery,' in order that they could take civilization to Africa"; second was his firm conviction that the time was ripe for the continent to be "reclaimed for Christ."[52]

But more than that, Crummell believed that the Episcopal Church was particularly equipped for the task of converting the Liberians: "There is a place for the Episcopal Church in Liberia. The doctrine, discipline and polity of the Episcopal Church are special needs of the people of Liberia. There is a peculiar work for souls in this country, for which the Episcopal ritual and regimen are specially fitted."[53]

Although Crummell's ministry in Liberia was fraught with problems, which had to do both with his contentious relationship with Bishop Payne and his ongoing feud with the ruling elite class of mulatto Americo-Liberians, Crummell nevertheless laid a firm foundation for an indigenous church, which ultimately led to the consecration of Samuel David Ferguson, who had been born in Charleston, South Carolina, and reared in Liberia, as Payne's successor. Both Crummell and Stokes consistently challenged Payne's paternalistic stance. Like George Alexander McGuire, they wanted an autonomous, black-run church, "under their own fig tree," and resented the fact that the Episcopal Church was the only denomination in Liberia still under foreign control. In July 1864, they sent an open letter to the bishop, which declared in part, "We came to this country hoping to find one spot on earth, where an American black man could entertain feelings of self-respect. It is our right in this land as well, ecclesiastically and politically, and we cannot yield it."[54] Inspired by James Theodore Holly and with the support of Bishop Crowther of Nigeria, Crummell tried to establish an independent church, but the effort failed when the Episcopal Church's Board of Missions withdrew its financial support.

There is a touch of irony that can be detected as we examine this peculiar circular missionary route that linked Africa, the United States, England, and the West Indies. Owing to the racism, imperialism, and triumphalism of the day, the Episcopal Church in the U.S.A. found itself in a situation in which it was bereft of a supply of black pastors when it needed it most. Because the Church had warmly embraced the colonization movement and had exported most of its early black priests to the mission field, priests who might have served in American parishes and who would likely have fostered the vocations of other blacks were not available. American bishops, therefore, had to go, mitre in hand, as it were, to the West Indies in order to replenish the ranks. But, it must be remembered, blacks were forthcoming from those "isles of the Southern seas" not because there was a glut of black clergy in the Caribbean, but because the British ruling class in the West Indies, for its part, had labored to ensure that the Church of England parishes in the Caribbean would remain the preserve of white English clergy. To this end, it siphoned off black men to serve as missionaries to Africa. They were, we may surmise from the enthusiasm with which they received requests from American bishops, equally open to the possibility of black West Indians serving in the United States.

It is instructive to examine the legacy of this missionary strategy. Today, 130 years later, there are no black American priests in West Africa. The Episcopal Church in Liberia, having transferred to the jurisdiction of the Province of West Africa in 1982, is no longer a missionary diocese of the American Episcopal Church.[55] Moreover, it is now served entirely by indigenous clergy.[56] The Church in the Province of the West Indies, since the independence of Caribbean nations a generation ago, "is firmly in the hands of the descendants of those whose very existence was grossly despised less than a century ago because of their African ancestry."[57] In the United States, "there has been a reticence . . . to ordain blacks because they were considered inferior morally and intellectually [which has] existed well into this century,"[58] causing, in turn, the discouragement of several generations of black vocations.[59] What is more, the Church has historically practiced overt discrimination in the deployment of those blacks who were ordained. Partly as a result of these factors, the Episcopal Church's pattern of importation of West Indian clergy, and more recently of African clergy, has, of necessity, continued apace.

Conference of Church Workers among Colored People, St. James' Church, Baltimore, 1916. Dr. John R. Logan Sr. (*top row, second from left*); Archdeacon Delany (*second row, third from left*). (*Source:* Collection of the Reverend Thomas W. S. Logan Sr.)

The Right Reverend Bravid Washington Harris, secretary for Negro work, 1943–46; consecrated bishop of Liberia, 1946. (*Source:* Logan collection.)

The Right Reverend Dillard Brown, consecrated bishop of Liberia, 1961.

Provincial Conference for Workers among Colored People, Philadelphia, 1939. At center is George Freeman Bragg Jr., secretary of the conference. To his right, with cane, is Archdeacon Henry Laird Phillips. (*Source:* Logan collection.)

The Seventh Triennial Conference of the Church Workers among Colored People, Kansas City, Missouri, October 1940. Bishop Edward Thomas Demby is seated seventh from left. (*Source:* Logan collection.)

Three generations of priests: The Reverend John R. Logan Sr. (*Source:* Logan collection); the Reverend Thomas W. S. Logan Sr. with the Reverend Thomas W. S. Logan Jr. (*Source:* Paul Smith.)

The Venerable Henry Laird Phillips (1847–1947), the "energetic, patriarchal Jamaican" who founded several black congregations in the Diocese of Pennsylvania. (*Source:* Logan collection.)

The Right Reverend Edward Thomas Demby, consecrated "suffragan bishop for colored work" in the Diocese of Arkansas and the Province of the Southwest in 1918, and his wife, Mrs. Antoinette Riggs Demby. (*Source:* Logan collection.)

Summer school at St. Augustine's College, 1950. Dr. Tollie Caution is in the first row, second from left. To his right is the Reverend Dr. Odell Harris, warden of the Bishop Payne Divinity School. (*Source:* Logan collection.)

Graduates of the Bishop Payne Divinity School at an alumni gathering, c. 1930. (*Left to right*): Fr. Alonzo King, Meade Memorial Chapel, Alexandria, Va.; Fr. Jackson, Coatesville, Pa.; Fr. Boyd, Gordensville, Va.; Fr. D. W. Grice, warden, Bishop Payne Divinity School; the Venerable James D. Russell, principal, St. Paul's School, Lawrenceville, Va.; Fr. George Freeman Bragg Jr., St. James', Baltimore; Fr. E. E. Miller, St. Stephen's, Petersburg; Fr. John Logan, St. Simon's, Philadelphia; Fr. R. M. Perry, St. Luke's, Columbia, S.C.; Fr. Jeffers, Charles Town, W.V.; Fr. Kent, Blackstone, Va. (*Source:* Logan collection.)

The Right Reverend John Melville Burgess, first black diocesan bishop in the United States. (*Source:* Paul Smith.)

The Reverend Pauli Murray, first black woman ordained priest in the Episcopal Church. (*Source:* Janet Charles.)

Black bishops of the Episcopal Church at a symposium in Santo Domingo in 1990. (*Standing*): Herbert Thompson, Southern Ohio; Richard Martin, retired suffragan, Long Island; Cornelius Wilson, Costa Rica; Orris Walker, Long Island; Henry Hucles, late suffragan of Long Island; Clarence Coleridge, Connecticut; Arthur Williams, suffragan, Ohio; E. Don Taylor, Virgin Islands; James Ottley, Panama. (*Seated*): Telesforo Isaac, Dominican Republic; John Walker, late of Washington; Barbara Harris, suffragan, Massachusetts; John Burgess, retired, Massachusetts; Quintin Primo, retired suffragan of Chicago; Jean-Rigal Elisée, retired, Gambia and the Rio Pongas; Herbert Edmonson, assistant, Central Florida (former bishop of Jamaica). (*Source:* Paul Smith.)

Presiding Bishop Edmond Lee Browning at the annual meeting of the Union of Black Episcopalians in Miami, 1987, with (*l. to r.*) the Reverend Jesse F. Anderson Jr.; Dr. Deborah Harmon Hines, national president; the Reverend Richard Chang, assistant to the presiding bishop; and the Reverend Canon Kwasi Thornell, Washington Cathedral. (*Source:* Harlee Little.)

The Rev. John Henry Edwards and members of the boys' choir of St. Luke's, New Haven, Easter, 1940. It was not uncommon for the Union Jack to be prominently displayed in parishes whose members came from the British West Indies. Fr. Edwards wrote several articles on the history of black Episcopalians. (*Source:* Archives of St. Luke's Church.)

The Right Reverend Orris G. Walker Jr., bishop of Long Island. He became the first black priest in the United States to be elected directly into jurisdiction (i.e., without having first been elected suffragan). (*Source:* Paul Smith.)

The Most Reverend John Maury Allin, presiding bishop, 1973–85, acceded to several requests made by the UBE, which resulted in increased participation on the part of African Americans in the life of the Church. (*Source:* Bachrach.)

Diane Marie Porter, senior executive for program at the Episcopal Church Center and vice-president of the Domestic and Foreign Missionary Society.

Dr. Charles Radford Lawrence, first black president of the House of Deputies.

The Rt. Rev. Barbara C. Harris, Bishop Suffragan for Massachusetts, the first woman consecrated bishop in the Anglican Communion (*Source:* Paul Smith.)

The Rev. Canon Harold T. Lewis and Mrs. Lewis present a copy of *Lift Every Voice and Sing* to the Most Rev. Robert Runcie, archbishop of Canterbury, Lambeth Palace, London, 1984. (*Source:* Paul Smith.)

Part Three

Contenders for the Gospel

Chapter 8

Renewed Efforts to Evangelize African Americans

Fling out the banner! Let it float.

—George Washington Doane (hymn text, 1848)

With the dawn of the twentieth century, the Episcopal Church continued to show limited concern for its black constituency. The Protestant Episcopal Freedman's Commission to the Colored People had been established immediately after the Civil War (and underwent two name changes, becoming known as the Commission on Work among Colored People, and then simply the Commission on Negro Work). Despite the outlay of funds from the Board of Missions,[1] the deployment of missionaries, and the erection of schools and churches and other efforts, in 1900 the commission could claim only 15,000 blacks among the Episcopal Church's faithful. Dissatisfied with the meager results of four decades of what it deemed to be concentrated missionary endeavor and, indeed, experiencing a "sense of shame for shortcoming and inadequate work"[2] among blacks, the Church dissolved the Commission on Negro Work in 1904.[3] Then, after commissioning a study on the subject, it "reached the conclusion that to best serve the Negro population a small autonomous body of twelve churchmen would be established to make a *specialty* of Negro work and to be called 'The American Church Institute for Negroes'" (hereinafter ACIN).[4] Part of the Church's shame, it should be pointed out, was that its woeful inadequacy in ministering to blacks stood in stark contrast to its much heralded successes in its missionary enterprises abroad:

> [The Church] has stronger heart, higher courage and clearer vision; hence she has surer touch, deeper insight, and enlarged confidence. Problems vast and complex do not now stun her into silence, or difficulties turn her into sloughs of hesitation. China, Japan, the Philippines, Alaska are no longer the stuff out of which dreams are made but the open promises of a working day; they are distinctly set within the horizon of the possible to a calculating sense as well as to an obedient faith.[5]

The same document goes on to lament the fact that "only in one field does there seem to be uncertainty of touch, hesitating judgment and faltering effort. About the Negro and about the methods of appeal to him we seem divided in mind, troubled in heart, and confused in action." The ACIN was founded, therefore, as a corrective to this anomalous situation in the life of the Church. Ironically, it went about its chosen course of action in a curious way, which bore little if any resemblance to a missionary enterprise or even a religious undertaking. For the founders of the ACIN subscribed to the view, prevalent at the time, that "education was the essential prelude to advancement of the race in citizenship and economic position as well as religious development."[6] Although the founders' stated objective was "the Christian education of Negroes,"[7] its 1912 annual report specified that its primary concern was for the "religiously inspired education of practical workers in the world—farmers, industrial workers, homemakers, etc."[8]

The ACIN was perhaps most accurately described in a later document as "a corporation devoted to the education of Negroes in the Southern states, under the auspices of the Episcopal Church."[9] Indeed, in another document promulgated soon after the establishment of the ACIN, the Episcopal Church, apparently believing that a traditional "religious" approach toward education would hamper its fundraising efforts, seemed to take pride in its commitment to a thoroughly secular venture. It distanced itself from the perception that the Church in its educational enterprises should be about the business of imparting "religion," stating that the ACIN

> is an attempt to use the religious motive in education, not after the old fashion of substituting ecclesiastical theory or piousness for good educational work, but in the *scientific* spirit and according to the best educational methods. Ecclesiastically inspired or controlled education has been in the past largely vitiated by the fault of the substitution before mentioned, and has consequently in large degree *forfeited the confidence both of scientific educators and of the giving public.* Indeed it may perhaps be said that the reaction against religious education in the higher as well as the public schools of the country has been due somewhat to this unfortunate substitution.[10]

Cognizant of the fact that considerable lay support was being given to the Hampton Institute in Virginia, and to the Tuskegee Institute in Alabama, the Episcopal Church believed that it, too, should be able to garner funds into an institute under its own auspices. To this end, the ACIN either adopted or founded "one school in each [Southern] state, so central to the Negro population within the state that it would be capable, sooner or later, of exercising at least a state-wide influence upon race relationships and upon the Negro population in general." The larger objective of the institute was "a constant effort to make good citizens who will raise the standards of living in the communities to which they return."[11]

A 1958 brochure provided an even more blunt description of its work, which is in some ways reminiscent of the language used to justify the exportation of black missionaries to Africa:

> The farsighted plan was not only to provide instruction, but also to *send students back to their people* as teachers, nurses or social workers in order that they might work toward the betterment of their own home communities. This concept still permeates each school's program. Results have been gratifying.[12]

It can be said that the ACIN proved somewhat successful in its stated purpose, namely educating blacks and equipping them to serve in their communities; but as a missionary endeavor the ACIN proved no more successful than the Freedman's Commission. This is because from the outset, by its own admission, there was neither the intention nor the desire, despite the presence of chaplains and the conduct of worship at the schools, to incorporate Negroes thus equipped into the life of the Episcopal Church.[13] The ACIN, then, was by no stretch of the imagination an example of missionary outreach. It was *social* outreach, however laudable, done in the name of the Church, but not for the purpose of bringing blacks into the fold. Indeed, J. Carleton Hayden comments that the establishment of the ACIN "marked a perceptible, although at first unrecognized, shift in Episcopal racial strategy." He writes:

> The Institute increasingly treated the schools as primarily educational institutions whose purpose was to provide general education, *employable skills* and some moral training. No longer would students at St. Augustine's be required to attend chapel twice daily, hear a daily instruction by the priest-principal, and learn the catechism.[14]

The ACIN, then, seemed especially adept at identifying the problem, namely that blacks were in need of spiritual, educational, and moral uplift, yet were particularly inept at providing the solution. It firmly believed that the Church had a moral obligation to address the "Negro problem," but maintained that its duty lay entirely in enabling blacks to be instrumental in determining their own destiny, as a separate and discrete entity within the broader society. In its rationale for the establishment of the ACIN, it states that "Christian forces in the country [must] awaken to the fact that this problem requires not so much a solvent as a solver. That Solver we believe to be Jesus Christ; and notwithstanding the smallness of our numbers we believe our church has a peculiar work to do."[15]

But that peculiar work did not envision Jesus the Solver as one who welcomed blacks into the Church in the same way that He had welcomed those who had been beneficiaries of the Church's missionary largess overseas. The Episcopal Church felt morally bound, because of "her organization, her ethical standards, her appeal to a normal sense of form and her medial position among the churches," to do an honorable thing on behalf of blacks, but that did not include making them integral members of the Episcopal Church. In commending the ACIN for its efforts six years after its founding, a clergyman wrote: "I wish I could give you $500, because every cent of it would be an investment in human uplift. *You are doing a scientific sociological work.*"[16] Even the Bishop Payne Divinity School, one of the schools "adopted" by the ACIN, which had come into existence largely because of the unwillingness on the part of the Church's official seminaries to admit black students, was seen as an institution whose very existence was a further example of the Church's intention to marginalize its black members.

Moreover, in its founding, the ACIN was suffused with the paternalism that marked the age in which it came into being. The "twelve churchmen" who constituted its board and determined its policy were all white — bishops, priests, and laymen; only the general agent and field agents who visited the ACIN member colleges to implement board policy were black. But the trustees of the institute firmly believed that because they were successful in extracting financial support for black education from white Episcopalians on both sides of the Mason-Dixon Line that this was *prima facie* evidence that the ACIN had been instrumental in tearing down racial barriers:

> The generosity of our southern bishops and educational leaders, the spirit of intelligent and fraternal cooperation which now obtains between north and south, the combination of direct southern knowledge and feeling with northern perspective and sense of proportion, the application to missionary work of proper standards of business and educational efficiency, and the mighty opportunity open to the Church is a well-equipped ecclesiastical agency uniting the intelligent and Christian men and women, both white and colored, of the whole land in this great work for God and man.[17]

The trustees' statement would suggest that they perceived whites' willingness to provide pecuniary assistance for the "advancement of the Negro" as evidence of a renewed racial harmony. They ignored the fact that, as in the case of the establishment and support of African colonization and missionary societies (see chapter 7), the education of the

Negro was considered a worthy cause so long as such education would ensure the continued separation of the races.

The irony that belied the efforts of the ACIN was that it purported to be an instrument for Negro uplift at the same time that the Episcopal Church remained unswervingly committed to segregationist policies at every level of its life. Deployment of black clergy was carried out along strictly racial lines. Scores of black congregations, North and South, were established either by dioceses or by white parishes in order to keep black Episcopalians separate but very much unequal. Bishop Burgess comments:

> From the turn of the century we find in many of the larger cities of the North and East the effort to found what were called "Missions for Colored people." There is much first-hand evidence that these Chapels were not so much an expression of a missionary outreach, as they were an effort to ward off, like a plague, any possibility that the increasing Colored populations from the South and the West Indies might want to find spiritual refreshment in the older established churches of the community.[18]

The Church had repeatedly rejected the idea of blacks in the episcopate. Most significantly, in the South, the colored convocation, a system that barred blacks from participation in diocesan conventions by setting up a parallel and powerless legislative system for black communicants, stood as a monument to an institutionalized racism that flourished in a church whose white and black members often boasted that the Episcopal Church had not split along racial lines, as had other denominations, after the Civil War.

Upon closer examination, then, it becomes evident that the ACIN's motives were consistent with the Church's attitude toward blacks in other spheres of its life. A century before, many white Episcopalians believed that the solution to the surfeit of blacks was to establish colonies for them in Africa. As this movement had been successful in removing only a small fraction of the free black population, American society and the Church so closely identified with its founding fathers now had to concede to the fact that the Negro was to be a permanent feature of the landscape. Given the historical reasons for the presence of blacks in their midst, many whites found it difficult if not impossible to accord them equal footing in society; blacks were seen as an anomaly, indeed as a problem:

> Now there stands over against the Anglo-Saxon or the Teutonic race in America another race in the presence of which constitutes the *greatest problem in American life, namely the negro race.* Brought here by our compulsion, not by their request, but determined and necessitated by reason

> of the facts of the situation to remain here, what have they to contribute to the coming of the human civilization for which our present dissatisfaction stimulates us to seek?[19]

The concern over the "Negro problem" was expressed in another document, which put forward the *raison d'être* of the ACIN, and which further explains why the Church chose education as the solution to that problem:

> Perhaps the most admirable elements in the Church's attitude toward the Negro are her sense of shame for shortcomings and inadequate work, and her repentance and desire to do better; but there is still a curious paralysis which affects her thought and her activity with reference to this immediate and urgent missionary task. We use the word curious advisedly; for to the general student of the social and moral welfare of our country what we call *the Negro problem*—which is fully as much the problem of the white man as of the Negro—is intensely interesting and critically important; and *no outpouring of thought and energy in modern times has been more splendid or more hopeful than that which issued in the great Negro schools.*[20]

We would like to suggest that the "curious paralysis" with which the Church found itself afflicted was attributable to an inability on the part of the founders of the ACIN in particular and white Episcopalians in general to conceive of the Negro as potentially an integral part of the Church. This is evidenced by the fact that blacks were seen in the first place as a group to be missionized. Like Filipinos, or Africans, or Alaskan Indians, blacks were considered as foreigners, as "other," as a group inherently different[21] who demanded special treatment, and who required a tailor-made missionary strategy. The only difference was that the group in question in this case was to be found across town, and not across the ocean.

Anna Julia Cooper, writing at the turn of the century, in a particularly insightful analysis of the situation put it this way:

> As a Mission field for the Church the Southern Negro is in some aspects most promising; in others perplexing. Aliens neither in language and customs, nor in associations and sympathies, naturally of deeply rooted religious instincts and taking most readily and kindly to the worship and teachings of the Church, surely the task of proselytizing the American Negro is infinitely less formidable than that which confronted the Church in the Barbarians of Europe. Besides, this people already look to the Church as the hope of their race. Thinking colored men almost uniformly admit that the Protestant Episcopal Church with its quiet, chaste dignity and decorous solemnity, its instructive and elevating ritual, its bright chanting and joyous hymning, is eminently fitted

> to correct the peculiar faults of worship — the rank exuberance and often ludicrous demonstrativeness of their people. Yet, strange to say, *the Church, claiming to be missionary and Catholic, urging that schism is sin and denominationalism inexcusable,* has made in all these years almost no inroads upon this semi-civilized religionism.[22]

Moreover, since in order to "qualify" as potential recipients of missionary beneficence, the missionized, traditionally, have had to be perceived as inherently different from the missionaries, the ACIN developed, accordingly, a folklore that spoke to the "romance" of the Negro. Thus, its founders could attribute to the Negro the following characteristics:

> a faith which has the power of including... detailed, complete, ultimate adversity... secondly,... a cheer which is boundless in its effects upon character,... thirdly, an emotional use of religion which is perhaps one of the most important contributions a race can make. Underneath the immorality and inconsistency into which the emotional nature of the Negro has led him, there is yet something in the Negro's insistence upon the necessary emotional character which is vital to healthful and permanent religious life.... [And] of course there will occur to every one who has observed the Negro character and accomplishment the music of the race. There can be no question in the mind of one who has listened to Negro music and who has studied it with any care that there are musical themes and motifs in the Negro's mind and heart which are unique and ultimate, integral and peculiar to him.[23]

The belief on the part of the Church that such stereotypical characteristics as moral laxity, cheerful disposition, and musical aptitude were inherent in the black race made it very clear that churchpeople by and large were not interested in incorporating such people into their fellowship; indeed, many believed that Negroes' "natural" characteristics rendered them undesirable for such fellowship.

The Church's "Negro problem" was that it insisted upon regarding blacks in their midst as an "alien race" who were treated, despite their propinquity, as if they were upon "a foreign shore." So long as such an attitude prevailed, any appreciable growth among black Episcopalians would be unlikely. Such dynamics set the stage for relationships between blacks and whites in the Episcopal Church at the outset of the twentieth century; and it is essential to understand them as we trace the evolution of those relationships in the decades that ensued.

The ACIN was an official agency of the Episcopal Church, with offices at the denominational headquarters in New York. The staff, then as now, were charged with carrying out the directives of, and implementing the programs approved by the General Convention and the

National (now Executive) Council.[24] It would be instructive, therefore, to examine the decisions made by General Convention regarding the Church's relationship with its black membership, as the fruit of those deliberations reflect the mind of the Church and its collective wisdom, or lack thereof, in such matters.

In its pronouncements, the General Convention developed a rhetoric reflective of a keen sense of mission. The Church's "press" suggests that it saw itself as a standard-bearer, committed to no less a goal than the salvation of the world. Moreover, its deeds were to stand as a shining example for all to see and emulate. Consider, for example, the report of the Committee on the State of the Church at the 1944 convention:

> The Church refuses to become a weak imitation of the expediencies and compromises of the worldly-wise. With stalwart faith and clear-cut loyalty she adheres to her ancient gospel which is in this and as in every age has been, the Light of the World. The Church is the spiritual Arsenal of Democracy, her gospel is the power unto salvation and her only charter of true freedom.[25]

Nevertheless, in its actions, it normally fell far short of the standard it set for itself and for others. This was especially true in its dealings with blacks. For example, at the 1919 convention, in the Church's response to a memorial presented by the CCWACP on social justice for Negroes, it was quick to shirk its responsibility to uphold democracy and freedom, and to declare the Negro problem outside of its realm of interest:

> As touching the matter of Social Justice for colored people and the securing of Christian treatment for them as full citizens of this Republic, your Committee, as a step towards a better understanding between the races, recommends the formation in every city of Local Committees of representative citizens of both races who shall constitute a Committee or Conference with a view to obtaining the sympathetic and intelligent co-operation of men and women of both races in the settlement of racial problems. Such committees would undoubtedly lead to a better understanding between the races and could be quickly called together for the purpose of considering special problems or acute conditions as they arise.[26]

It is noteworthy that the General Convention was content to reject the appeal of the CCWACP and to return the ball to their court. The CCWACP, whose members experienced social injustice first-hand, had hoped that the Church would bring its moral suasion to bear on the society in which such injustice was being meted out, and would, moreover, serve as an advocate to their fellow Episcopalians who were the victims of that injustice. Instead, the Church in effect said that this was not its problem, and suggested that interracial committees be set up in those very local communities rife with racial tension; and placed on communities the responsibility of working through the problems themselves.

The CCWACP introduced a similar resolution fifteen years later, and the Church once again referred the matter to other bodies for consideration:

> This Committee has read with interest and sympathy the communication and appeal for social justice made by the Conference of Church Workers Among Colored People. We note that this appeal has also been sent to the President of the United States, the Secretary of Labor, the Secretary of the Interior, and the Secretary of the Federal Relief Administration. *As the grievances recited in the appeal are for a correction of governmental administration,* your Committee feels no definite recommendation should be made to the House in this matter. We urge the co-operation of Churchmen in helping to eliminate *any injustice that may exist* against the colored people.[27]

It is ironic, moreover, that on the same page of the convention *Journal,* the report of the Joint Commission on the Status of the Negro

> urges the National Council and all diocesan authorities to emphasize the recognition of the Negroes as constituent members of the Church, to promote in every way possible their spiritual welfare by supporting and increasing missionary work among them and by giving them increased opportunities for service [and] recommends that the Negroes be welcomed to a freer and more active participation in legislation, and that they be accorded every possible opportunity for developing leadership in Diocesan, Provincial and National administration, in the office of Archdeacon and in the Episcopate as Suffragan Bishops, where conditions make such office useful and advisable; and that they be called in consultation in matters concerning the spiritual welfare of the race.[28]

To consider these two statements in apposition is to give us considerable insight into the racial attitudes of the Episcopal Church. It is clear that it was not interested, despite its unabashed claims of "clear-cut loyalty to the Gospel," in the status of the Negro in society. The report of the commission made this point explicit:

> The vast question of the social, economic, and industrial status of the Negro in the country is not within the province of this Commission. It is utterly beyond the capacity of the Commission to consider and to secure the information necessary to arrive at any adequate conclusion. It is a question for specialized scholars and experts. What the Commission is charged with is to consider and report upon the status of the Negro

> *in the Church,* and to recommend methods by which a fuller measure of leadership may be developed among them.[29]

Its purported interest in his status in the Church, therefore, was but lip-service, for if we read the second statement carefully, it is noncommittal and nonspecific in its stated support of blacks, and specific in mentioning only those roles that in fact function to limit the Negro's effectiveness and impact on the life of the Church, such as archdeacon or suffragan bishop for colored work. Moreover, the Negro's sphere of influence was seen to be limited, partly by his intellectual ability, and partly by the extent to which the white establishment accorded him privileges:

> The Church wishes to *give to the Negro* assurance of its sense of its *responsibility to his race* for their spiritual growth in the Christian life, and for their development in leadership *in accordance with their ability,* under the Catholic order of its government and administration.[30]

In the full report of the Commission on the Status of the Negro, its members, while conceding the existence of some problems between the races in the Church's life, declared such circumstances to be few and "sectional," that is, pertaining only in Southern dioceses.[31] In the same spirit that allowed the Church a century before to turn a blind eye to the fact that many Southern Episcopalians were slaveholders, the committee maintained "whatever may be our differing opinions as to the equity or legality of his position in the South, it must be recognized that there are practical difficulties which cannot be remedied by legislation." The report continued: "It would seem to be questionable wisdom to insist in our legislation upon a remedy for what is considered a defect in the Church's policy, but which exists only in so small a part of the Church. Is it wise to pass general laws to apply only to special and sectional conditions?"[32]

Despite evidence to the contrary everywhere in the Church's life, the commission came to the remarkable conclusion that "the Negro is now a constituent member of the Church. With a limited exception, he possesses the same status as the white people." Declaring that "great leaders do not wait for office or opportunity," the document challenged "our Negro brethren among clergy and laity [to] demonstrate" their leadership qualities and thus receive recognition.[33]

The Episcopal Church's penchant for being ambiguous on matters of race manifested itself in subsequent conventions as well. In 1940, for example, a delegate from the Diocese of Bethlehem pointed out that colored delegates "frequently suffer at the General Convention from the fact that they are excluded from convenient hotels and from attendance and conferences held in conjunction with meals" and moved that "the Committee on Arrangements *strive* to make arrangements that will allow the colored delegates and visitors to be accorded the same treatment as the white delegates." However, when the resolution was passed, it read that the arrangements committee "be asked to *give due consideration* to the matter of *possible* discrimination in the accommodation of delegates because of race."[34]

But the 1940 convention was also marked by a shift in the Church's strategies regarding race relations. Having been less than successful in reaching the Negro masses through the establishment of the ACIN and the appointment of various commissions and committees, the Church established the position of secretary for Negro work, reflective of the opinion "that a greater share in the responsibility for the progress of the Negro Work must be placed upon the shoulders of the Negroes themselves."[35] This was brought about out of a realization on the part of the Church that its efforts until that date had not proved especially effective. Moreover, by entrusting the advancement of Negro work to blacks themselves (albeit under white control and subject to the budgetary restrictions imposed by a virtually all-white General Convention), it placed the onus on black churchmen to "stimulate the work." But although the office of Secretary for Negro Work was to report to an interracial Joint Commission for Negro Work, a revolutionary idea in its time,[36] the development of Negro work was still understood to be an enterprise designed to treat black Episcopalians, to use McGuire's term, as an *ecclesiola in ecclesia* (see chapter 6), and not an attempt to bring blacks closer to the bosom of the Church. There was also a vestige of the "noblesse oblige" that had characterized the Church's attitude toward blacks in previous eras in the Church's life: "The tremendously significant thing is that the Church is showing herself awake to the opportunity and duty *we owe to the thirteen million Negroes in the United States.* There is no limit to the opportunity and no escape from duty."[37]

As we have seen, the Episcopal Church, in the first half of this century, continued to make efforts, some halfhearted, some sincere, but almost always ineffective, to reach out to the Negro. The Church was motivated at times by a perceived need to address the "Negro problem." At other times, it felt obliged to do something, since the "problem" would not go away. If its attempts failed to ensure the Negro a secure place in the life of the Church, it is possibly because that was not the Church's intention. To accord blacks equality and respect, to recognize black clergy and laypeople as equal in every respect to their white counterparts, would have been to imbue them with rights that they did not enjoy in the secular arena, and therefore such acts would have been, for the Episcopal Church, an uncharacteristically prophetic act. Commissions, committees, councils, and General Convention itself issued statements that "assured," "encouraged," "urged," and "recommended" action to "promote," "prosecute," and "stimulate" work on the Negro's behalf. Some of those statements even smacked of penitence and remorse for the evils perpetrated on blacks by generations of whites. But with the notable exception of the establishment of the office of Secretary for Negro Work, such resolutions seldom resulted in concrete actions, or in a demonstrable improvement of the Negro's lot.

Chapter 9

The Witness of the Conference of Church Workers among Colored People and the Secretaries for Negro Work

Awake thou Spirit of the watchmen
Who never held their peace by day or night.

—Karl Heinrich von Bagatzky (hymn text, 1749)

The principal reason for the ongoing friction between the CCWACP and the Church establishment was simply that the two entities possessed different world views, or at the very least espoused radically different agendas. The Church saw as its role the provision of sacramental and pastoral ministrations for its black members, to be carried out for the most part in a segregated ecclesiastical environment. The Church expressed its support of such a view in the finding of the study of the Joint Commission on the Status of the Negro in 1934 that "the status of the Negro as regards the spiritual privileges in the Church are the same as those of white clergy and congregations." The CCWACP, on the other hand, understood its role as seeking to improve the conditions under which black people existed in church *and* in society. It saw the Church, which according to both its doctrine and constitution was committed to such equality within its own ranks, as an advocate for its black members who sought justice both within and without the Church. Indeed, one of the CCWACP's many memorials stated as one of its goals "to take such steps as will greatly aid in bringing about social justice for the Colored People of the United States and securing for them Christian treatment as full citizens of this Republic."[1] For example, in 1907, the conference spoke to issues in both arenas. In reference to the racial disturbances, and more particularly to lynchings, the CCWACP voiced an "appeal . . . to the more numerous race to co-operate with the best classes, in efforts to restrain the disorderly classes of both races, and to moderate their lawless passions."[2] Concerning their status in the Church, the conference, addressing the issue of black leadership, pressed for missionary districts under black bishops, putting forward their requests in terms that underscored not only their commitment to full participation in the Church's life, but their belief that the plan would best serve the cause of the mission of the whole Church:

> To re-affirm, ratify and emphasize our conviction that in view of the social and racial conditions of our country, some adaptation of the Episcopate is imperative if the Church is to make adequate progress among our people.... We would express our unshaken confidence and belief that the Church is so solicitous and anxious for the Evangelization of our people that under the guidance and inspiration of the Holy Spirit we can look to her representatives gathered in the General Convention to take wise and statesmanlike action.[3]

The CCWACP, throughout its existence, was lavish in its praise of the Church for its accomplishments; at the same time it never failed to urge the Church to "go a second mile." For example, in response to the establishment of the ACIN, it observed:

> We express our unqualified and enthusiastic approval of Industrial education, but we hope the day is not far distant when we may have a college for the higher education of approved grade and standard, and that the Theological Seminary founded for the race may offer as advanced training as that of any Seminary in the land.[4]

And in those instances, as was most often the case, that the General Convention did not see fit to grant their requests, the members of the CCWACP, like a Greek chorus commenting on the action in the play, were quick to remonstrate. When, for example, a committee of the General Convention charged with studying the racial episcopate asked to be discharged, having deemed that the elections of Demby and Delany "seemed to meet with reasonable fullness the emergency which the proposed amendment was intended to provide for," the CCWACP commented: "This is most pathetic indeed.... It is extremely ludicrous to imagine that the present two Suffragans could prove equal to the task."[5]

Although the distinction of founding the CCWACP belongs to Alexander Crummell, the renown of the organization and its influence on the life of the Episcopal Church are attributable to the indefatigable efforts of George Freeman Bragg Jr., who as the conference's secretary and historiographer for thirty-five years wielded the power of the pen, both in terms of shaping its present and preserving its history. In addition to chronicling the conference's activities in the *Church Advocate,* Bragg was a prolific writer, with numerous books, pamphlets, and articles to his credit. In his writings, he never shirked from being critical of the Church if it did not live up to his expectations. J. Carleton Hayden's comment sums up Bragg's theology and ministry:

> Bragg was thoroughly devoted to Anglicanism which he believed the most scriptural ancient branch of the Catholic Church, and to the Episcopal Church which he regarded as the leading national institution where acceptance and cooperation by the best of both races occurred. Bragg believed that the faith and practice of the Church rightly and systematically applied would result in sizeable numbers of educated Blacks drawn to it. He vigorously denounced racial discrimination within the Church. "For Zion's sake, I will not hold my peace" was the motto of *The Church Advocate.* He believed that the Church was in its foundation catholic, inclusive, and egalitarian and that the fight for racial justice was essential to its renewal and reformation.[6]

But in addition to challenging the institutional church, Bragg was relentless in his challenge to his black clerical colleagues to enable their congregations to become self-supporting. He believed that the pride that comes from self-determination and self-actualization could only be realized if black Episcopalians could stand on their own feet financially. He was of the opinion that the lack of militancy on the part of black clergy was directly attributable "to their failure to grasp the prophetic nature of their ministries and to the fact that they were dependent upon white bishops for their salaries."[7] He believed that the most effective vehicle for self-determination was a solvent black congregation under black clerical leadership.

Moreover, Bragg, through the organs of the CCWACP, did much to foster an *esprit de corps* among black Episcopalians. Since typically black clergy were isolated, ministering to those few black congregations in which they were permitted to minister, the *Church Advocate* and, more important, the annual meetings of the conference served to foster a sense of confidence among blacks, which, in turn, emboldened them to challenge the white power structure of the Church in ways that they could not have accomplished individually. Bragg further believed that black Episcopalians, who were among the most educated and privileged blacks in the United States, should set an example for other African Americans. Thus, the masthead of the *Church Advocate* carried the slogan "Published on or about the first of each Month, *in the interest of the Colored Race, in general,* and of the Episcopal Church."

As the twentieth century approached its midpoint, a gradual but perceptible shift in the Episcopal Church's racial policy was beginning to become evident. With the establishment of the office of the Secretary for Negro Work, and the appointment of the Venerable Bravid

Washington Harris as its first incumbent, blacks for the first time began to exert some influence on the policies affecting their participation in the Church's life, from a position within the Church's official structure. These and other accomplishments were due in large measure to the dogged determination of George Freeman Bragg Jr. and other leaders in the CCWACP. Like the persistent widow, the organization pressed for recognition and justice. Like clockwork, memorials to General Convention were presented for consideration at virtually every triennial gathering for three-quarters of a century, beginning in 1883 when the CCWACP prevailed in thwarting the passage of the "Sewanee canon."

The genius behind establishing the office, although perhaps not envisioned by the Church's hierarchy, was not merely that there would be a black person who would have some say in shaping the Church's strategy on behalf of blacks, but that his efforts would complement the work of the Church Workers Conference. The CCWACP was a caucus whose job it was to speak *to* the Church; the office of the Secretary for Negro Work, operating out of "Pharaoh's house," had as its responsibility to speak *on behalf of* the Church. The CCWACP would have a friend at court, an advocate, someone who could represent their interests at the highest echelons of the Church's life. These functions were spelled out in a 1942 document entitled "The Value and Function of an Executive Secretary for a Division on Negro Work" by Mrs. Fannie Gross:

> The Secretary would be expected to evaluate and interpret the church's work among Negroes, and to represent and present the point of view of the Negro. In the field, he would be expected to consult with Bishops and other officials on problems relative to their Negro work; to interpret to the Negro clergy and churchmen the general program and policy of the National Church, and to promote increased participation on the part of the Negro in every phase of the Church's program.[8]

During the years in which Bravid Harris and Tollie Caution served as secretary for Negro work, black Episcopalians were cared for in ways they had not been before. The secretaries helped to sponsor and were always present at the annual meeting of the Church Workers Conference. In addition, under their aegis, a summer school for Christian education was held annually, either at St. Paul's School or St. Augustine's College. Regional conferences for clergy were held. But the bulk of their work involved establishing, maintaining, or improving "Negro work" in the dioceses of the Episcopal Church, especially in the South.

Harris and Caution were highly respected, among blacks as well as whites. Edwards observed that during the tenures of the two secretaries,

> a complete survey of the Negro work throughout the country was made. The Bishop Payne Divinity School was merged with the Virginia Seminary; the property was sold and the proceeds set up as a trust fund for the... training of Negro clergy. Increased interest and support for the work in Liberia with qualified American Negro priests and workers in the field was secured.[9]

Moreover, Harris and Caution were pontifical in the true sense of being "bridge-builders." Bishop Burgess wrote of Harris's work: "Bravid Harris was Secretary for Negro Work in the National Council, an office which he discharged with such vigor as to inspire and accelerate the church's work in this important field."[10]

Bishop Walter Dennis commented on Caution's accomplishments by describing him as "the precursor, the forerunner, the pathfinder, the stalking horse, the prophet (sometimes without honor)."[11] Bishop Turner echoes those remarks:

> Dr. Caution laid a firm and sure foundation in his ministry. Because of him, blacks today are more active in the church and hold significant positions in its life and ministry. Once, when someone asked Dr. Caution about his success, he replied; "If I have achieved anything, it is because I have stood on the shoulders of giants." We now stand on Tollie's shoulders, and because of his living legacy we are striving toward and achieving greater goals than ever before.[12]

But it must be kept in mind that despite their valiant witness, neither the secretaries for Negro work themselves nor the Church establishment saw it as the secretaries' job to effect integration of church facilities or services. "Negro work" was still seen as a separate and distinct entity. That work was to be strengthened, but by no means was it understood that it should be incorporated into the work of the Church at large. The racial climate in the United States at that time made such actions highly unlikely. But the secretaries and the Bi-racial Committees to whom they reported were not unmindful of that dynamic, and they never flagged in urging the Church to take a stand. Perhaps the most significant document to come out of this area was "Guiding Principles," adopted by National Council in February 1943. Inspired by the report of the 1937 Oxford conference, which declared that "the Church is a divine society that transcends all national and racial limitations and divisions and that in its own life and worship there can be no place for barriers because of race or color," the council adopted four principles:

1. *Fellowship is essential to Christian worship....* We dare not break our Christian fellowship by any attitude or act in the House of God which marks other brethren of our races as unequal or inferior.

2. *Fellowship is essential in Church administration....* Negro Churchmen [are] assured that their fellowship in the Episcopal Church is valid and secure.

3. *High standards must be maintained in every department of our work with the Negro....* This principle applies to buildings, equipment, personnel. ... *Where separate facilities are still maintained, they should provide the same opportunities as those which are available to other racial groups.*

4. *It is both the function and the task of the Church to set the spiritual and moral goals for society....* In these ways the Church will demonstrate her belief that God "has made of one blood all nations of men for to dwell on the face of the whole earth."

It is interesting to note that part of the document was the caveat that "the fact that all these principles cannot be realized at once in their fullness should not prevent us from keeping them before us as the Christian goal." The document was bold for its day, and clearly was worded so as to minimize possible offense. The Bi-Racial Committee, armed with the statement, passed a resolution that "the entire Church be encouraged to implement these principles in its various departments of activity." It was further suggested that the Guiding Principles be used to try to convince bishops of dioceses with segregated conventions to change their policies, "but [it] was later decided by the Committee that such a step might cause friction in view of the fact that all bishops concerned are anxious to bring this about without outside pressure."[13] This proved to be a strategic error, since, as would become abundantly clear over the next several years, "outside pressure" was the only stimulus to which the Church would respond.

In the mid-fifties, changes were taking place in the nation which through a ripple effect began to have ramifications on the life of the Church, and to exert the very kind of pressure the Bi-racial Sub-committee wished to avoid. In 1954, according to David Sumner,

> the Diocese of South Carolina became the last Episcopal diocese to remove the racial barrier for representation at diocesan conventions. That same year, John T. Walker [later to become bishop of Washington] was the first black to graduate from Virginia Theological Seminary.... A year earlier, the School of Theology at the University of the South [Sewanee, Tennessee] was integrated. In 1955, the church moved its General Convention from Houston to Honolulu to ensure that all facilities would be fully integrated.... A group of black Episcopalians, including Supreme Court Justice Thurgood Marshall, the Reverend Tollie L. Caution, and the chief counsel for the NAACP, met with [Presiding] Bishop Sherrill and urged a change in the Convention site.[14]

In light of such developments, the CCWACP began to assess its life and mission. A special meeting of the Church Workers was held in Washington in 1954, under the chairmanship of the Reverend Thomas W. S. Logan, who served as president from 1952 to 1961. Its principal agenda was the "procurement of a sample of opinion concerning the continued existence of the Conference as a Church organization."[15] At that time, white and black Episcopalians, buoyed by what they perceived as substantive changes on the landscape, cherished the belief that such breakthroughs as described above signaled the nation's and the Church's commitment to integration, and they feared that maintaining an all-black organization might impede progress. The Venerable Richard B. Martin, archdeacon for colored work in the Diocese of Southern Virginia and the rector of Grace Church, Norfolk (and later bishop suffragan of Long Island), "voiced the generally accepted opinion when he said, 'the conference should not just be a watch-dog group for things concerning Negroes. There is a danger of making desegregation the goal instead of integration.'"[16] He even went so far as to suggest that the purposes of the conference's founding had been almost all realized, and that therefore it should be integrated "because any problems worthy of consideration at all are worthy of it by the whole American Church." The Reverend John Milton Coleman, rector of St. Philip's, Brooklyn, New York, suggested that "the Conference does have a place, but should be revamped."[17]

Virtually no participants in the special meeting believed the CCWACP should be disbanded, but felt that it should continue to exist as a vehicle for integration. It was clear from the comments that clergy whose professional careers were in the Church believed that the organization in its historical form would be an impediment to their advancement. They clearly did not want to be seen as being out of step with the times, or worse, recalcitrant or even ungrateful in light of the Church's "progress." The ironic twist in this development, however, is that even as black churchmen praised the Church for its enlightened racial attitude, the General Convention of 1955 was slated to take place in Houston, where the bishop of Texas "claimed to give no countenance to segregation, *while he yet expected the attendance of the clergy at a dinner with separate, but equal facilities.*"[18]

It should be noted that black Episcopalians so embraced the idea of integration at that time that St. Luke's, Houston, a black congregation that was to be the host for the conference when it met in that city in conjunction with the General Convention, presumably believing that they could not protest the segregation of the convention while engaging in a similar practice, "declined to provide hospitality for a segregated Church workers meeting."[19] Such thinking predominated for several years. In 1961, when the convention was scheduled to meet in Detroit, the Reverend Malcolm Dade, rector of St. Cyprian's Church in that city, resigned from the organization, declined to host its meeting, and wrote to Father Logan that it was his opinion "that the Church Workers Conference should come to a cessation of activities in whatever way your wise judgment sees, except by way of public meeting in Detroit, 1961."[20]

Although the CCWACP would continue until the founding of the Union of Black Clergy and Laity (UBCL) in 1968, the elusive promise of integration meant that its political agenda became less focused. It still functioned, however, as a means of uplift and fellowship for black Episcopalians, in much the same way as Bragg had envisioned it:

> Many have been the benefits of these annual conferences. They have interpreted to both races the black man at his best. Through these conferences the colored people have come to know and somewhat understand the purpose of the Episcopal Church. They have proved the means of introducing to each other our own colored laity and linking them together for constructive work. The Conference has furnished to our own colored clergy the opportunity for practice, and imparted an ecclesiastical education which could not have been realized elsewhere. By means of it many of them have found themselves, and have been inspired and rendered more helpful in their difficult work. They have learnt to do by doing. Their entire life, social, intellectual and ecclesiastical has felt the invigorating influence of the forces inseparably connected with such meetings.[21]

But the rank and file of black Episcopalians, believing that "new occasions teach new duties," had begun to cast their lot with the Episcopal Society for Cultural and Racial Unity. In retrospect, this period of history proved in many ways to be a hiatus in the struggle for catholicity and recognition on the part of black Episcopalians. Believing that the Promised Land was in view, black Episcopalians declared that their long labors could come to a halt. They did not know then that in the short space of a decade, in the light of broken promises, the premature cessation of their efforts would be relegated to but a brief respite, and that they would redouble their efforts with a vengeance. In the race for justice, the baton would be handed on to the UBCL, which would pick up where the *old* CCWACP left off.

Part Four

Interpreters of the Gospel

Chapter 10

The Episcopal Church and the Civil Rights Movement

In Christ all races meet their ancient feuds forgetting.
—George Wallace Briggs (hymn text, 1933)

The adage *Qualis patria, talis ecclesia* ("As the nation goes, so goes the church") seems an especially fitting description of the *modus operandi* of the Episcopal Church in every age. We have elsewhere described the Episcopal Church as "a non-prophet organization,"[1] that is to say, a body that has not, historically, set a moral example for the nation to follow but rather has taken its lead from the mores of the nation with which it has had a unique, symbiotic relationship since they both came into existence, almost simultaneously, at the end of the eighteenth century. John Kater, an Episcopal priest-professor, describes the phenomenon in this way:

> The [Episcopal] Church [believes] that order is the primary social goal and value. Hence, the Church can be expected in principle to view unrest with alarm, and in general to side with the powers which enforce that order. So it was that up to the time of the Civil War most Episcopalians... accepted slavery as preferable to the anarchy which they assumed was the only alternative. Episcopalians tended to be set apart from other Christians, however, by their understanding of the Church as a divinely-appointed agent of social unity. When it becomes apparent that order cannot be maintained without altering social structures to meet the demands of the discontented, *the Church possesses the potential to become the champion of new relationships*—for the purpose of creating a *new* order. The Episcopal Church's mysteriously active place in the social gospel movement of the nineteenth century is not really a mystery; it occurred when the Church's leadership realized that unless labor were mollified, endless social unrest would be the consequence.[2]

During the early days of the freedom movement, the Church's actions followed a similar pattern: "As long as a relative calm blanketed black-white relationships in the U.S., the Church acquiesced in and tacitly approved a *de facto* segregated church in a segregated society." But when it became clear that such an arrangement would no longer be tolerated, "the Episcopal Church became an advocate for racial equality as the social order demanded by Christian faith."[3] Thus, the Episcopal Church, in whose congregations, institutions, and even diocesan conventions segregation had long been *de rigueur*, gradually began to adopt an integrationist policy only after the U.S. Supreme Court's historic *Brown v. Board of Education* decision in 1954.[4] Indeed, the 1955 General Convention "issued the strongest statement the Church had made to that date on the racial issue."[5] It urged Episcopalians to "accept and support the ruling of the Supreme Court and . . . to anticipate constructively the local implementation of this ruling as the law of the land." Moreover, stating that "discrimination and segregation are contrary to the mind of Christ and the will of God," the convention affirmed that "in the work of the church we should welcome people of any race at any service conducted by a priest or layman of any ethnic origin, and bring them into the full fellowship of the congregation and its organizations."[6]

John Burgess, in commenting on this phenomenon, said:

> Though we have had a bad conscience about segregated education, especially in church schools, we must admit that it is the United States Supreme Court that has driven home the necessity of free access to education in a free society. It does not really trouble me that men are not inspired by Christian Faith to do great things for men, I am only troubled that Christians do not yet find in their Gospel the power to do likewise.[7]

The civil rights movement, during which "Episcopalians were jolted out of their complacency,"[8] made new and more stringent demands on the Church. Because there was "an undercurrent of tension [that] warned of danger if equality did not come soon,"[9] the Church was challenged to a greater extent than it had ever been before. But the chameleon-like Episcopal Church proved equal to the task yet again, creatively adapting to a new terrain. The sit-ins and other peaceful civil rights demonstrations, often countered with violence on the part of law enforcement officials; the murders of civil rights workers in the South; the growing resistance to American involvement in Southeast Asia;[10] urban riots; and other events, especially those occurring during the "long hot summers," as they became known, prompted the Episcopal Church, at every level of its life, to take action, or at least to mount a reaction.

The perceived need to react stemmed from the Church's realization, or perhaps more accurately, admission of the fact that its own members, both as individuals and in the Church's name, had participated in the oppression of racial minorities. As John Booty expresses it: "The Episcopal Church was forced by the course of events to recognize the existence of a deep-rooted racial prejudice in its midst."[11] The incongruity between such practices and the principles for which the Church claimed that it stood became painfully obvious. The Episcopal Church, therefore, began, by its actions, to acknowledge what black Episcopalians had claimed for nearly two centuries — that there had long been a disparity between the Church's catholic claims and the unjust treatment of some of its members.

This climate prompted Presiding Bishop Arthur Lichtenberger to issue a statement on May 26, 1963, asking Episcopalians to involve themselves in the struggle for the Negro's rights, to make financial contributions, and to take appropriate action. Stating that "present events reveal the possible imminence of catastrophe," he wrote:

> Discrimination within the Body of the Church itself is an intolerable scandal. Every congregation has a continuing need to examine its own life and to renew those efforts necessary to insure its inclusiveness fully. Diocesan and church-related agencies, schools and other institutions also have a considerable distance to go in bringing their practices up to the standard of the clear position of the Church on race.[12]

The House of Bishops, meeting in August of that year, urged passage of effective civil rights legislation. Several dioceses established commissions on race relations or similar bodies to address such problems in their common life. The action of the Diocese of Southern Ohio was typical. Its commission on race relations was set up

> to seek by various means further understanding between Negro and White Christians within the Church. The Commission will encourage the creation throughout all parishes of the Diocese of local study groups involving both White and Negro persons, to deepen understanding of the present social revolution and to provide an opportunity for meaningful contact between people of different races;... seek to encourage the participation of clergy and laity in bi-racial civil action and study groups in local communities... seek to establish guide-lines for the clergy and laity of the Diocese as they seek to witness or demonstrate for civil rights.[13]

Despite these actions, however, the church establishment, restrained, if unconsciously, by their penchant to preserve the status quo, were loath to move "with all deliberate speed." Presiding Bishop John Hines, for example, declared that "he had great sympathy for the Negro, because of the wrongs done him and that those wrongs ought to be corrected," but further observed that "the structure of the church at present does not afford for rapid change." Bishop Burrill of Chicago commented that "change must come slowly, as the Episcopal Church is congregational in nature and the Bishops have no power to do more than to invoke change." Bishop Jones of Louisiana, citing the existence of "some integrated parishes and day schools [in his diocese] and the beginning of a change of attitude," suggested that "pressure at this time might damage the progress and harden attitudes."[14]

Black Episcopalians, however, embraced the urgency that characterized the civil rights movement. Bishop Burgess spoke for the group when he stated, "We can no longer depend upon gradualism. Tokenism tends to give the impression that all is well. All is not well and time has just about run out! We must have a crash program to correct the inequities that are the shame of our church.... Something must be done quickly."[15]

It was partly out of a desire to urge the Church to move more quickly than it would if left to its own devices that the Episcopal Society for Cultural and Racial Unity (hereinafter ESCRU) was formed. While not an official organization of the Church,[16] it represented an effort on the part of a widely based cross-section of Episcopalians[17] to attempt to raise the Church's consciousness around the issue of integration, in order that it might be brought into line, so to speak, with policies in the secular arena. Bishop (then Canon) Walter Dennis, who served on ESCRU's first board of directors, commented that "ESCRU believed the church wasn't moving fast enough, and thought that it could help it along."[18] ESCRU had its initial meeting in late December 1959 on the campus of St. Augustine's College, Raleigh, North Carolina. It is clear from its statement of purpose that it was concerned with encouraging the Church to be a more prophetic institution than it had been previously:

> [ESCRU will] promote increased acceptance and demonstration of the Church's policies of racial inclusiveness in its own life, as well as its role in providing leadership in the community and nation in establishing full opportunities for all persons, without racial discrimination, in fields such as education, housing, employment and public accommodation.[19]

Indeed, the policies that ESCRU espoused caused *The Living Church* to report that it "adopted a militant statement of purpose," which resulted in the resignation of one board member immediately following his election because it had become apparent to him that "the group chose to become a protest sect instead of a strategical organization for implementing throughout the Church the official pronouncements and policies of Church councils."[20]

The principal founders of ESCRU were white churchmen,[21] who by and large were desirous of empowering the Church to do no less than the nation in the arena of race relations. It was a black priest, however, it should be noted, subsequently elected ESCRU's first vice-president and later president, who saw the organization's formation in terms of the prophetic and catholic witness that had long characterized black Episcopalians' agenda:

> The problem of racial and cultural relations is the number one social problem of our day. As such it is the number one challenge before the Christian Church. And our Lord is judging His Church, testing its loyalty to Him and its obedience to His word in terms of what it is doing to heal the divisions between men.... If, through God's grace, we rise to this challenge, future generations may look back on our day and declare, "it was then that the Christian Church began to live the Faith it proclaims."[22]

In its actions during its eleven years of existence, ESCRU commended and supported clergy in their struggle for civil rights at the local level; protested policies that discriminated in the areas of employment and housing; decried school segregation and antimiscegenation laws in the South; condemned the practice of discrimination and segregation at the University of the South and other church-related schools;[23] and organized sit-ins and kneel-ins, the latter being a conscious effort to end segregation in parishes through encouraging its members to "transfer to the church nearest to their residence whose congregation is of a color and culture other than their own," such persons being designated as "missionaries."[24] In 1969, it sponsored, on Ash Wednesday, a public book burning of Episcopal Church school curricula that it considered racist in nature.[25]

Toward the end of its short life, ESCRU's black president, the Reverend Jesse Anderson Sr., expressed the concern that ESCRU was an organization run by and reflective of the theology of white liberals. Understandably, its black membership became "increasingly restive under what they perceived as white dominance." They believed, moreover, that "a largely white organization could never result in the empowerment of black Episcopalians nor unite with other black groups in the all-out attack on racism."[26] Or, as Kater expressed it, "numbers of blacks once active in the integration movement began to doubt the willingness, and more seriously, the ability of the dominant (white) society to reform itself."[27] ESCRU quite honestly attempted to effect integration in the life of the Church, a goal reflective of one of the principal aims of the civil rights movement. The Church discovered, however, as the nation had, that such a goal was not always attainable and not necessarily desirable. Good will alone, the Church learned, could not ensure harmony between the races. As in the nation at large, the enactment of laws did not necessarily turn people's hearts.[28] It soon became clear that the idea of "cultural and racial unity" denoted cultural and racial *sameness.* What is more, the respective cultural characteristics of the races were often obliterated in the process.[29] The sameness that resulted was more often than not dictated by the mores of the majority culture; "cultural unity," therefore, was achieved at the expense of minority, and particularly black, culture.[30]

Black parishes, for example, seen as vestiges of an age of segregation, were viewed as painful reminders of an unenlightened era; it was considered a more Christian enterprise to have integrated parishes. Even John Burgess, then archdeacon of Massachusetts, could advocate:

> Today, these churches must be prepared to die. Neighborhoods, we maintain, will reflect more closely the American ideal of true community. Churches, we maintain, will reflect more truly the Gospel that is their base. The props that have upheld these segregated churches will thereby be removed. But to die is not easy; the history of their organization, their struggle to maintain themselves and their status within the Church's life and their community's life — these have given them a vested, even a selfish, interest in their continuance.... *When they come into the more inclusive fellowship of the Church's life,* they come with a wealth of experience, devotion and faith that stands us majestically above the flippancy that judges them merely as anachronistic and dated.[31]

In the phrase "the more inclusive fellowship of the Church's life" is the implicit suggestion that the black congregations should be the ones willing to sacrifice their identity by assimilating into white congregations in order to achieve integration. In the attempted implementation of this goal a number of black congregations in the North were merged into white congregations,[32] but black parishioners in many such cases either found a cool welcome, or discovered that they became second-class citizens in the merged parish.[33] This resulted, as often as not, in their "defecting" to black denominations. But perhaps most important they learned that the power base they had in the black congregation had been relinquished, depriving them of that "social meeting place" where, according to Maloney, "the talent for racial leadership is developed."[34]

Within the ranks of ESCRU, blacks felt more and more marginalized, believing that the organization was having a more profound effect on race relations in society than in the Church itself. Thus, as early as 1965, six prominent black clergymen[35] shared with the fifth annual meeting of ESCRU held in Jackson, Mississippi, the text of their "Declaration of Concern," which they had presented in protest at a meeting of the House of Bishops in Montana a few days earlier. The document addressed the question of the Church's unchanging deployment practices. Its language echoes previous statements by black Episcopal Church leaders. Its reference to being considered aliens; the declaration of black Episcopalians' loyalty to the Church despite the mistreatment they had received at its hands; its reminding the Church of its catholic principles — are perennial themes reminiscent of the declarations of the CCWACP:

> Today, no noticeable changes have been made in the continuing custom of our church, and the silent sanction of our bishops, of the practice of recommending Negro priests for "Negro" parishes and missions and white priests for "white" parishes and missions.... As Priests of Negro ancestry, treated as *aliens and strangers* within this church... we demand as loyal and faithful sons of this branch of Christ's One Holy Catholic and Apostolic Church the end of a restricted ministry within the Episcopal Church. While the walls of segregation have come tumbling down in every institution — in government, in business, in sports, in entertainment, in education, in science — the Church continues to be the last bulwark of segregation in our society.... As a consequence of this blatant racism within the household of faith the Church has ceased to be catholic and has become a racially uncatholic structure scorned by those who have been kept out of it or who refuse to enter it on segregated terms. The evangelistic task of the Church is scandalously impaired and even openly denied in both North and South, not to speak of the effects of the hypocritical association of white domination in Christianity upon our mission in Asia and Africa.[36]

At the 1966 annual meeting, black members of ESCRU felt the need to prod their white counterparts to support them in their efforts to "welcome the assertion of black power as a sign of maturity and as a recognition by American citizens who are Negroes of the reality that only in the assembly and commitment of strategic but still latent economic and political power can social change be accomplished which resembles justice."[37] More significantly, blacks urged ESCRU to mount "a relentless assault upon the ethos and ethics of white supremacy... and paternalism in the Episcopal Church."[38] The growing tension between whites and blacks in ESCRU led the Reverend Quinland Gordon to entitle his keynote speech at the 1967 annual meeting, "ESCRU: In Transition, or on Its Deathbed?" A September 1967 editorial in the *Christian Century* was entitled "ESCRU at the

Crossroads." By the 1968 annual meeting, the organization that less than a decade before had dedicated itself to unity was divided into a black caucus and a white caucus. The minutes of the black caucus's meeting held on November 16 of that year reported: "There was much frank discussion as to whether Black Episcopalians should continue to remain in ESCRU in its present form."[39] It is not coincidental that the Union of Black Clergy and Laity (later the Union of Black Episcopalians) had already been formed that year in the belief that it could be a more effective agent of change for black Episcopalians.

It was at the ESCRU banquet held in Houston during the 1970 General Convention that the announcement was made by Vice-President Barbara Harris that the organization had been disbanded.[40] The executive director, the Reverend Albert R. Dreisbach Jr., indicated that sufficient funds were not forthcoming which would enable the society's continuance. Two of his comments, in which he reflected on changing times, are especially telling. The first had to do with financial realities:

> All attempts to gain funding outside our own ranks were equally futile; for it is now quite clear that minority self-empowerment is "the" number one priority for both the foundations and other similar funding sources like GCSP.[41]

The second comment had to do with the ideological shift that had taken place during the decade since ESCRU's founding (and which, it can be argued, accounted for the decrease in financial support):

> I still remain as firmly convinced today as I did in 1964 when I joined the staff that Cultural and Racial Unity are valid goals. However, I do admit that my definition of these terms has been altered considerably in the intervening years. The culture which will unite us in the future will be one counter to the one which we thought merely stood in need of reform during those beautifully naive days when we walked hand-in-hand through the "Civil Whites Movement." And the unity which, God willing, we will someday achieve will be a unity of purpose wherein one's ideology is his or her most distinguishing characteristic.[42]

ESCRU came to the realization that the 1960s had subscribed to a "melting pot" theory of racial equality; by the 1970s the nation was moving on to a more honest "salad bowl" theory.[43] ESCRU, inextricably caught in the web of the old paradigm, could not shift, and therefore died a natural, if dignified death. While ESCRU may have been somewhat successful in its attempt "to arouse the conscience of the Episcopal Church and lead it into effective action with its own life,"[44] black Episcopalians found that such effective action as was implemented did not result in an appreciable improvement of their lot, which in the 1960s had been of necessity subsumed in the white liberal agenda.

The Union of Black Clergy and Laity (UBCL), then, in some ways was the phoenix that arose out of ESCRU's ashes. Edward Rodman sees its coming into being as a common manifestation of the times. He points out that "every major denomination saw similar groups emerge, each seeking attention of the decision-makers within their institutions to the black agenda, which spoke to the urgency of the situation as its black members saw it."[45] James Findlay also sees the emergence of the UBCL as reflective of the times, and specifically as an outgrowth of the black power movement. His comments would suggest that, given their divergent goals, ESCRU and the UBCL could not have coexisted in the same church:

> The black power movement almost immediately led to the creation of black caucuses within predominantly white churches. Black power provided a strong sense of identity instead of a constant ambiguity of being neither members in independent [black] churches nor full participants in a truly inclusive church. These developments in the Episcopal Church led to the rapid disintegration and demise of the Episcopal Society for Cultural and Racial Unity.[46]

But more significantly, the UBCL was formed because it was strongly believed that only a united black voice could exert the pressure needed to bring about needed change and, more specifically, the eradication of racism. Too, the UBCL's founders believed that it was incumbent upon them to speak directly to the Church's leadership regarding matters pertaining to them. For example, while black Episcopalians endorsed, in principle, the General Convention's actions in 1967 which established the General Convention Special Program (GCSP) designed to redress the problems of blacks and other minorities in the inner cities, they nonetheless took umbrage at the action because it empowered black groups in local communities, an action that, as Rodman observed, "completely ignored the role of the black Episcopal Church as a focus for this new program by giving money directly to secular groups, many of whom were openly hostile to religious institutions."[47]

Such an affront did not go unnoticed. The decision of the special General Convention held in South Bend, Indiana, in 1969 to make $200,000 available through GCSP to the Black Economic Development Conference and not to the Episcopal group, the Committee of Black Churchmen, was repudiated by black Episcopalians and further served to embolden them, and to make them even more firm in their resolve to mobilize in and act through a caucus rather than to attempt to effect change through "the system." After General Convention made its intention clear, the Reverend Junius Carter declared "I'm sick . . . and I'm sick of you. You don't trust me, you don't trust black priests."[48] The *Journal of the General Convention* reported that reaction somewhat more diplomatically: "The Rev. Mr. Carter of Pittsburgh and the Rev. Mr. Casson of Delaware, on behalf of black clergymen, expressed their disappointment at the action just taken."[49]

It is crucial that we grasp the significance of the official actions on the part of the Episcopal Church in this regard. Through those actions, the Church displayed an unabashed lack of confidence in its own black membership. Because the most vocal activists in the black community were in the secular arena, the Church acceded to *their* demands. Believing them to be a more authentic and representative voice for blacks, the Church did not recognize in black Episcopalians the possibility that they whose parishes, in most instances, were in the heart of the urban centers wracked with violence and unrest could be instrumental in addressing the problem.

The Church's action in this regard was consistent with its historical attitude. This was but a variation on an old theme of marginalization. It would appear that the Episcopal Church had so condescended to blacks in its midst that to the mind of the Church they were neither fish nor fowl — that is, neither an integral part of the Episcopal Church, nor an authentic component of the black community. Blacks, as always, had been relegated to an ecclesiastical and societal limbo. Moreover, so committed was the Church to this new way of doing business with the black community that it began to take steps to remove the Reverend Dr. Tollie Caution from his position as secretary of the Division of Racial Minorities at its national headquarters, in the belief that he could not make the necessary adjustments to conform to the new paradigm of racial strategy that the Church was adopting during the throes of the civil rights movement.[50] This added insult to injury, and served as a catalyst for the founding of the UBCL. The Union's founding, it can be said, "fulfilled the prophecy" of Bishop Burgess, who had indicated that in light of Caution's dismissal he was "sure that there are enough concerned Negro churchmen who will organize outside the official structure to promote our interests."[51]

But according to the Right Reverend Quintin E. Primo Jr., a founder and first president of the Union, now retired bishop suffragan of Chicago,[52] the indignation of the Ad Hoc Committee of Negro Clergy[53] did not center on the act itself, but on the way it was carried out. Bishop Primo reports that Dr. Caution was given a letter of resignation composed and written by the Right Reverend Daniel Corrigan, then head of the Home Department on the presiding bishop's staff. Caution was asked simply to sign it. This act was looked upon by the committee as unconscionable. It was, in the first instance, a personal affront to Caution, who had served the national Church in various capacities for nearly a quarter of a century. But moreover, the insensitive action was perceived by extension to be an insult to all black clergy (since Dr. Caution had long been regarded as their "friend at court"). Therefore, the slight came to represent, to the mind of the committee, the contempt that the Church held for all of its black clergy.

The incident was related to Primo in a telephone conversation with Caution. Primo admonished Caution not to sign the letter and not to resign his position. Primo then convened the Ad Hoc Committee for a special meeting at St. Luke's Church, Washington, D.C., on January 5, 1968.[54] At that meeting it was decided that a delegation of black priests would meet with Presiding Bishop Hines. The delegation, made up of the Reverend Messrs. Austin Cooper, Thomas Gibbs, Quinland Gordon, Kenneth Hughes, Clifford Lauder, Joseph Nicholson, and Quintin Primo, met with Presiding Bishop Hines on January 17, and voiced their displeasure about the way Tollie Caution had been dismissed. They further demanded that he be retained for at least one year, in order that he be able to leave with dignity. The presiding bishop acceded to most of their demands. Dr. Caution remained on staff until June 1968, and a fitting celebration of his ministry was held at St. Martin's Church in New York City, but these developments notwithstanding, according to Primo, "Tollie was crushed."[55]

The black priests' protest was fueled by a sense of betrayal. In April 1967, a delegation from the Ad Hoc Committee had met with the Presiding Bishop and five other bishops to discuss what the committee perceived as the Church's iniquitous practices in relation to its black members, especially its clergy.[56] A further meeting was held two months later in order that the dialogue might continue.[57] At that meeting, the specific question of clergy deployment was addressed, and the Church's policies and intentions in this area were reflected in the agenda. Of the comments made, it is interesting to note that the black clergy cited incidences in which such practices as the "old boys' network" militated against fair practices in black clergy deployment, *especially at the Executive Council.* In this connection, Dr. Nicholson queried: "Why must Negroes always have so much training, when others (i.e., whites) with so little or no training or experience are considered for openings and are subsequently given on-the-job training?" The Reverend Harold Louis Wright, a black priest from the Diocese of Long Island who later became bishop suffragan of New York, linked the limited employment opportunities for Negro priests to the "difficulties experienced [by them] in recruiting other Negroes for the priesthood. He said that other institutions in our society are getting young Negroes, simply because the young Negro sees no opportunity for growth and advancement in the Episcopal priesthood. To this all Negro priests can well attest."

Similarly, "Bishop Burgess gave names of prominent Negroes in the civil rights arena, who have left the Church (and even Christ) because the Church was not progressive enough in pressing for social change." In light of the testimony presented by black clergy, "Father Charlton [a white priest] suggested that the elected officials of Executive Council should publicly embrace a statement to the effect that they would attempt to compensate for past oversights and exclusions of Negroes, where there are openings in Executive Council."[58] To this end, a resolution that had been passed by Executive Council earlier that year was read and discussed.[59] In light of these developments, Dr. Caution's summary dismissal was, for the black clergy, a bitter pill to swallow. It sent a signal to them that the Church's hierarchy did not take their plight seriously, and was only giving lip-service to their demands.

On February 8, 1968, the Ad Hoc Committee gathered at historic St. Philip's Church in Harlem to form the Union of Black Clergy and Laity. The founders "decided to focus on the desperate need of blacks and on the existence of racism in the church."[60] According to the Reverend Austin Cooper, who served as secretary to the Ad Hoc Committee, the group had received word that Presiding Bishop Hines would "take a hard look" at the firing of Tollie Caution. He recounts that the Reverend St. Julian Simpkins was deputized to place a telephone call to the presiding bishop's office, and upon reporting to the group that he had learned that no further consideration had been given to this matter, the motion to organize the Union was made immediately.[61] Accordingly, upon passage of the motion, the Reverend Dr. M. Moran Weston, St. Philip's rector, moved that the presiding bishop be informed that the new organization was the successor of the Ad Hoc Committee of Negro Clergy.[62] It was also Dr. Weston who, recognizing the historicity of the occasion, notified the press. The following day, the *New York Times* reported that a statement issued by the founders

> said the main goal of the Union was to "remove racism in the church and in the community by any means necessary to achieve full participation on the basis of equality in policy making, decision making, program and staffing on the parochial, diocesan and national levels." Other announced goals were to stimulate the growth of "black membership" throughout

> the church, to promote the placement of Negro professionals within the church without regard to race and at "all levels" and to protect Negro clergymen from "racist practices."[63]

The UBCL set about the business of organizing its work. Although the founders were all prominent clergymen,[64] the group, which according to Primo realized that "the layfolk had the power," made a conscious decision (as evidenced by its new name) to recast the organization to ensure that its membership (and power base) would be lay as well as clerical.[65] They wanted to make it clear that they had been transformed from a exclusively clerical group concerned with the mistreatment of a colleague to a more broadly based group whose role it was to address not a specific grievance, but an endemic problem. That endemic problem was addressed in the words of the preamble to the "Purposes" of the Union drawn up at its inaugural meeting, which made it very clear that it was again a *catholic* agenda, a concern for the *whole* Church of which blacks believed themselves to be an integral part, which inspired them to act: "Since the cause of Jesus Christ is hindered in our own time by racism within the Church and community (making it difficult for many to accept and causing others to reject Him) this Union of Black Clergy and Laymen of the Episcopal Church is established."[66]

Through a mass solicitation, in which black congregations were asked to contribute $100 each, funds were raised to place ads in three major church publications, *The Witness, The Episcopalian,* and *The Living Church.*[67] This move succeeded in drawing the attention of a large cross-section of Episcopalians.[68] In addition to raising money, the Union's new leadership sent cards to black clergy throughout the country, asking them to sign them as an indication of their support of the Union's principles. Further, in an effort "to counter black Episcopalians who thought the UBE was divisive, the Union took its show on the road," and held regional conferences.[69]

Not surprisingly, the birth of the UBCL was not universally heralded as a joyous event. Many people (some blacks as well as whites) saw it as a separatist, racist, or even communist organization. Another UBCL founder, the Right Reverend Walter Dennis, bishop suffragan of New York, comments that at a very basic level, at a time in history when the term "Negro" was in common parlance, many black Episcopalians did not want to be called black, and therefore objected to the union for no other reason than its name. These developments "frightened comfortable black Episcopalians," he observed; "even Tollie felt the UBE was sometimes too radical."[70] Bishop Primo recounts that the bishop of Alabama threatened a black vicar in his diocese with dismissal for encouraging his congregation to make financial contributions to the Union.[71] But despite setbacks, from within the ranks as well as without, the UBCL early in its history found itself woven into the fabric of the Church's life.

Its excellent and inspired leadership, its timely formation, the fact that the Caution incident had served as a catalyst in its establishment, and the fact that the Union saw itself from the beginning as a caucus "whose primary function was to encourage blacks to come together in order to present a united front to fight racism,"[72] all account in part for its rapid (and, as history has shown, permanent) absorption into the Church's life.[73] But the major reason that the UBCL got off to such a "flying start" is that it was not really a new organization at all, for it had emerged not only from the ashes of ESCRU, but also from the ashes of the Conference of Church Workers among Colored People, which, according to Rodman, "had run out of gas in 1967, and was leaderless with the departure of Dr. Caution."[74]

The campus of St. Augustine's College, Raleigh, where many of the Church Workers' conferences had taken place, and where ESCRU had its inaugural meeting, in 1968 became the site of the first annual meeting of the UBCL. Its first elected president, the Reverend Quintin Primo Jr., then rector of St. Matthew's, Wilmington, Delaware, called together a disparate (and to a certain extent, desperate) group of blacks who roughly fell into three categories. The first of these were old "church workers," who epitomized black middle-class respectability, and who were historically committed to "working within the system." They were the spiritual sons and daughters of Alexander Crummell, who eighty-five years earlier had mobilized clergy to protest the proposed "Sewanee canon." The group had continued to meet to register their protests against the Church's treatment of blacks. The second group were disillusioned ESCRUites, who had previously bought into the dreams of an integrated society, but who were now convinced that integration was not the answer. The third group, whom Rodman dubs "the young turks," were principally newly ordained clergy who had been emboldened and inspired by the rhetoric of the civil rights and black power movements.[75] They constituted a demonstrably radical element, impatient with the Church's response to the plight of blacks, and were committed to revolutionizing it "by any means necessary." The UBCL, then, was aptly named. Its coming into being marked a *union of black Episcopalians* (which later became its name) from different backgrounds. They were all united in a common purpose, a common vision. As Rodman succinctly described the new movement, "1968 marked the arrival of Black consciousness within the Episcopal Church, and as a result, it would never be the same again."[76]

The emergence of the UBCL points to an interesting phenomenon. Its founding members were effective in their attempts to challenge the Church to be responsive to the black agenda because they could ride on the wave of the civil rights movement, which provided an "implicit challenge to reform and renew the church as a fellowship in the love of God."[77] The Church, then, which historically had turned a deaf ear to the complaints of blacks and had moved slowly and reticently when it did act, now found itself making major concessions.[78] This could take place because although the *pressure* to change came from black leaders within the Church, the actual *motivation* to change originated outside the Church, where the societal order was undergoing a virtual metamorphosis. The union's founders, it can be argued, were able to capitalize on the (admittedly short-lived) period of "white guilt" which was operative at that time in the nation at large, in general, and, characteristically, in the Episcopal Church in particular.

Primo, Cooper, Mayson, Simpkins, Weston, and the others were no less prophetic in their witness than such pioneers as Crummell, Bragg, Miller, Holly, and Frazier, but the protests raised during the civil rights movement emerged at that precise kairotic moment when the Church, desperately seeking to accommodate itself to the expectations of the broader community and eager to win its approbation, was at its most receptive. As we have pointed out elsewhere:

> God, from time to time, raised up prophets within the bosom of our church — men like James Theodore Holly... George Freeman Bragg... and Tollie LeRoy Caution.... But they were often dismissed, placated or patronized; or ways were found to lessen their potential impact. It was not until prophets arose from without, in the society in which the church was so integral a part; it was not until the terrain... had begun to shift irreversibly, that we began to see action.[79]

Thus the society to whose drumbeat the Church had consistently marched was once again dictating the Episcopal Church's moral and social agenda.

Conclusion

The African American Struggle for Recognition in the Episcopal Church, Revisited

Join hands then, brothers of the faith whate'er your race may be.

—John Oxenham (hymn text, 1908)

If it is true, as W. E. B. Du Bois alleged, that "the Episcopal Church has probably done less for black people than any other aggregation of Christians,"[1] it is no less true that what little has been done was done not of the Church's own volition, but as a result of pressure exerted on the Church from within and without. It can be argued, then, that the Episcopal Church, in addressing matters concerning its black constituency, has been given more to reaction than action, more to response than initiative, more to acquiescence than advocacy. Such acts, born solely of a sense of obligation, have been carried out with reticence, reluctance and reserve. The Church's approach has been minimalist—that is, it did no more than it felt it absolutely had to do, with the result that in most instances the Church did far less than it could have done.

The Reverend Dalton Downs, in a letter to black bishops and General Convention deputies in 1973, put it this way:

> During the 60s, some of the leaders dragged pieces of the Church along by the ears, but the basic core of the Church's constituency *never* was committed to anything involving fundamental changes in society that would result, for example, in the redistribution of power and resources. ... It makes little sense today to say the Church is beginning to suffer from a failure of nerve. That would imply that there is a large number of people in the Church who want to do something but were afraid. The reality is that most churchmen are status-quo oriented.... They are doing exactly what they want to do, and in most cases their "thing" is divorced completely from the hard world in which our people live and suffer and die.[2]

Examples of this phenomenon abound, occurring as early as the founding of St. Thomas', Philadelphia, and as recently as last week.

St. Thomas' was established not because the Diocese of Pennsylvania willed it into existence but because free blacks in Philadelphia petitioned the diocese. When the parish was founded, it was established on the condition that it relinquish its right to representation in the councils of the diocese, a stipulation that was not removed for seventy years. Such a practice, as we have seen, was replicated in the founding of most black parishes, North and South, during the next hundred years.

Black bishops were first consecrated not because the Church thought it was a good idea, but because of the pressure exerted by its black leadership through the CCWACP, whose members demanded that they be represented in the Church's hierarchy. But when consecrated, such bishops were limited in their ministrations to "their own people." Indeed, the CCWACP was instrumental not only in lobbying on behalf of blacks, but in heading off action on the part of the Church that would have greatly diminished their effect on its life; notably, it was successful in preventing the Church from officially dividing along racial lines by sending a memorial to the 1883 General Convention, which in effect thwarted the passage of the "Sewanee canon." Their original gambit having met with success, the conference made it a practice to meet during each succeeding General Convention year to present or transmit memorials — for example, on the racial episcopate, or social justice for blacks. Since black deputies to General Convention were virtually nonexistent until the 1960s,[3] CCWACP visits to the triennial gatherings served to remind the Church of the existence of African American members in its ranks.

When, in the 1930s black churchmen brought to the Church's attention the fact that they were consistently mistreated, demeaned, and marginalized, the General Convention responded by establishing a Commission on Negro Work, but as soon as a secretary for Negro work was put in place, the committee asked to be discharged. During the civil rights era, the Church made concessions to the demands of its black members only after an ad hoc committee of black clergy, who later formed the UBCL, registered a protest centered around the dismissal of the secretary for Negro Work.

The Episcopal Church, at various stages in its history, has been prodded into action not by a particular group, but by a societal condition so prevalent that to ignore it would render the Church liable to allegations of imperviousness. Thus, when faced, for example, with a new population of freed blacks in the South after the Civil War (many of whom had remained in the church in which they had previously worshipped in slave chapels) the Church felt obliged to found the Freedman's Commission in order to provide some outreach to that group. Early in this century, the Church, concerned about the "Negro problem," founded the American Church Institute for Negroes.

One major exception to this norm concerns the initiatives taken by the Church to evangelize slaves. As we have demonstrated, it was a conditional evangelization process at best, designed not to assist in a removal of the state of bondage, but rather to reinforce it; to remind slaves, in the unforgettable words of Bishop Gibson, that baptism "lays them under stronger obligation to perform [their] duties with the greatest diligence and fidelity."[4]

The researcher who conducts even a perfunctory survey of the historical relationship between black Episcopalians and the white power structure of the Episcopal Church is at once struck by the *déjà vu* nature of the data. This should not be surprising, since the Church, given its tendency to regard as suspect those who challenge or threaten the established order, is more likely to placate such persons, and to apply temporary or narrow remedies where more comprehensive, radical, long-term remedies were indicated.[5] The Church has been most successful, therefore, in treating the most prevalent symptoms of the disorder in question, and not the disorder itself. Given such inadequate treatment, if we may belabor the metaphor, a chronic recurrence of the disease is inevitable. Perhaps this phenomenon is nowhere more evident than it is in the arena of clergy deployment. A *leitmotif* of black Episcopal Church history has been the observation on the part of the CCWACP, the UBE, and various individuals and ad hoc groups that the Episcopal Church discriminates in its appointment practices, that is, that it has traditionally been a foregone conclusion that black priests can only serve in black congregations.

In 1889, Seth Low, the president of Columbia University, commented: "We have in our diocese of Long Island a colored presbyter of marked ability, but what is his outlook? He has reached the acme of his opportunity now. He is at the head of a colored congregation. He may accept the call to some other colored congregation, but that is all."[6] In 1965, as we have noted, a group of black clergy decried the Church's long practice of "restricted ministry."[7]

In 1967, the Reverend Robert E. Hood's study about deployment patterns found that the Church has acted as if there were two ordinals, one for black priests and one for white priests: "As such the church is a party to perpetuating a fraud upon its Negro clergy. As such, the church is a party . . . to a felt sense of betrayal on the part of Negro clergy and indeed, many whites."[8]

In 1968, the UBCL was founded in the hope that it could help the Church "achieve full participation on the basis of equality in policy-making, decision making, program and staffing on parochial, diocesan and national levels."[9] In the same year, in a declaration of Negro clergy addressed to Presiding Bishop John Hines, black priests lamented their "subtle and well-nigh systematic exclusion... from the heart of the church's life." They further stated that

> doubt... is cast upon the integrity of the whole church, when it accepts Negroes... as postulants for the sacred ministry only if their work is to be in a limited area in contrast to the "God-desired areas where there are no bounds" and the use of one set of criteria by the bishops in missions and by vestries in parishes for the placement of Negro clergy and of another set of criteria for the placement of white clergy.[10]

In 1973 John Edwards observed, "The Negro applicant for the ministry in the Episcopal Church is forced with the problem of where he can exercise his vocation. Continuing integration of Negroes into white parishes and the closing of Negro churches mean that there is no place or future for Negro clergymen."[11] In 1979, Adair Lumis wrote, "A pervasive source of frustration of black clergy is the relative lack of opportunities for occupational mobility within the Episcopal Church."[12]

As recently as 1992, the Reverend Canon Edward Rodman, in an open letter, brought to the attention of Presiding Bishop Edmond Browning that several senior black clergy had been relieved of their positions.[13] Among those dismissed were the Reverend Canon Lloyd S. Casson, as vicar of Trinity Parish, New York City, reputedly the wealthiest parish in the Episcopal Church; the Venerable Enrique R. Brown, archdeacon of Region II, a predominantly white and affluent section in the Diocese of New York; and the Reverend Dr. J. Carleton Hayden, associate dean of the School of Theology at the University of the South, Sewanee, Tennessee, an institution that a generation earlier had not even admitted black students! These and other appointments had been heralded as precedent-setting breakthroughs, but in the end proved to be anomalous and short-lived exceptions to a long-established norm.

In response to Rodman's letter, the presiding bishop commissioned a study to look into the "role of black males in the Episcopal Church."[14] The study, however, failed to address the endemic problem, focusing instead on tangential issues among black Episcopalians. In the end, the presiding bishop, after sharing the document with black bishops, suppressed it, an action that clearly demonstrated that the issue of black clergy deployment was not, for him, a high priority. While in previous generations the Church would at least have issued a platitudinous statement deploring the evils of the system, in this instance the Church, by its silence, betrayed an official lack of interest in the matter altogether.

The unfortunate dénouement of this episode must be seen in light of a broader development. First it must be remembered that in the space of a generation, the Episcopal Church, never known for its "staying power," had exhibited marked signs of shifting interests in the causes it championed. During the civil rights movement, racism was the only "-ism" with which the Church had to contend and, accordingly, put virtually all of its eggs in that one ideological basket. Jolted out of complacency, as we have seen, the Church, sometimes deftly and sometimes clumsily, sought to work with and through black groups in order that it might appear to have some credibility outside of the white, privileged circles with which it had so long been identified. Initially, those black groups were often outside the Episcopal Church, and even the faith community.

John Maury Allin, who was elected presiding bishop in 1973, aware that such alliances both raised questions about the Church's integrity and alienated its black constituency, sought to regain the trust of African Americans in the Episcopal Church. Rodman reports that Bishop Allin, immediately after his election, conceded to virtually all of the requests made by the Union of Black Episcopalians.[15] To each petition in the UBE's litany, the newly elected presiding bishop dutifully intoned "Amen." Accordingly, the Office of Black Ministries (the "black desk") was established, and the Reverend Franklin D. Turner (now bishop suffragan of Pennsylvania) was appointed as its first incumbent. This ended the five-year hiatus in a black programmatic thrust which had existed since the dismissal of Tollie Caution. Allin further acceded to a request for a more secure basis for funding for the three black Episcopal colleges (St. Augustine's, St. Paul's, and Voorhees). The presiding bishop also assured the UBE that a black priest would be appointed to his senior staff[16] and that other blacks already on the national Church's staff would be retained. Allin promised the UBE that any successor to the General Convention Special Program would include the black Church in its strategic planning and grant-making, and made a commitment to implement an affirmative-action hiring program at Executive Council.

Moreover, he told the UBE that he would see to the appointment of black bishops and deputies to the important standing committees of the Church. This last pledge was facilitated by the fact that halfway through Allin's term Dr. Charles Radford Lawrence was elected president of the House of Deputies, marking the first time that an African American held that post. In this role, Dr. Lawrence enjoyed the power of appointment of all clergy and laypersons to interim commissions and committees of General Convention, and exercised that prerogative in such a way as to ensure that virtually all of those committees became racially inclusive.

Edmond Lee Browning, a descendent of Robert E. Lee, became presiding bishop in 1985. Although he shared with his predecessor both Southern provenance and alma mater (the University of the South at Sewanee) their ministerial careers followed very different paths. Allin spent his entire ministry in the South, becoming bishop coadjutor of Mississippi in 1961, and had an intimate involvement — some would say a baptism by fire — in the civil rights movement. Browning, however, spent only five years in Texas parishes before being appointed an overseas missionary to Okinawa in 1959, where he was consecrated bishop nine years later. He was successively appointed bishop of the American Convocation in Europe, then Executive for World Mission at the Church headquarters in New York, and was later translated to the missionary diocese of Hawaii, from which see he was elected twenty-fourth presiding bishop.

At the time of Browning's election, African Americans in the Episcopal Church were still basking in the sunshine created by the fact that the presidents of both houses had been their friends at court. More than a score of African Americans held appointed positions at church headquarters; and owing to the Lawrence legacy, black Episcopalians sat on virtually every commission and committee in the life of the Church. Browning's promise at the 1985 General Convention in Anaheim that there would be "no outcasts" in the Church was, therefore, well received by blacks, who were confident that what had essentially amounted to a "favored status" for them would continue into the new administration. They believed this although John Thomas Walker, bishop and dean of Washington, the candidate whom most blacks had hoped would be elected, had been defeated.

But their hopes were dashed by the end of the first triennium of Browning's primacy. Many black Episcopalians saw themselves as the very outcasts whom Browning had indicated would not exist in the Church. By the time of the Indianapolis General Convention in 1994, it was clear that with the exception of the retention of (an eviscerated version of) the Office of Black Ministries, all the other advances achieved by blacks at Louisville two decades earlier had been effectively eliminated.[17] This overall development can be traced to two sources. First, Browning, owing to a series of overseas appointments, had had virtually no contact with African Americans during his ministry. He had not lived through the civil rights movement, and had little basic understanding of African Americans or their struggles. While black Episcopalians do not fault him for his lack of experience, they have expressed concern that unlike his predecessor, he has not sought the counsel of or even listened to the black leadership of the Church who had borne the burden in the heat of the day. Hence, he could, for instance, fly in the face of the virtually unanimous advice and counsel of his black constituency, representatives of which had been summoned to a meeting in New York (and that of a goodly number of white Episcopalians as well) and insist that the 1991 General Convention take place in Phoenix, at a time when almost every thinking organization in America was boycotting the State of Arizona because of its failure to make Martin Luther King Day a holiday. Second, Browning had returned to the mainland at a time when new "-isms" were holding sway. Other groups, had, after all, piggy-backed on the success of the civil rights movement and had started revolutions of their own. So although racism had by no means been eradicated, interest in it in the 1980s and '90s has been largely eclipsed in the nation, and therefore in the Episcopal Church, by concerns around sexism and heterosexism, with the Church throwing in clericalism for good measure. So while Browning gave lip service to the evils of racism, even railing against it on occasion, his passion was confined to problems inherent in sexism and clericalism, doubtless accounting for the absence of clergy and the predominance of laywomen on his senior staff.

Bishop Browning has preached at two national conventions of the UBE. He has appointed three black bishops — John Walker, James Ottley, and Arthur Williams — to the largely ceremonial post of vice-president of the House of Bishops.[18] In 1992, accompanied by his staff officer for black ministries, he made a national tour of black congregations and outreach programs. He has invited the Reverend Michael Curry, the rector of St. James', Baltimore, to preach to the House of Bishops; he has invited the Rev. Dr. Kortright Davis of the Howard University School of Divinity to provide theological reflection for the same body. While such acts have been laudable, they have been at best fleeting honors. Browning has been less than assiduous, however, in looking after issues that have long-term implications for blacks in the life of the Church, such as the deployment of black clergy, which, as we have seen, has been of constant concern to black Episcopalians. The suppression of the report on the status of black males in the Episcopal Church bespeaks a penchant of the Browning administration for treating the black agenda with indifference. Moreover, it may well be that in light of his own track record, he was loath to circulate a document that reported that black males "have little influence or power with the

Presiding Bishop's office"; and which called for the creation of "special monitoring from deployment offices on the calling, hiring and termination of ethnic minorities."[19] In May 1995, only six blacks remained on his appointed staff, a 75 percent decrease of the number at the time of his election. Of these, none was an African American male, the first time that this has been the case since the appointment of Bravid Harris in 1943.[20]

It should also be noted, however, that one black person, a new wave of black marginalization notwithstanding, has exercised both influence and power with the presiding bishop's office. She is Diane Marie Porter. Ms. Porter joined the staff in 1988 as deputy for public policy, in the Advocacy, Witness and Justice Ministries unit. She brought to the position a distinguished record in public service, having worked in the Department of Housing and Urban Development, and, immediately prior to her appointment, as chief of staff to a prominent U.S. congressman. A lifelong Episcopalian, she had also exercised a significant lay ministry, principally in the Diocese of Long Island, where she served as a trustee both of the diocese and of the George Mercer School of Theology, a member of the Standing Committee, and chairperson of the Mercer Scholarship Fund. Ms. Porter's rise through the ranks at the Episcopal Church Center can only be described as meteoric. She became acting executive, and then executive of the unit. She was later named senior executive for program, while remaining in her previous post as executive, placing her in the enviable position of being her own boss, and in the ambiguous position of being both supervisor and peer to other unit executives. In the fall of 1994, Bishop Browning appointed Ms. Porter vice-president of the Domestic and Foreign Missionary Society, making her the second highest–ranking officer in the Episcopal Church, and the first African American, male or female, clerical or lay, to occupy that or any comparable post in the Episcopal Church's hierarchy. *Ebony,* which has been chronicling the achievements of African Americans for half a century, featured Ms. Porter in its April 1995 issue in an article entitled "Amazing Grace: Fifty Years of the Black Church." In it, she was pictured with the heads of black denominations as well as other African American executives in predominantly white churches.

But the true measure of Ms. Porter's influence cannot be discerned by referring to the organizational flow chart. At an unofficial level she has been confidante to the presiding bishop, and has advised him on matters pertaining to race and gender, international affairs, staffing, the Church's budget, and a host of other issues. She has accompanied the presiding bishop and Mrs. Browning in their travels, both in the United

States and abroad, particularly to the Middle East. Ms. Porter's position is unique both because the breadth of her influence on the Primate is unprecedented, and because she has been the sole person in such a role. In a church that has been justifiably accused of racism, sexism, and clericalism, Ms. Porter is to be commended for having risen to so prestigious and pivotal a position in its governance. Indeed, in a recent interview, she described herself as having succeeded despite having "three strikes" against her.[21]

But while Ms. Porter's achievements can be applauded as a personal victory, one that has successfully challenged the "-isms" with which the Church is beset, it is widely believed that history will show that from the point of view of the struggle of blacks for recognition in the Episcopal Church, it is a pyrrhic victory at best. For one thing, her succession of appointments took place during precisely the same period of time in which the number of other black staff at the Church's headquarters decreased drastically, through demotions, dismissals, and resignations. Diane Porter has been duly rewarded for her loyalty and tenacity, but other blacks did not share in her recognition, and it is unlikely, therefore, that a foundation has been laid or a legacy provided for subsequent generations. Because Ms. Porter was appointed by the presiding bishop because of her personal loyalty to him, and not, like Allin's black appointees, for their commitment to the movement, her role, therefore, represents a paradigm shift, away from the examples of other African Americans who worked for the national Church and whose exercise of ministry served as an invitation to others to stand on their shoulders.

To return to the overall question of black deployment, many persons, when made aware of the statistics showing that black rectors of predominantly white congregations have been a rarity, have pointed out that the election of a large number of blacks to the episcopate[22] should be regarded as a more significant accomplishment than the election of rectors, and therefore should be seen as a greater gain. Such a view betrays a woeful misunderstanding of the Church's polity. The power base of the Episcopal Church is the rector and vestry of a parish. Although called "episcopal," the Church is actually congregational in its structure. The bishop's rights and prerogatives are limited by canon.[23] The power of moral suasion that the office might have enjoyed in an earlier generation has been greatly diminished in an era in which such concepts as "total ministry" and "lay empowerment" and the catechetical declaration that "the ministers of the Church are lay persons, bishops, priests and deacons"[24] bespeak a decentralization of clerical power and influence. And if a finding of the Church's 1991 racial audit is correct, black bishops are accorded even less respect than their white counterparts.[25] Many of the bishop's roles are ceremonial, administrative, and, more recently (given the prevalence of sexual misconduct and abuse cases), judicial. These roles tend to set the bishop at a remove from the rank and file. Parishioners, therefore, perceive the bishop as a somewhat remote figure who makes an annual visitation to the parish; and, accordingly, it has proved far easier to elect blacks to such positions than to rectorships of white congregations where their interaction with the flock is on a daily basis. At the House of Bishops meeting held in Panama in 1993, the Right Reverend Orris G. Walker Jr., the first black bishop to head the Diocese of Long Island, startled his colleagues by announcing that while pleased to have been elected to that see, he knows that there are a goodly number of parishes in his own diocese which would not have been disposed to electing him as rector!

In a similar vein, Bishop Primo remarked, "The Church doesn't want us... in positions of authority."[26] Bishop Dennis, while recognizing that there has been an increase in the number of blacks elected to the episcopate and to the deanships of cathedrals, commented:

> Blacks in the Episcopal Church are not seated where the *real* power is. We'll *never* have it. We can be the "raven over the door," but never in power because we are not part of the establishment. For a black bishop or priest, the power of personal integrity is the greatest power we can possess.[27]

Such comments raise serious doubts as to the validity of the contention that blacks seek out the Episcopal Church because of the status that membership in it purportedly confers. Because of its close identification with the American power establishment, the status of black members in the Episcopal Church is analogous to the status of blacks in society as a whole. Sara Lawrence-Lightfoot, herself the granddaughter of a black Episcopal priest, in her recent study of the black middle class makes comments on the dilemma faced by blacks in white American society which bear no less relevance to the issue of blacks' struggle for catholicity and recognition in the Episcopal Church:

> The losses that accompany privilege are felt more fully by blacks because the predominantly white worlds we enter tend to be so unwelcoming. We strive to arrive at a secure place only to discover the quicksand of subtle exclusion. We work hard to amass the credentials and signs of status even as we recognize that our status will never assure a sense of belonging, or full membership in the white world. We feel ourselves moving toward the center of power even as we feel inextricably tied to the periphery; our outsider status becomes clearer as we work to claim

> an insider's place. For... African-Americans, these contradictory experiences of insider/outsider, power/impotence, security/uncertainty are felt, I think, with particular force.[28]

The outlook for systemic change within the Church is bleak. In March 1994, the House of Bishops issued a pastoral letter entitled "The Sin of Racism." In it the bishops admit that the Episcopal Church's practices have continued to mirror the nation's racial attitudes and policies:

> For decades this church has issued statements, passed resolutions and taken actions which have addressed many aspects of racism and racial justice. *While positive changes have occurred at certain times in various situations, racism not only persists in our world, but in many places is powerfully resurgent.*[29]

And even as the bishops cause a resounding *nostra maxima culpa* to echo throughout the Church, promising to "make an inventory of racist attitudes in our feelings... [and] refusing to participate in racially discriminatory clubs, or... engage in racially denigrating stories and humor,"[30] Episcopalians, by and large, if correspondence in the church press is any indication, find the subject of racism distasteful, primarily because most white Episcopalians take exception to the Church's working definition of racism, cited in the document, which asserts that only the racial group wielding power in a society can be racism's perpetrators. Many Episcopalians, therefore, embrace instead a new so-called multiculturalism, allowing them to "celebrate diversity," thereby running the risk of glossing over racial differences and the reality of racism.[31] The bishops, in their pastoral letter, may well have been inspired by the 1961 General Convention resolution, which stated

> that this Church, expressing penitence for marks of racial discrimination and segregation, both in her past and present life and structure, take what steps she can to conform herself to the reconciling comprehensiveness of the Body of Christ, specifically *recognizing ability in whomsoever it may be found, for example, in considering persons for positions at national, diocesan and parochial levels here and abroad.*[32]

More than thirty years later, there having been little progress in this area, the Church's bishops, giving new definition to the adage *plus ça change, plus la même chose,* felt the need to make the same impassioned plea: "We place a high priority on the development of strategies for the recruitment, deployment and support of persons of color... at every level — congregational, diocesan, national — and their inclusion in decision-making positions throughout."[33] But even as these words were being read in every congregation in the Episcopal Church, the ethnic desks' commissions (the successors to the commissions and biracial committees on Negro work)[34] had been eliminated; and, as we have shown, the number of minority staff at the Church's headquarters in New York had been decimated.

The questions that we raised in the introduction seem even more compelling now. We have documented a history of black Episcopalians which has shown that such gains as they have attained have been achieved principally through their own persistence and initiative. Their evangelization was carried out for the primary purpose of ensuring their bondage, and when their fetters were broken, those former slaves who remained in their masters' church were met with reactions ranging from astonishment to discouragement to benign neglect to abandonment. When their numbers grew despite the Church's indifference, the Church, again following the nation's example, invented a theology to justify their "return" to Africa. Loath to foster vocations among African Americans, the Church looked to the Caribbean to seek black clergy who could serve in newly established black congregations, but got more than it bargained for. For in addition to being well-trained, dyed-in-the-wool Anglicans, West Indian clergy proved to be among the Church's most militant advocates for change. It was a priest from the Virgin Islands, Paulus Moort, who encouraged black Episcopalians to press for suffragan bishops. It was a Trinidadian priest, Edmund Oxley, who provided the blueprint for the establishment of the Joint Commission on Negro Work and the office of Secretary for Negro Work. It was the son of a Guyanese priest, Quintin Primo, who became the first president of the UBCL.

Unsuccessful in its attempts to create "a drain to carry off our surplus coloured population," the Church made various attempts at a virtual Bantustanization of its black communicants. The Freedman's Commission and, later, the American Church Institute for Negroes were established to provide blacks with *limited and specialized* education, in order that they could function in and uplift members of their own community (the Bishop Payne Divinity School fell into this category as much as the "normal schools" in the South) and even be of *service* to the white community, but there was never any expectation that blacks would through such education enter the mainstream. The Church, unsuccessful in its efforts to Jim Crow the Church nationally through the Sewanee canon, invented the "colored convocation" as a diocesan alternative, to ensure that in the Church, as in society, there would be virtually no opportunity for the races to commingle as equals. And the creation of "colored missions" on both sides of the Mason-Dixon Line, dedicated to such patrons as Monica, Augustine, Cyprian, Simon of

Cyrene, and Philip the Evangelist,[35] attested to the Church's commitment to a separate-but-unequal existence for its black members, giving substantiation to a saying attributed to Dr. Martin Luther King Jr., that "eleven o'clock Sunday morning is the most segregated hour in America."

At the outset of this study we asked why blacks have remained in the Episcopal Church. We have both more and less reason to pose that question now. For despite the fact that the Church, as regards its racial policies, has had a blemished history and faces a rather gloomy future; despite the fact that in the Church's hierarchy there have in recent years "arisen Pharaohs who knew not Joseph" who have been instrumental in turning the clock back in the arena of race relations; despite the fact that a new political climate and a less-than-salubrious economic climate have affected the Church in such a way that it seems to have less concern for oppressed minorities and more concern for the environment — the black Church shows signs of vitality. Nearly 1,000 African Americans (of whom more than a third were youth and young adults) gathered in St. James' Cathedral in Chicago in 1993 for the twenty-fifth anniversary of the Union of Black Episcopalians, at whose opening mass ten black bishops (including three diocesan bishops) concelebrated with the presiding bishop. There are more than thirty black men and women in the Church's seminaries preparing for ordination. Black congregations in major urban areas are sponsoring programs that are making a difference in their communities.

Why have blacks remained in the Episcopal Church? We would like to offer the following hypotheses by way of explanation. In the first instance, it is because they have no illusion about their historical relationship to or the way in which they are perceived in the Episcopal Church. In a 1990 statement, the black bishops expressed it this way:

> Our existence as Afro-Anglican members of the Community of Faith, in the One, Holy, Catholic, and Apostolic Church, has always been marked by ambiguous conditions. We have confessed Jesus Christ as Lord and Savior, but our confession has not always been sufficient to accord us full acceptance among others who make a similar confession. Our Episcopal church has not in itself been a shelter from the stormy blasts of racism, oppression, sexism, or other forms of assault on the dignity of our personhood. Our blackness has not always blessed us with a stronger sense of God's justice at the hands, or in the faces of, others more powerful than ourselves. Yet we have struggled to maintain our rights to fullness of life and human dignity in the face of countervailing circumstances. Through it all, God has been "our help in ages past"; we

> remain convinced that God will continue to be "our hope for years to come."[36]

The black bishops' statement is reflective of a theology of hope born of suffering, which is a common theme in black and third world theologies written from the vantage point of the disadvantaged. A similar theme was addressed in "The Codrington Consensus:"

> We recognize that the Anglican tradition was not originally designed for persons of other cultural traditions, and that the attendant attitudes of human equality and inter-cultural acceptance within Anglicanism are still to be established.... These and other contradictions we regard as challenges to our faith in Christ, and we are prepared to confront them all in search of the practice of love, peace and joy, which are in very truth the gift of the Holy Spirit.[37]

Nor is this a new theme. A churchwoman who was a member of the CCWACP, writing in a 1924 issue of *The Church Advocate,* struck a similar chord:

> My heart is full of hope for the future. Pain and suffering are but crucibles out of which come gold more fine than the pavements of heaven, and gems more precious than the foundations of the Holy City. If pain and suffering are factors in human development, surely we have not been counted too worthless to suffer.... Has the Negro been poor and homeless?... Has our name been a synonym for contempt?... Have we been despised and trodden under foot?...
>
> Have we been beaten and bruised in the prison-house of bondage? ... Today that cross of shame is a throne of power.[38]

Blacks have remained in the Episcopal Church because they have distinguished the essential message of the Gospel from its original packaging. They intuitively recognized that the Church of England missionaries, in bringing *fides anglicana* to American shores, were, like most Western missionaries, "unconscious of the fact that their theology was culturally conditioned... [and] simply assumed that this culture had to be exported together with the Christian faith." Black Episcopalians further rejected the assumption that "missionary outreach... meant a movement from the civilized to 'savages' and from a 'superior' culture to 'inferior' cultures — a process in which the latter had to be subdued, if not eradicated." Black Episcopalians have clearly understood that, as David Bosch has observed, "the Christian faith never exists except as 'translated' into a culture," and that this "has been an integral feature of Christianity from the very beginning."[39] Therefore, they set about the task of interpreting the Gospel in terms of the needs of the missionized and not in terms of the needs of the missionaries. As Gray has observed:

> the Gospel carries implications which transcend the understanding of those who proclaim it. Christian scriptures and sacraments have, as it were, escaped from the hands and minds of those who brought them, and have spoken directly to the various and very differing needs of Africans . . . and their diaspora descendants.[40]

Black Episcopalians, to use Bosch's phrase, have "transformed mission." The Gospel has been understood by black Episcopalians as empowering, not subjugating; as liberating, not controlling. The Christian faith, and more particularly the Anglican expression of it, was not dismissed simply because it was deemed a "white man's religion." The revolutionary nature of such a movement should not be underestimated. It thwarts the efforts at "conditional Anglicanization" that characterized the Church's actions, predicated on the cultural assumptions of the missionaries, and substitutes for it a new paradigm, based on a catholic understanding of the faith that transcends such cultural imperialism. For as we have noted, "catholic" to the black Episcopalian denoted a church that predated the racist practices of an institutional church. It was to the ancient Church to which blacks appealed and on which they staked their claim. In a reference to the conversion of the Ethiopian eunuch, Bragg points out:

> the first person, other than a Jew, received into the Christian Church was a black man. . . . It seemed to be the will of God that such should be the case; for Almighty God sent St. Philip on a special mission to meet this great black man, the prime minister of a black queen, and impart to him the necessary information with respect to the existence of the Catholic Church.[41]

Blacks have remained in the Episcopal Church, moreover, not only because they believe in their inherent right to be in it, but because they believe they have unique gifts to offer the Church which will accrue to its benefit. At the 64th General Convention, held in Louisville, Kentucky, in 1973, the Reverend Joseph Green, on behalf of his fellow black deputies, stated:

> Black Episcopalians are a minority within this Church. We bring special gifts and talents to the legitimacy of our collective witness. As the largest minority in our Church we have special needs and are the advocates of special concerns that the larger majority often takes for granted because of the very nature of our social order or disorder.[42]

But as early as 1920, Bragg had written in a similar vein:

> [The Black man] is simply unconquerable. From his first presence in America, until now, he has steadily gone forward, and advanced under oppression and persecution. And why? He has a God-appointed work for humanity to perform.... God is making a race, through suffering, to give the highest interpretation to the spirit of the Sermon on the Mount and the Decalogue.[43]

Black Episcopalians have remained in the Episcopal Church because they believe that they are in a unique position to be agents for change. As the Codrington Consensus expressed it:

> We firmly believe that God has called us as Afro-Anglicans to be part of the salt of the earth, and that we are richly endowed with many gifts of grace and human virtue to persevere in our Christian calling... and to become what God would have us become in our own cultural and historical contexts. Our endowments of warmth and feeling, of movement and beauty... of a spirituality of endurance, survival and hope, are by no means marks of a divine mistake.[44]

We would like to suggest further that behind almost every page of this study we find the specter of shame and guilt, emotions that, in the arena of race relations, have characterized the attitudes and actions of the Episcopal Church since its founding. After deriving considerable benefit from the institution of slavery, many white Episcopalians expressed remorse (at a time in history when the increase in the numbers of free blacks threatened the status quo) that they had brought Africans to the shores of the new world, and vowed to atone for the rape of Africa by sending black missionaries thither to bring the light of the Gospel to that "dark continent." The bishop of Pennsylvania and others instrumental in the establishment of black congregations did so out of a residual guilt on their part for not having made provision for free blacks (but they were not penitent enough to admit them as full-fledged parishes with the rights of white parishes). The Episcopal Church was ashamed that blacks had fled the fold after Emancipation, and out of that sense of shame went about the business of providing for their sheep thus lost through the establishment of the Freedman's Commission.

The church hierarchy was shamed into consecrating black bishops, because it was forced to recognize the fact that those men would help to usher in the Kingdom among Negro Episcopalians. It was out of a sense of shame, coupled with self-interest, that the Church of England in the West Indies shipped its black clergy to North America and to Africa, in order that they would not have to be deployed at home.

It was because the Episcopal Church was ashamed that home missions among blacks were faring so poorly, while overseas missions flourished, that they attempted at the turn of the century to redouble their evangelistic efforts among the colored population. A recognition that even this renewed effort was unsuccessful led to the turning over of the operation to black hands. It was the collective guilt of white America, justifiably shared by the Episcopal Church, which provided the impetus for the Church to accede to the demands of black Episcopalians during the civil rights movement. And it has been a sense of shame that has compelled the General Convention, the Executive Council, diocesan conventions, and the House of Bishops to issue statement after statement lamenting the sorry state of race relations in the Episcopal Church, of which the House of Bishops' 1994 pastoral letter on racism is but the most recent example.

Black Episcopalians, then, have remained in the Church to be partners with their white counterparts in an effort to "cast out their pride and shame that hinder to enthrone" Jesus Christ as King, and Lord of the whole Church.[45] Bishop Wilfred Wood, a native of Barbados who is the only black in the House of Bishops in the Church of England, speaks of the necessity of black inclusion in the life of the Church in words that bear equal relevance to the struggle of blacks in the Episcopal Church:

> In any forum which genuinely seeks meaningful black participation there can be no substitute for the presence of black people. I use the word *participation* advisedly, and I would draw your attention to the fact that this is the word used... in preference to "representation." Parliament, local government, trade unions, clubs and democratic institutions may order themselves on the basis of *representation* and therefore talk of quotas, lobbies, majority votes and so on may rightly be applied to them. But... the Catholic Church of Jesus Christ is like nothing else on earth. What empire, nation, parliament or borough council has there ever been where the supreme motivation in all things and at all times is meant to be *love?* And what institution is there whose members derive their sense of worth from the claim that "while we were yet sinners Christ died for us" and therefore lay claim not to *rights* but to privileges?[46]

Bishop Wood is making the obvious point that the Church must be made up of different groups in order to provide an arena in which the Church can put its catholic principles of love and universal brotherhood into action.[47] In the same way that the quality of a marriage cannot be improved through the separation of husband and wife, so must the races live together in the Church in order to realize the claims of unity that the Church professes. This is precisely what black Episcopalians have contended for 200 years. Believing that freedom is not possible unless all members of a society share it equally, and being of the further opinion that white people's freedom is seriously hampered, indeed is rendered false by the fact that other groups do not enjoy it, black Episcopalians have seen as their responsibility the offering to the Church of the ultimate missionary opportunity. They have issued a standing invitation to the Church in the words of the missionary hymn, "In Christ there is no East or West":

> Join hands then, brothers of the faith
> Whate'er your race may be!
> Who serves my Father as a son
> Is surely kin to me.[48]

We return, then, to Booker T. Washington's quip, cited in the first line of this study, namely, "If a black man is anything but a Baptist or a Methodist, someone has been tampering with his religion." The remark was not only stupid, as Bishop Burgess has rightly observed;[49] it is insulting, insensitive, and at its core, racist, for it presumes to proscribe the nature of black religion and to declare as off-limits to blacks the forms of religious expression that the Episcopal Church has found meaningful. But most significantly, the statement is erroneous and must be turned on its head. We would suggest that a more accurate rendering of the aphorism would be: *If a black man is an Episcopalian, he has been tampering with the white man's religion!* That white man's religion, as we have shown, has historically been predicated on providing an ecclesiastical arena in which the dominant culture could enjoy privileges in the same way that its members enjoyed them in the secular arena, and therefore proceeded to establish colored congregations, colored convocations, and deputies, archdeacons, and suffragan bishoprics for colored work. That white man's religion has accepted uncritically the racist assumptions that informed the thinking of the nation's founders, and provided for those assumptions a theological justification. That white man's religion, so identified with America's ruling class, has seen as its purpose, as Maloney has suggested, "to pay a call to God to offer Him help in the difficult problem of guiding the course of the world."[50] That religion's purpose, in short, has been to preserve the status quo, and not to champion the cause of the oppressed.

It has been black Episcopalians who, with a steady beat, have faithfully provided a corrective. It has been black Episcopalians who, with a steady beat, have pointed out the theological inconsistencies, indeed the heresy of a church many of whose members have been regarded, for no other reason than their race, as lesser members of the Body of Christ. Black Episcopalians have offered to become those very neighbors whom the broader Church could love as themselves. Black Episcopalians have offered themselves as partners in the Gospel who together with whites and others can, in the words of Tweedy's hymn:

> help to spread thy gracious reign, till greed and hate shall cease,
> And kindness dwell in human hearts, and all the earth find peace![51]

In their witness to the Faith, black Episcopalians in every age have taken up the refrain of Anna Julia Cooper. They have believed in the Holy Catholic Church. They have believed that "the church will go on conquering and to conquer till the kingdom of this world, *not excepting the black man and the black woman*... shall have become the Kingdom of the Lord and of His Christ."[52] Black Episcopalians have cherished the hope that they could be recognized neither as an alien race, nor as coming from a foreign shore, but as integral and bona fide members of the Church at whose fonts they have been made inheritors of Christ's everlasting kingdom, and at whose altars they have ministered and been nurtured in the sacraments for 200 years.

Notes

Introduction

Epigraph: H. H. Tweedy, "Eternal God whose power upholds," No. 265 (hymn text, 1929), *The Hymnal 1940* (New York: Church Hymnal Corporation, 1940).

1. Gavin White, "Patriarch McGuire and the Episcopal Church," *Historical Magazine of the Episcopal Church* 38 (1969): 120.

2. C. Eric Lincoln and Lawrence H. Mamiya, *The Black Church in the African-American Experience* (Durham, N.C.: Duke University Press, 1993), 1. They write:

> In general usage any black Christian person is included in "the Black Church" if he or she is a member of a black congregation. In this study, however, while we recognized that there are predominantly black local churches in white denominations such as the United Methodist Church, the Episcopal Church, and the Roman Catholic Church, among others, we chose to limit our operational definition of "the Black Church" to those independent, historical and totally black controlled denominations, which were founded after the Free African Society of 1787 and which constituted the core of black Christians.

3. E. Franklin Frazier, *The Negro Church in America* (New York: Schocken Books, 1963), 27. The organization formed by both Jones and Allen was the Free African Society, which predated both St. Thomas' Episcopal Church and Mother Bethel A.M.E. Church. A majority of the members of the FAS followed Jones, not Allen. For a thorough discussion of the significance of the incident, including Frazier's inaccuracies, see chapter 2.

4. Ibid.

5. Ann C. Lammers, "The Rev. Absalom Jones and the Episcopal Church: Christian Theology and Black Consciousness in a New Alliance," *Historical Magazine of the Episcopal Church* 51 (1982): 164.

6. Forrest G. Wood, *The Arrogance of Faith: Christianity and Race in America from the Colonial Era to the Twentieth Century* (New York: Knopf, 1990), 318.

7. James Cone, *A Black Theology of Liberation* (Philadelphia: Lippincott, 1970), 130.

8. Lincoln and Mamiya, *Black Church in the African-American Experience,* xii. The Right Reverend John Melville Burgess, in a sermon delivered at the Institution of the Very Reverend Quinland Gordon as dean of the Absalom Jones Theological Institute, Atlanta, April 11, 1972, concurs: "The idea of

black churchmen within the white church structure will probably never appeal to great numbers of black people in America" (Archives of the Episcopal Church, Austin, Texas, RG159.1.24).

9. Burgess, sermon, Absalom Jones Theological Institute, 5. The Absalom Jones Theological Institute was an innovation in theological education. It was established to provide an Episcopal presence at the predominantly black Interdenominational Theological Center in Atlanta. It provided a place for seminarians, black and white, from Episcopal seminaries to spend a semester or a year concentrating on black studies. It functioned for approximately a decade.

10. American Institute of Public Opinion, *Gallup Opinion Index, Special Report on Religion* (1967), 23. Figures as low as 3.7 percent in J. Nicholson, *What Is Happening to the Negro in the Protestant Episcopal Church?* and Hood, "The Placement and Deployment of Negro Clergy in the Episcopal Church," published by the Episcopal Society for Cultural and Racial Unity (1967), 14. Archives, PP7.

11. M. Moran Weston, *Social Policy of the Episcopal Church in the Twentieth Century* (New York: Seabury, 1964), 138. Dr. Weston, the first black on the Episcopal Church's national staff to serve in a "nonethnic" post, was coordinator of the Office of Christian Citizenship from 1951 to 1954. He later served as rector of St. Philip's, Harlem, from 1954 until his retirement in 1982.

12. Kortright Davis, "Afro-Anglicanism and the Ecumenical Imperative," *Linkage,* no. 6 (October 1986): 2.

13. George Freeman Bragg, *The Episcopal Church and the Black Man* (Baltimore: Church Advocate Press, 1908), 7. It is interesting to note that Bragg takes especial delight that black Episcopalians are recognized for their refinement (and therefore not lumped with the "Negro masses"). In reporting on a meeting of the CCWACP, he writes:

> In the Sunday edition of the [Charleston] *News and Courier,* Nov. 1, an extended "write up" of the personnel of the Conference [included] . . . this most significant paragraph: "The recent Conference of Church Workers Among Colored Peopled has created a great deal of interest among all classes in this community and has shown clearly that though the masses of the Colored People care little for the Episcopal Church, that this small body of Churchmen and women contained possibly more culture, more learning and more refinement than any other body of colored people that ever assembled in South Carolina."

14. John Henry Edwards, *The Negro Churchman's Upward Climb* (Hartford: Church Missions Publishing, 1936), 36.

15. John Henry Edwards, "The Episcopal Church and the Black Man in the United States," Archives RG159.1.17.

16. J. Carleton Hayden, "Let My People Go: The Role of Blacks in the Episcopal Church," Archives RG159. Hayden is alluding here to St. Mark's, Charleston; St. Stephen's (later St. Matthew's), Savannah; All Saints, St. Louis; and St. Matthew's (later St. Matthew & St. Joseph), Detroit.

17. Wallace Thurman, *Negro Life in New York's Harlem* (Kansas City, Mo.: Girard, 1928), 55.

18. Burgess, sermon, Absalom Jones Theological Institute, 5.

19. Willard Gatewood, *Aristocrats of Color: The Black Elite, 1880–1920* (Bloomington: University of Indiana Press, 1990), 276.

20. J. Carleton Hayden, "Black Episcopal Preaching in the Nineteenth Century: Intellect and Will," *Journal of Religious Thought* 39 (1982): 12.

21. Bishop Holly was consecrated in 1874 as a bishop of the Eglise Orthodoxe Apostolique d'Haiti. It later became a diocese of the Episcopal Church; today it is the church's largest missionary diocese.

22. J. Robert Love, "Needs and Claims of Haiti and a Missionary Field," cited in Hayden, "Black Preaching." Love was born in Nassau, Bahamas, in 1839. In 1869, he became the first black to be ordained deacon in Florida. Unlike many black candidates at the time, he did not request a dispensation from Latin and Greek in his ordination examinations. He previously had served in the Diocese of Georgia. After three years (1869–72) at St. Stephen's, Savannah, a majority of whose members belonged to the blue-veined aristocracy, Love, who was jet-black in complexion, founded St. Augustine's Church, which became a mission for blacks of darker complexion. St. Matthew's, Savannah, still in existence, was founded in 1944 as a merger of the two congregations (see Charles Hoskins, *Black Episcopalians in Georgia: Strife, Struggle and Salvation* [Savannah: St. Matthew's Episcopal Church, 1980]).

23. Anna Julia Cooper, "Womanhood: A Vital Element in the Regeneration and Progress of a Race," in *A Voice from the South* (New York: Oxford University Press, 1988), 4.

24. John Thomas Walker, bishop of Washington, cited in Harold T. Lewis, "Black and Anglican Traditions: How Can They Co-exist?" in *College of Preachers Newsletter* 23, no. 3 (Fall 1977).

25. Van S. Bird, "Christian Witness and Social Transformation — I," *St. Luke's Journal of Theology* 22, no. 4 (September 1979): 294.

26. Weston, *Social Policy of the Episcopal Church,* 138.

27. Bragg, *The Episcopal Church and the Black Man.*

28. Weston, *Social Policy of the Episcopal Church.*

29. James Theodore Holly, in a letter to black clergy in Virginia, June 1, 1889, cited in Bragg, *The First Negro Priest on Southern Soil* (Baltimore: Church Advocate Press, 1909), 64.

30. Eleanor S. Harrison, "'One Holy, Catholic, and Apostolic Church?' The African American Struggle for Incorporation in the Episcopal Church: A Case Study of St. John's Church, Savannah, Georgia." B.A. thesis, Princeton University, 1992, 5.

31. Memorial of the CCWACP, 1906, cited in Bragg, *The Attitude of the Church Workers among Colored People Towards the Adaptation of the Episcopal Church to the Needs of the Colored Race* (Baltimore: Church Advocate Press, 1906).

32. John Melville Burgess, opening address delivered at Convocation of Black Episcopalians, 1979, in *St. Luke's Journal of Theology* 22, no. 4 (September 1979): 245–46, italics mine.

33. Cf. John Pobee, "Newer Dioceses of the Anglican Communion — Movement and Prospect," in Stephen Sykes and John Booty, eds., *The Study of Anglicanism* (Philadelphia: SPCK/Fortress, 1988), 398:

> The story of the English Reformation which brought into being the Church of England has been encapsulated in the phrase 'Catholicism without the pope.' Anglicans claim to retain the Catholic tradition shorn of its medieval accretions and abuses. One side of it is that *ecclesia anglicana* claims to preserve the tradition of the ancient Church.

34. Cf. William Beveridge, bishop of St. Asaph, 1704–8: "The 'Apostolical office' of the episcopate marks out the Church itself as 'truly Apostolical' and is thus a guarantee of its identity as Christ's Church, but it does this because in fact it is a mediating sign of the sanctifying presence of the Spirit of the Church (*Works* [Oxford, 1841], 1:11). The doctrine was also given prominence during the Oxford Movement, especially by Newman, as a proof of the church's authority: "The real ground upon which our authority is built [is] our *Apostolical descent*" (*Tracts of the Times,* 1883).

35. See Massey Shepherd, ed., *The Oxford American Prayer Book Commentary:*

> However inadequate this terminology has seemed to later generations — and there have been many attempts to change it, or at least to remove it from the title page of the Prayer Book — it corresponded to the actual situation and to the accepted usage of words at the time it was first adopted. "Protestant" distinguished it from Roman Catholic; "Episcopal" from Nonconformist. The Revolution had dissolved its legal connection with "The Church," as then understood, the Church of England. (i)

36. Bird, "Christian Witness and Social Transformation," 295.

37. John S. Pobee, "Afro-Anglican: Meaning and Movement," a paper delivered at the first Conference on Afro-Anglicanism, Barbados, 1985, published in the *Journal of Religious Thought* 44, no. 1 (1987): 35.

38. Richard Gray, *Black Christians and White Missionaries* (London: Yale University Press, 1990), 1.

39. Kortright Davis, *Emancipation Still Comin'* (Maryknoll, N.Y.: Orbis Books, 1990), 118.

40. Shelton Hale Bishop, cited in Edwards, "Episcopal Church and the Black Man," 49.

41. James Theodore Holly, in a letter to black clergy in Virginia, June 1, 1889, cited in Bragg, *First Negro Priest on Southern Soil,* 64.

42. Cf. *New York Times,* February 9, 1968, "Negro Episcopal Priests Form Union." "One of the Union's first actions was to protest what it called the 'involuntary' retirement of the Reverend Dr. Tollie L. Caution, associate secretary of special ministries of the church's Executive Council."

43. See biographical sketch of Maloney in Randall Burkett, *Black Redemption: Churchmen Speak for the Garvey Movement* (Philadelphia: Temple University Press, 1978). General Theological Seminary's first black graduate was Hutchens Chew Bishop in 1882. He became rector of St. Philip's Church, Harlem, and was succeeded by his son, Shelton Hale Bishop.

44. Cf., e.g., James H. Cone, *God of the Oppressed* (New York: Seabury Press, 1975).

45. Arnold Hamilton Maloney, "Whites Strive to Keep the Colored Race Divided," in *Negro World* (July 1922), italics mine. This is part of a speech delivered in Liberty Hall, the headquarters of the Universal Negro Improvement Association, italics mine. *Negro World* was the UNIA's official organ.

The writings of a contemporary black theologian bears a striking resemblance to Maloney's:

> For Blacks, "going to church" was never as much a matter of social custom and convention as it has been for white people. It was a necessity. The church has been the one impregnable corner of the world where consolation, solidarity and mutual aid could be found and from which the master and the bossman—at least in the North—could be effectively barred.

Gayraud Wilmore, *Black Religion and Black Radicalism* (Garden City, N.Y.: Doubleday, 1972), 106.

46. Among the findings of the 1934 Joint Commission on the Status of the Negro were that there were at least four dioceses in which Negroes had neither seat nor voice at diocesan conventions; there were eight in which there were "separate convocations and councils for the colored clergy and lay representatives"; 70 percent of the colored clergy believed "they did not think the Negro had a fair representation in the councils of the church" (*Journal of the General Convention of the Episcopal Church,* 1934).

Among the findings of the racial audit in 1991: 79 percent of black Episcopalians believe that a specific portion of leadership positions is reserved for whites; 65 percent believe that white Episcopalians feel superior to other groups; and 72 percent believe that "respect accorded to bishops is different for non-white bishops than for white bishops." Among *all* Episcopalians, 90 percent believe that the Episcopal Church is more likely to refer racial issues to committee for further study than to initiate direct action. Only 22 percent believe that the Church has done enough to support cultural diversity; and 80 percent believe the Episcopal Church should develop more programs to develop an appreciation for the experience and contributions of racial and ethnic minorities (NTL Institute for Applied Behavioral Science, "Overview of Race and Ethnic Relations in the Episcopal Church Audit," July 16, 1991).

47. George Freeman Bragg, "The Episcopal Church and the Negro Race," *Historical Magazine of the Episcopal Church* 4, no. 1 (1935): 52.

48. Burgess, sermon, Absalom Jones Theological Institute.

49. Alexander Crummell, notably, had been denied admission to General Seminary in 1839. John Jay, in his book *Caste and Slavery in the American Church,* chronicles the incident:

> In the month of June, 1839, the Board of Trustees of the General Theological Seminary [met in New York City]. . . . From the minutes, it appears that a candidate for Holy Orders in the diocese of New-York, now the Rev. Alexander Crummell, applied to them by petition, to be allowed to enter the Seminary as a student; that the petition was referred to a committee . . . who, after deliberate consideration, recommended a resolution of rejection. . . . The true cause which led the Trustees to nullify the constitution [of the Episcopal Church] and deny

> the right of the candidate, and which they were ashamed to acknowledge, was, that he was a coloured man.... Nothing can be clearer than that the Trustees, by that act, not only exceeded their powers and violated the trust reposed in them, but deliberately established a system of Caste in the Church — not among its lower members only — not among the laity, alone, but among the very clergy who approach us as ambassadors of God, and minister at his altars.... They establish a principle which would justify us in regarding the coloured man as an inferior being, intended to occupy a lower sphere in the scale of creation; which designates him as one whose constitutional privilege we may innocently annul, whom we may, without shame, insult, injure, and oppress, even though he be one arrayed by Episcopal hands in the robes of the priesthood, who walks forth a messenger of the Most High.

50. J. Carleton Hayden, "Different Names but the Same Agenda," 1968, Archives RG159.1.

51. Ibid.

52. Cf. Harold T. Lewis, "Centenary of a Black Caucus" in *Ministry Development Journal* (1983). Originally called the Convocation of Colored Clergy, it changed its name when several black laity and two white priests joined their ranks (Hayden, "Different Names but the Same Agenda"). It should be noted that the integration of the organization was not universally regarded as beneficial. the Reverend Harry Rahming, who as a newly ordained priest was chosen to be the preacher at the CCWACP meeting in 1919, addresses the issue in letter to the Reverend Canon Thomas W. S. Logan, dated May 10, 1978. It is especially instructive given the fact that the problem is a perennial one, having been discussed at several annual meetings of the Union of Black Episcopalians, as recently as 1994:

> Up until the time of the change, the membership of the Conference was limited to colored clergy, and colored congregations, which meant that if a colored congregation had a white priest, while the congregation could belong to the Conference of Colored Church Workers, its white priest could not.... Two colored congregations in this condition... challenged the composition of the Conference, on the basis that it discriminated against white clergy illegally, because it was a Conference of Colored Church Workers, and any priest who worked among colored people, regardless of race, was entitled to membership, and the Conference accept their contention. Well, there was one thing that... your father [the Rev. John R. Logan, Sr.]... always impressed on me, and that is that 'whenever colored people and white people get together in a situation, the white people always... run the situation, and I knew from then from my experience at Brown University, and General Theological Seminary... I learned that regardless of how nice white people are to colored people, they never forget that they are white, and the colored people are colored.... After the change in the composition of the Conference of Colored Church Workers, I lost interest and didn't go, as I had enough bother with poor ambitious white priests in Colorado to travel miles to a conference, where there were some ambitious, egotistical self-seeking poor, middle-class white priests, who felt they knew all about colored work and had all the answers, so I didn't go after the change was made. (Logan papers.)

53. White, "Patriarch McGuire and the Episcopal Church," 140.

54. The singing of hymns (and spirituals among African Americans) has also been an important aspect of black worship. Davis comments: "The hymns and songs learned from early childhood (through regular attendance at worship)

provide simple means of release and relaxation for the burdened heart" (*Emancipation Still Comin',* 112). Many of the Victorian missionary hymns, though smacking of a racist imperialism, were nevertheless adapted and sung lustily by blacks in the United States and the Caribbean. Burkett points out (*Garveyism as a Religious Movement: The Institutionalization of Black Civil Religion* [Metuchen, N.J.: Scarecrow Press, 1978], 102) that Heber's "From Greenland's icy mountains" was the official hymn of Garvey's Universal Negro Improvement Association, which saw as one of its principal duties the evangelization of the African continent. However, the stanza, containing the words, "Can we, whose souls are lighted / With wisdom from on high / Can we to men benighted / The lamp of life deny?" was omitted from the UNIA hymnal.

55. George Washington Doane, "Fling out the banner," No. 259 (hymn text, 1848); Jane Borthwick, "Hasten the time appointed," No. 257 (hymn text, 1859); and Mary Ann Thompson, "O Sion haste," No. 261 (hymn text, 1870); and Reginald Heber, "From Greenland's icy mountains," No. 254 (hymn text, 1819), in *The Hymnal 1940.*

56. See note for epigraph, above. In 1929, the hymn won a prize offered by the Hymn Society of America for a new missionary hymn (*The Hymnal 1940 Companion,* 3rd ed. [New York: The Church Hymnal Corporation, 1951]).

57. Heber, "From Greenland's icy mountains."

58. Hayden, "Let My People Go."

59. Bishop Burgess, in commenting on the Booker T. Washington quotation, quipped: "It was a stupid remark when it was made, and it does little credit to those scholars in the field of the black church who seem to hold this view" (Burgess, address to the Convocation of Black Episcopalians, 245).

60. Burgess, sermon at Absalom Jones Theological Institute.

61. Bragg, *Episcopal Church and the Black Man,* 3, 4.

Chapter 1. The Conditional Anglicanization of Negro Slaves

Epigraph: John Morrison, "The race that long in darkness pined," No. 43 (hymn text, c. 1770), in *The English Hymnal* (London: Mowbray & Co., 1933).

1. Kit Konolige and Frederica Konolige, *The Power of Their Glory—America's Ruling Class: The Episcopalians* (New York: Wyden Books, 1978), 27. Emphasis added.

2. George Hodges, *Three Hundred Years of the Episcopal Church in America* (Philadelphia: George W. Jacobs & Co., 1906), 21.

3. Powel Mills Dawley, *Our Christian Heritage: Church History and the Episcopal Church* (New York: Morehouse Gorham, 1959), 128.

4. Ibid., 130.

5. Robert W. Prichard, *Readings from the History of the Episcopal Church* (Wilton, Conn.: Morehouse-Barlow, 1986), 2.

6. Samuel Wilberforce, Lord Bishop of Oxford, *A History of the Protestant Episcopal Church in America,* 2nd ed. (London: Francis & John Rivington, 1846), 426ff.

7. de Tocqueville, cited in Andrew Hacker, *Two Nations: Black, White, Separate, Hostile, Unequal* (New York: Scribner's, 1992), 18.

8. Prichard, *Readings from the History of the Episcopal Church.*

9. J. Carleton Hayden, "Reading, Religion and Racism: The Mission of the Episcopal Church to Blacks in Virginia, 1865–1877," Ph.D. dissertation, Washington, D.C.: Howard University, 1972, 1.

10. J. Carleton Hayden, "Afro-Anglican Linkages, 1701–1900: Ethiopia Shall Soon Stretch Out Her Hands Unto God," *Journal of Religious Thought* 44, no. 1 (1987): 25.

11. Edmund Gibson, bishop of London, "To the Masters and Mistresses of Families in the English Plantations Abroad," 1727, cited in Wood, *The Arrogance of Faith,* 119. For the full text of Gibson's letter, see Frederick Dalcho, *Historical Account of the Protestant Episcopal Church in South Carolina* (Charleston, 1820), 104–12.

12. See Wood, *The Arrogance of Faith.*

13. William Wilson Manross, *A History of the American Episcopal Church* (New York: Morehouse-Gorham, 1950), 147.

14. Albert J. Raboteau, *Slave Religion: The "Invisible Institution" in the Antebellum South* (New York: Oxford University Press, 1978), 99, 103.

15. Gibson, "To the Masters and Mistresses of Families in the English Plantations Abroad."

16. The Reverend Francis Le Jau, St. James', Goose Creek, South Carolina, cited in Edgar L. Pennington, *Thomas Bray's Associates and Their Work among Negroes* (Worcester, Mass.: American Antiquarian Society, 1939), 25.

17. Phyllis Barr, "Learning the Lessons of Freedom: Black History at Trinity Church [New York City]," in *Trinity News* (Lent 1992): 20.

18. H. Richard Niebuhr, *The Social Sources of Denominationalism* (New York: World Publishing, 1957), 248.

19. George Freeman Bragg Jr., *History of the Afro-American Group in the Episcopal Church* (hereinafter *Afro-American Group*) (Baltimore: Church Advocate Press, 1922), 29.

20. Manross, *A History of the American Episcopal Church,* 146.

21. The Virginia House of Burgesses in a letter to Col. Francis Nicholson, governor of Virginia, 1699, quoted in Pennington, *Thomas Bray's Associates and Their Work among Negroes,* 38–39.

22. Raboteau, *Slave Religion,* 100.

23. The Reverend Francis Le Jau, minister of St. James' Church, Goose Creek, South Carolina, in a letter to the Secretary of the Society for the Propagation of the Gospel, June 13, 1710, cited in Raboteau, *Slave Religion,* 103.

24. Ibid., 102.

25. Hacker, *Two Nations,* 57.

26. Manross, *A History of the American Episcopal Church,* 153.

27. David Humphreys, quoted in Edwards, "Episcopal Church and the Black Man," 13.

28. Bragg, "The Episcopal Church and the Negro Race," 49.

29. Racial Audit of the Episcopal Church, 1991 (New York: Domestic and Foreign Missionary Society, 1993).

30. Davis, *Emancipation Still Comin',* 24. Although Dr. Davis is here referring to the institution of slavery in the Caribbean, it is no less applicable to the North American situation. This shows a basic similarity in the imperialistic missionary strategy of the Church of England, regardless of where it held sway.

31. Prichard, *Readings from the History of the Episcopal Church,* 59.

32. There is a certain irony in this fact, given that Whitfield (according to Hoskins, *Black Episcopalians in Georgia*) was one of the chief supporters of the introduction of slavery into Georgia.

33. Ibid., 60, 61

34. Robert A. Bennett, "Black Episcopalians: A History from the Colonial Period to the Present," *Historical Magazine of the Episcopal Church* 43 (September 1974): 236.

Chapter 2. The Struggle for the Ordination of Black Priests and the Establishment of Black Congregations

Epigraph: From J. Rippon's *Selection:* "How firm a foundation ye saints of the Lord," No. 564 (hymn text), *The Hymnal 1940.*

1. Gatewood, *Aristocrats of Color,* 275.

2. George Freeman Bragg, "Beginnings of Negro Work in the South," in the *Living Church,* August 20, 1921, 505.

3. Bragg, *Afro-American Group,* 42. Holly, too, sees Absalom Jones's ordination as a sign of the church's catholicity. He writes: "A catholic minded prelate in the person of the first bishop of Pennsylvania had the Christian courage to ordain Absalom Jones, a man of the Negro Race, to the sacred ministry of the Church of Christ" (from a testimonial written on the occasion of Alexander Crummell's fiftieth anniversary of ordination, 1894). The comments of Bragg and Holly also bear a striking resemblance to a statement made by the delegates of the fourth Black [Roman] Catholic Congress held in Chicago in 1893:

> Public opinion has moulded the sentiment that a negro could not be a priest of the Roman Catholic Church. The Catholic Church has rebuked this sentiment by ordaining the Reverend Father A. Tolton, the first negro priest in America, and the Rev. C. R. Uncles to the exalted state of Catholic priesthood. We desire to say every encouragement, every fraternal greeting extended the priests of our race are in our opinion so many more proofs of the divine truth of Catholic religion. (Cited in Cyprian Davis, *The History of Black Catholics in the United States* [New York: Crossroad Publishing Co., 1993], 188.)

Tolton was ordained in 1854, and Uncles in 1891. Clearly, the Roman Catholic Church moved far more slowly than the Episcopal Church in the ordination of blacks to the priesthood.

4. Bragg, *Afro-American Group,* 30.

5. Ibid., 39.

6. W. E. B. Du Bois, *The Philadelphia Negro: A Social Study* (1898; New York: Schocken Books, 1969), 47. Cf. Warner Traynham, "A Theological Perspective on the Last Two Hundred Years of the Black Presence in the Episcopal Church," *Journal of Religious Thought* 50, nos. 1 and 2 (Fall-Spring 1993–94): 94:

> W. E. B. Du Bois spoke of this ambiguity as we perceive it internally. He called it a twoness — a sense of being the same and other, of being American and black when to be American seems to deny our blackness and blackness is denigrated and spat upon. Our situation is peculiar and particular, but it may have in it the seeds for some understanding of the human predicament universally.

7. Kyle Haselden, *The Racial Problem in Christian Perspective* (New York: Sheed and Ward, 1960).

8. See introduction.

9. Cited in Bragg, *Richard Allen and Absalom Jones* (Baltimore: Church Advocate Press, 1915).

10. Lammers, "Rev. Absalom Jones and the Episcopal Church," 168.

11. Richard Bardolph, *The Negro Vanguard* (New York: Random House, 1961), 46.

12. Wilmore, *Black Religion and Black Radicalism,* 113.

13. Ibid.

14. Lammers, "Rev. Absalom Jones and the Episcopal Church," 168.

15. Bragg, *Afro-American Group,* 51.

16. Ibid.

17. Ibid.

18. Robert W. Prichard, *A History of the Episcopal Church* (Harrisburg, Pa.: Morehouse Publishing, 1991), 111.

19. Bragg, *Afro-American Group,* 60.

20. Lammers, "Rev. Absalom Jones and the Episcopal Church," 173, 176.

21. Bennett, "Black Episcopalians," 235.

22. *Proceedings of the Convention of the Diocese of Pennsylvania,* June 2, 1795, quoted in Bragg, *Afro-American Group,* 63.

23. Ibid.

24. Lammers points out that the phrase "peculiar circumstances" is used in diocesan documents "without precise definition." The record indicates that Jones was approved for ordination "without the knowledge of the Latin and Greek languages agreeably to canon." In other words, the waiver of the language requirement, a not uncommon practice for which at the time of Jones's ordination there was ample precedent, was unrelated to St. Thomas' "peculiar circumstances at present." Nevertheless, the convention worded its minute so as to make it seem that the dispensation from the language requirement was related to the withholding of representation at convention.

25. The Free African Society was consistently engaged in works of uplift and empowerment of the black community in Philadelphia. With Allen, Jones founded the first black insurance company in the United States. During the

yellow fever epidemic in Philadelphia, Jones and his parishioners ministered to black and white victims alike (see *Lesser Feasts and Fasts* [New York: Church Hymnal Corp., 1980]).

26. Carol V. R. George, *Segregated Sabbaths: Richard Allen and the Rise of Independent Black Churches 1760–1840* (London: Oxford University Press, 1973), 63. George's facts are correct, but her interpretation of them is erroneous, and again betrays a certain revisionist approach to history common among members of black denominations who typically regard black Episcopalians as somehow less than authentic. Bragg makes it clear (*Richard Allen and Absalom Jones*) that the only reason that the founders of St. Thomas' made it possible for there to be white clerical leadership was that at the time of their founding, that is, prior to the ordination of Absalom Jones, there were no black priests in the Episcopal Church.

27. Bennett, "Black Episcopalians," 240.

28. George, *Segregated Sabbaths,* 15, 236.

29. Ibid., 49–50.

30. George, *Segregated Sabbaths.*

31. *Journal of the Convention of the Diocese of New York* (1841).

32. Carter Woodson, *History of the Negro Church* (Washington, D.C.: Association Publishers, 1921), 95.

33. *Journal of the Convention of the Diocese of New York* (1846): 76, italics mine. See James Elliott Lindsley, *This Planted Vine: A Narrative History of the Episcopal Diocese of New York* (New York: Harper and Row, 1984), 66ff.

34. Bragg, *Afro-American Group,* 91.

35. Bravid W. Harris, Archdeacon for Colored Work in the Diocese of North Carolina, "A Study of Our Work," a paper delivered at the St. Augustine's Conference, St. Augustine's College, Raleigh, N.C., June 1, 1939, Archives RG159.1, 6.

36. The Right Reverend James Kemp, bishop of Maryland, quoted in Bragg, *Afro-American Group,* 94, 93.

37. Randall K. Burkett, "The Reverend Harry Croswell and Black Episcopalians in New Haven, 1815–1860," a paper delivered at the Biennial Convention of the American Studies Association, San Diego, Calif., November 1, 1985, 15.

38. Ibid.

39. *Journal of the Convention of the Diocese of Connecticut* (1844).

40. Edwards, "The Story of a Negro Parish" (1936), Archives of St. Luke's Church, New Haven, Conn., 49.

41. Cf. Edwards, "Episcopal Church and the Black Man."

42. Ibid., 20. Stokes later assumed the rectorship of Christ Church, Providence, R.I., after which he became a missionary to Liberia, where he died in 1867 (see chapter 7).

43. Ibid., 22.

44. Christ Church, Providence, R.I., founded in 1843; Crucifixion, Philadelphia, begun in 1847; and St. Philip's, Newark, N.J., founded in 1856,

should be added to this list. See Robert Bennett, "Black Episcopalians"; also Prichard, *Readings from the History of the Episcopal Church.* It should be noted that of the antebellum congregations herein mentioned, most are still extant. St. Thomas', Philadelphia; St. Philip's, New York City; St. James', Baltimore; and St. Luke's, New Haven, are flourishing congregations, numbering among their membership some of the most prominent African Americans in their respective cities. Only one of the parishes, Christ Church, Providence, R.I., was closed outright, in the 1950s. While no official merger took place, many of its members affiliated with a white parish, St. Stephen's. St. Philip's, Newark, N.J., was destroyed by fire, and was merged with Trinity Cathedral, a largely white congregation. St. Matthew's, Detroit, also merged, in the late 1960s, with a white congregation, St. Joseph's. In both the latter cases, the urban phenomenon known as "white flight" resulted in those integrated parishes becoming virtually all-black congregations.

45. Crucifixion, Philadelphia, was the exception. According to Bragg (*Afro-American Group*), it was founded by a white layman who was a member of St. Paul's Church. There was also some confusion over the date of the church's founding, since "this parish seems to have been *admitted* at one Convention, then informally *omitted* from the regular list." This was due to the congregation's ambivalent status stemming from the fact that although constituted almost entirely of blacks, the vestry were white. "From this viewpoint," according to Bragg, "the fight was exceedingly interesting." The fight, of course, centered on the fact that by admitting the congregation, the Convention of the Diocese of Pennsylvania ran the "risk" of being faced with the prospect of having to seat black delegates. It will be remembered that it was not until 1863 that St. Thomas', the only other black congregation in the diocese, was admitted with full rights to the Convention, even though it had been founded in 1794.

46. Bragg, "Episcopal Church and the Negro Race," 50.

47. Bennett, "Black Episcopalians," 236.

48. A "separate congregation" differed from a "parish" in that the latter was an independent and duly constituted church with "metes and bounds" (i.e., a geographical area) as in the English parish system. Separate congregations were churches or chapels within the geographical area of the parish and under its administration.

49. J. Carleton Hayden, "After the War: The Mission and Growth of the Episcopal Church among Blacks in the South, 1865–1877," *Historical Magazine of the Episcopal Church,* 1972), 4.

50. Gatewood, *Aristocrats of Color.* It should be noted that although the number of black Episcopalians was disproportionately high compared to white Episcopalians, it was still true that the number of black Episcopalians was infinitesimal compared to the overall number of black Christians.

51. Hayden, "After the War," 404.

52. Ibid., 408.

53. Harris, "A Study of Our Work."

54. John Hope Franklin, "Negro Episcopalians in Ante-Bellum North Carolina," *Historical Magazine of the Episcopal Church* 13 (1944): 228, italics mine.
55. Ibid., 230.
56. Ibid., 231.
57. Robert Strange, *Church Work among the Negroes in the South,* cited in Franklin, "Negro Episcopalians in Ante-Bellum North Carolina."
58. Franklin, "Negro Episcopalians in Ante-Bellum North Carolina," 217.
59. J. Carleton Hayden, "Conversion and Control: Dilemma of Episcopalians in Providing for the Religious Instructions of Slaves, Charleston, South Carolina, 1845–1860," *Historical Magazine of the Episcopal Church* (1972): 144.
60. Pastoral letter promulgated by the bishops of the Episcopal Church in the Confederate States of America, Augusta, Ga., November 22, 1862, italics mine.
61. Charles Cotesworth Pinckney, in an 1829 address to the Charlestown Agricultural Society of South Carolina, cited in Hayden, "Conversion and Control."
62. Wood, *Arrogance of Faith,* 140.
63. Edwards, "Episcopal Church and the Black Man," 16.
64. George, *Segregated Sabbaths,* 13.
65. W. E. B. Du Bois, *The Negro Church* (1903).
66. Bragg, "Episcopal Church and the Negro Race," 52.

Chapter 3. The Defection of Black Episcopalians after Emancipation

Epigraph: William Harry Turton, "Thou who at thy first Eucharist didst pray," no. 191 (hymn text, 1881), *The Hymnal 1940,* 191.

1. Bishop Henry C. Potter, cited in Bragg, *Afro-American Group.*
2. George Freeman Bragg, *The Episcopal Church and the Black Man* (Baltimore, 1908), 12.
3. *Journal of the Diocese of South Carolina* (1868): 127.
4. Hayden. "After the War," 410.
5. *Journal of the Diocese of Maryland* (1867): 40.
6. *Journal of the General Convention* (1877).
7. Hayden, "After the War," 411.
8. Bragg, "Episcopal Church and the Black Man," 12.
9. John Hope Franklin, *From Slavery to Freedom,* 7th ed. (New York: McGraw-Hill, 1994), 310.
10. Hayden, "After the War," 412.
11. Ibid.
12. *Spirit of Missions* (1866): 407.
13. Bishop Atkinson, cited in Bragg, *Afro-American Group,* 129, italics mine.
14. *Journal of the Diocese of Louisiana* (1867).
15. Niebuhr, *Social Sources of Denominationalism,* p. 248.
16. Hayden, "After the War," 412.

17. Bragg, cited in Alexander Crummell, "The Best Methods of Church Work among the Colored People," *The Church Magazine* (June 1887): 555–56.

18. Crummell, in ibid.

19. Edwards, "Episcopal Church and the Black Man," 60.

20. Frazier, *Negro Church in America,* 8.

21. Bishops' Biographical files, Archives.

22. Cone, *A Black Theology of Liberation.* It should be pointed out that many whites saw the inherent value of black clergy ministering to blacks, but feared they (the whites) would lose control of the situation if such a practice were observed:

> I am persuaded that nothing would be easier than to swell my list of communicants to an almost indefinite extent, if I would but invest men of their own color with something of spiritual power, and send them forth as missionaries in our cause amongst their fellows. But in such a constitution of society as ours, to make slaves the religious instructors of slaves, is a proceeding pregnant with mischief as much so to the slaves themselves, as to the order and happiness of the community. The extent of influence possessed by such preachers is almost incredible; and I fear that the abuse of the influence is everywhere equal to its extent. (the Reverend T. H. Taylor, St. John's Church, Collection, South Carolina, cited in *Journal of the Diocese of South Carolina* [1834]: 22.)

23. White, "Patriarch McGuire and the Episcopal Church," 121. It should be noted, however that Bragg interprets this situation in its most favorable light, arguing that the Episcopal Church's refusal to split showed that it was committed to the idea of racial equality. Bragg was not so naive as to think that there was no racial discrimination in the church; rather, his quotation is another example of how he and other black leaders held the church to its official position, even if its actions did not always reflect that position.

24. See Wood, *Arrogance of Faith,* 277.

25. John M. Burgess, "The Role of ESCRU in the Life of the Church," keynote address delivered at the opening of the second annual meeting of the Episcopal Society for Cultural and Racial Unity, Chicago, June 22, 1962, the Records of the Episcopal Society for Cultural and Racial Unity, Archives PP7.

26. We are indebted for information regarding the Confederate Church to Joseph Blount Cheshire, *The Church in the Confederate States* (New York: Longmans, Green, 1912), 114 and passim.

27. Cecil Frances Alexander, "All things bright and beautiful," no. 311 (hymn text, 1848). Although found in *The Hymnal 1940,* the original third stanza, owing to changing social concepts, was omitted (see *The Hymnal Companion,* 202). It read:

> The rich man in his castle,
> The poor man at his gate,
> God made them high and lowly
> And ordered their estate.

28. S. B. Lines, "Slaves and Churchmen: The Work of the Episcopal Church among Southern Negroes, 1800–1860," Columbia University thesis, 1960, cited in White, "Patriarch McGuire and the Episcopal Church," 121.

29. Conference of Church Workers among Colored People, "Address to the Church at Large" (1906), 3.

30. "A term used to express the essentially objective mode of operation of the sacraments, and its independence of the subjective attitudes of either the minister or the recipient" (*Oxford Dictionary of the Christian Church*).

31. Pobee, "Newer Dioceses of the Anglican Communion."

Chapter 4. Efforts to Evangelize the Freedmen

Epigraph: Heber, "From Greenland's icy mountains."

1. Bragg, "Episcopal Church and the Negro Race," 49.

2. James Russell Lowell, "Once to ev'ry man and nation," No. 519 (hymn text, 1845), *The Hymnal 1940.*

3. Hayden, "After the War," 413.

4. *Spirit of Missions* (February 1869): 123. Despite the official name change, it continued to be known as the Freedman's Commission.

5. *Journal of the General Convention* (1868), italics mine.

6. Mary Ann Thompson, "O Sion haste."

> Proclaim to ev'ry people, tongue, and nation
> That God, in whom they live and move, is Love:
> Tell how he stooped to save his lost creation
> And died on earth that man might live above.

7. *Journal of the General Convention* (1865).

8. *Journal of the Convention of the Diocese of North Carolina* (1868), cited in Bragg, *Afro-American Group,* 129.

9. Ibid.

10. Ibid.

11. Raymond W. Albright, *A History of the Protestant Episcopal Church* (New York: Macmillan, 1964), 259.

12. The Right Reverend Thomas Atkinson, bishop of North Carolina, in the *Journal of the Diocese of North Carolina* (1868), cited in Bragg, *Afro-American Group,* 128.

13. *Journal of the General Convention* (1868), 149.

14. See above chap. 3, nn. 16 and 17.

15. *Spirit of Missions* (October 1866): 316.

16. *Spirit of Missions* (April 1868): 316.

17. Hayden, "After the War," 421. For a full discussion of the impact of West Indians on the Episcopal Church, refer to chapter 6.

18. Hayden, "Let My People Go."

19. Bragg, *Afro-American Group,* 247.

20. Bragg, "Episcopal Church and the Negro Race," 50.

21. *Spirit of Missions* (November 1868): 691.

22. *Journal of the General Convention* (1874): 505.

23. Weston, *Social Policy of the Episcopal Church,* 138. In this connection, it is interesting to note that the Right Reverend Alfred Lee, bishop of Delaware,

in his sermon at the consecration of Samuel Ferguson as bishop of Liberia commented: "If any branch of the evangelistic work of our Church has peculiar and sacred claims to generous support, it seems to me to be our African Mission, as well as our home Missions among our colored people" (*Spirit of Missions* [August 1885]: 437).

24. Weston, *Social Policy of the Episcopal Church.* Indeed, the report of the Freedman's Commission made specific reference to the church's missionary work in Africa, suggesting that in a like way, the church could minister to African Americans in its midst:

> Upon the western coast of the continent of Africa, where, a half century ago, only darkness was visible, there is now a fringe of light. In a region once devoted to idolatry and cruelty, a Christian civilization has taken up its abode, and bearers of the Cross, in the true spirit of martyrs, have carried thither its blessings. (Cited in Bragg, *Afro-American Group,* 130.)

25. Heber, "From Greenland's icy mountains."

26. Bragg, *Afro-American Group,* 247. By not admitting black congregations as self-supporting parishes, Southern dioceses precluded the possibility that black delegates from these parishes would be seated in diocesan conventions.

27. See chapter 2.

28. Bragg, *Afro-American Group,* 246.

29. Ibid., 241–42.

30. Weston, *Social Policy of the Episcopal Church.*

31. Ibid.

32. George Freeman Bragg, *Story of Old St. Stephen's Church, Petersburg, Va., and the Origin of the Bishop Payne Divinity School* (Baltimore: Church Advocate Press, 1917), 17, italics mine.

33. The Right Reverend Thomas Hubbard Vail, bishop of Kansas, in *Journal of the Convention of the Diocese of Kansas* (1877): 41.

34. Lincoln and Mamiya, *Black Church in the African-American Experience,* 3.

35. Edwards, "Episcopal Church and the Black Man," 70.

36. Bragg, *Afro-American Group,* 137.

37. The Reverend Harry Rahming, rector of Redeemer, Denver, Colo., cited in Edwards, "Episcopal Church and the Black Man," 137.

38. Bishop Thomas Hubbard Vail, first bishop of Arkansas, in an address to the Diocesan Convention, 1877, cited in Blanche Mercer Taylor, *Plenteous Harvest: The Episcopal Church in Kansas, 1837–1972* (Topeka: Diocese of Kansas, 1973), 237.

39. "The Negro in the South: His Economic Progress in Relation to his Moral and Religious Development" in Herbert Aptheker, ed., *Writings by W. E. B. Du Bois in Non-Periodical Literature edited by others* (Millwood, N.Y.: Kraus Thompson, 1982), 94.

40. Hayden, "After the War," 426.

41. Bragg, *Afro-American Group,* 238.

42. Hayden, "After the War," 426.

43. Ibid. Of this group, St. Peter's, Key West, was unique in that it was founded by recently migrated Anglicans from the Bahamas. It should be noted that all of these parishes are still in existence.

44. Thomas LaBar and Mary S. Wright, "The New Citizen: A Progress Report on the Negro and the Episcopal Church," in *The Episcopalian* (October 1957): 23.

45. Harris, "The Story of Our Work," 8. Note that Harris refers to Baptists, Methodists, and other Protestant churches as "the denominations." This is not uncommon in the writings of black clergy of his and previous periods who, believing the Episcopal Church to be neither Protestant nor a denomination but part of a universal catholic church, referred to it as "the church."

46. Bragg, "Beginnings of Negro Work in the South," 505. It is interesting to note that in the South Carolina situation the committee voted against admission allegedly because of the high proportion of mulattoes in the parish. When the matter came to the floor of Convention, the clergy voted for the admission of St. Mark's, the laity against. The situation was exacerbated when in 1881 a Negro deacon was ordained to serve St. Mark's, thereby changing the dynamic somewhat, for now the question was not simply the admission of a black parish, but the recognition and seating of a black clergyman in the Diocesan Convention.

47. *Journal of the General Convention* (1877): 491.

48. Gatewood, *Aristocrats of Color,* 273.

49. Lincoln and Mamiya, *Black Church in the African-American Experience,* 124, 159.

50. Weston, *Social Policy of the Episcopal Church,* 138.

51. LaBar and Wright, "The New Citizen," 22.

52. W. E. B. Du Bois, cited in Aptheker, ed., *Writings by W. E. B. Du Bois.*

53. E. Don Taylor, "Tensions and Opportunities between West Indian and American Blacks in the Episcopal Church — II," *St. Luke's Journal of Theology* 22, no. 4 (September 1979): 272–73. Note: At the time this speech was delivered, Taylor, a native of Jamaica, was rector of St. Philip's Church, Buffalo, a largely black American parish. From 1987 until 1994, he was bishop of the Virgin Islands. He is now the assistant bishop of New York.

54. Alexander Crummell, *Africa and America: Addresses and Discourses* (1891; Miami: Mnemosyne Publishing, 1969), 464, italics mine.

55. Edward Thomas Demby, in *The Colored Churchman,* Little Rock, Christmas 1930. Bishops' biographical files, Archives.

56. George Frazier Miller, "The Missionary Episcopate as a Method of Evangelism," in Burgess, ed., *Black Gospel/White Church,* 35. Cyprian Davis, in his study of black Roman Catholics, observes that "another aspect of black theology is the moral imperative to denounce racism within the church because it goes contrary to the authority of catholic belief and morality. They do not see themselves as rebels or even as a loyal opposition. Rather, they are entirely loyal and faithful to the church they love and are proud of." He cites a document of the 4th Black Catholic Congress, held in 1893:

> We thoroughly confide in the rectitude of our course in the enduring love of Mother Church, and the consciousness of our priesthood. We show our devotion to the church, our jealousy of her glory, and our love for her history. (Cf. Davis, *History of Black Catholics*, 189.)

57. George Alexander McGuire, in the *Church Advocate*, Baltimore (March 1908). McGuire, it is interesting to note, later founded the African Orthodox Church. For a full discussion of the AOC, see chapter 6.

58. "The Address to the Church at Large," included in the report of the 22nd annual Conference of Church Workers among Colored People, October 16, 1906, in St. James' Church, Baltimore, in George Freeman Bragg, ed., *The Attitude of the Conference of Church Workers among Colored People Towards the Adaptation of the Episcopate to the Needs of the Race* (Baltimore, 1906).

59. The Right Reverend John Melville Burgess, bishop of Massachusetts, "The Character of the Black Witness" in Burgess, ed., *Black Gospel/White Church*, 63–64, italics mine.

60. See introduction.

Chapter 5. The Question of a Racial Episcopate in a Catholic Church

Epigraph: Thompson, "O Sion haste."

1. Pobee, "Newer Dioceses of the Anglican Communion," 398.

2. Cyprian, *De Unitate Ecclesiae Catholicae* 5.1–14, ed. M. Bévenot, S.J. (Oxford: Clarendon Press, 1971).

> Now this oneness we must hold to firmly and insist on — especially we who are bishops and exercise authority in the Church — so as to demonstrate that the episcopal power is one and undivided too.... The authority of the bishops forms a unity, of which each holds his part in its totality.

3. The order of service for the consecration of a bishop, *Book of Common Prayer.*

4. Richard Hooker, *Of the Laws of Ecclesiastical Polity* (London: J. M. Dent, 1922).

5. David M. Reimers, "Negro Bishops and Diocesan Segregation in the Protestant Episcopal Church: 1870–1954," in *Historical Magazine of the Episcopal Church* 31 (September 1962): 233.

6. J. C. Hayden, "From Holly to Turner: Black Bishops in the American Succession," *Linkage*, no. 10 (December 1988): 4.

7. *Potestas* refers to the sacramental power conferred by virtue of consecration, such as the power to ordain or confirm; *auctoritas* refers to the authority inherent in the office, including, but not limited to jurisdiction and moral suasion.

8. Reimers, "Negro Bishops and Diocesan Segregation," 233.

9. *Journal of the General Convention* (1874).

10. *Journal of the General Convention* (1877). It should be noted that although, according to Reimers, "the office of suffragan was being reestablished

in part to allow the electing of Negro bishops," it was not solely for that purpose:

> Support for the plan also came from churchmen in the West and heavily populated Northeast who wanted suffragans to help supervise expanding church work. These suffragans were to be white. Thus a coalition formed because the new position could fill two different needs. The General Convention [eventually] hammered out the suffragan proposal which then became church law. (234)

Although it is widely held that Demby was the first suffragan bishop in the Episcopal Church, since the office was created partly to provide for colored suffragans that distinction belongs to Samuel Babcock, consecrated bishop suffragan of Massachusetts in 1913 (see *Episcopal Church Annual* [1994], 197.)

11. Weston, *Social Policy of the Episcopal Church*, 141.

12. *Journal of the General Convention of the Episcopal Church* (1883), appendix 11, p. 595.

13. Ibid.; letter written by Bishop Green on May 28, 1883, cited in ibid.

14. Ibid., 596–97. It should be noted that the desire to bring blacks into the fold of Christ does not mean that it was thought that blacks were, strictly speaking, in some other fold, that is, a member of some organized religion. They were thought to be godless heathen. An early missionary to the West Indies made the following comment about the religious activities of the natives, which strikes a resonant chord with like comments made of slaves in North America:

> The Indians and Negros have no manner of Religion by what I could observe of them. 'Tis true they have several Ceremonies, as Dances, Playing, &c, but these for the most part are so far from being Acts of Adoration of a God, that they are for the most part mixt with a great deal of Bawdry and Lewdness. (Hans Stone, cited in Davis, *Emancipation Still Comin'*, 60.)

Even when slaves had been converted, it must be observed, objection was made to their retaining vestiges of their old religion:

> They are the vices that have come down to them from the days of their African heathenism, or were incident to their condition previous to Christianity. Superstition of an abject and soul-enthralling kind, doubtless an indelible reminiscence of Africa, is widely prevalent among them.... Besides being enslaved by these iniquitous superstitions, the Negro Christian has too often a very limited practical belief in the sanctity of truth and honesty. (Mitcheson, bishop of Barbados, cited in Davis, *Emancipation Still Comin'*, 62.)

It must be remembered, too, that given the fact, as we have demonstrated, that evangelization on the part of the slaveholder was done for the purpose of exercising control over his slaves, aberrant behavior of any kind was seen as counterproductive, and therefore could not be tolerated.

15. Proposed canon, "Of missionary organizations within constituted episcopal jurisdictions," *Journal of the General Convention* (1883), 597.

16. *Journal of the General Convention* (1883), 595ff. It should be noted that the only Southern bishop who dissented from the Sewanee decision was Richard Hooker Wilmer, bishop of Alabama. Bishop Wilmer remained consistent in his views that the church had erred in its treatment of Negroes. He later wrote:

> For many years the Church's old time influence among this race had been waning and in several dioceses the Negro churches were practically extinct. The precipitate action of the General Convention of 1865 in committing all religious instructional of the Negro to the Protestant Episcopal Freedman's Commission was largely responsible for this decadence of work. It was felt by Southern bishops that this step, schismatic in nature, was taken in distrust of themselves, and they would have none of it. (Cited in Walter C. Whitaker, *Richard Hooker Wilmer* [Philadelphia, 1907], 232.)

17. It may well have been that the Southern bishops were especially angry, since the vote at General Convention passed in the House of Bishops, but failed in the House of Deputies, made up of clergy and laymen.

18. Reimers, "Negro Bishops and Diocesan Segregation," 233.

19. Hayden, "Let My People Go."

20. The Right Reverend Alfred M. Randolph, bishop of Virginia, in his address to Diocesan Council, 1899, cited in Odell Greenleaf Harris, *A History of the Seminary to Prepare Black Men for the Ministry of the Protestant Episcopal Church* (Alexandria: Virginia Theological Seminary, 1980), 46, italics mine. In light of such attitudes toward blacks, it is no wonder that George Freeman Bragg, then a priest in the Diocese of Virginia, and his brother clergy predicted that such actions would "put an end to the growth of the church among our people." If the statistics of the Bishop Payne Divinity School are any indication, those clerics proved to be prophetic. Enrollment at the all-black seminary in Virginia plummeted in the years immediately following the enactment of the diocesan canon. (Cf. Harris, *History of the Seminary.*)

A similar chord is struck by the Right Reverend Frederick F. Resse, bishop of Georgia, in an address to the tenth annual Council of Colored churchmen (referred to in most dioceses as the "colored convocation") in his diocese in 1916. In commenting on the suffragan bishop plan, he told the assembled delegates:

> I do not believe that our colored people as a race are yet prepared to minister an ecclesiastical organization in the church without the cooperation and assistance of their white brethren. Are you people ready to cut loose entirely from the white people in government, education, social betterment, and in the church, and face the whole tremendous problem of human life without any reliance on the white man? Would you do it if you could? I do not say this to disparage... you. God knows, I would not do this.... You may remember indeed that Anglo-Saxon churchmen have earned by centuries of toil and suffering the right to leadership in teaching and guarding the faith and order of the church. (Cited in Hoskins, *Black Episcopalians in Georgia,* 110.)

21. *The Churchman* 57 (May 12, 1888): 562.

22. Hayden, "From Holly to Turner," 4. It would appear, too, that where Jim Crow laws held sway, the most strenuous objections to according equal rights to blacks came from the laity. Bravid Harris points out that "generally, bishops and clergy were favorable to the reception of the members of our group, but the laity were not of the same view" ("The Story of Our Work," 9). Bragg, in an explanation of this phenomenon, offered the following: "It so happened that many Southern laymen who were prominent in state affairs were likewise prominent in the affairs of the Kingdom of God." (Bragg, *Afro-American*

Group, 152). In 1958, this theme is echoed by the Reverend Kenneth Hughes, rector of St. Bartholomew's, Cambridge, Mass., who writes:

> In such communities the "trouble is often not with the rectors but with powerful laymen who threaten economic boycott or dismissal if the status quo is tampered with. Many of these powerful laymen belong to the white citizens councils dedicated to preserve segregation." (Hughes, "Problems of Minorities Discussed by Negro Church Leaders," *The Witness* [October 23, 1958]: 6.)

23. Wilmore, *Black Religion and Black Radicalism*, 62.

24. Wood, *Arrogance of Faith*, 306. There continued to be resistance to the ordination of blacks, and many staunch segregationists lobbied for a totally separate black Presbyterian Church. This did not come to pass; indeed, in the last decades of the nineteenth century, northern Presbyterian missions moved into the South and organized black congregations in which blacks were given full equality in church governance. But it was a separate and parallel equality, similar to the colored convocation system in Episcopal dioceses, for such congregations, while not constituting a separate black denomination, nevertheless constituted separate black presbyteries.

25. Wood, *Arrogance of Faith*, 316.

26. the Reverend J. Benson Hamilton, pastor of Cornell Methodist Church, New York City, quoted in ibid., 317.

27. Ibid., 330.

28. Appendix XI, *Journal of the General Convention* (1883), 597.

29. *The Churchman* (August 25, 1883).

30. Ibid.

31. Ibid.

32. Hayden, "Let My People Go," 14.

33. Hayden, "From Holly to Turner," 4.

34. Reimers, "Negro Bishops and Diocesan Segregation," 234.

35. Hoskins, *Black Episcopalians in Georgia*, 109–10.

36. Hayden, "For Zion's Sake," 11.

37. Bragg, *Afro-American Group*, 152–53.

38. Bragg, "South Carolina: A Good Field for the Negro Missionary Bishop," *The Church Advocate* 22, no. 12 (April 1913): 2.

39. George Frazier Miller, "Missionary Episcopate as a Method of Evangelism," in *Black Gospel/White Church*, ed. John Melville Burgess (New York: Seabury Press, 1982), 33–34.

40. Ibid.

41. Statement drafted by the CCWACP, at St. Luke's Church, New Haven, Conn., 1903.

42. *Journal of the General Convention* (1916).

43. Ibid.

44. Ibid.

45. William Montgomery Brown, *The Crucial Race Question* (Little Rock: Arkansas Churchman's Publishing, 1907), 269–70.

46. Bragg, *Afro-American Group*, 156.

47. Bragg, *Episcopal Church and the Black Man*, 13.

48. Cf. Reimers, "Negro Bishops and Diocesan Segregation," 234.

49. George Freeman Bragg, in the *Church Advocate* (January 1918).

50. Miller, "The Missionary Episcopate as a Method of Evangelism," 34.

51. The canons of the Episcopal Church were changed to give to suffragan bishops the right to vote in the House of Bishops.

52. Reimers, "Negro Bishops and Diocesan Segregation," 235.

53. Cf. Hayden, "Afro-Anglican Linkages," 33, italics mine.

54. White, "Patriarch McGuire and the Episcopal Church," 113.

55. Reimers, "Negro Bishops and Diocesan Segregation," 236.

56. The Reverend Canon Edward W. Rodman, "Walk about Zion," an address delivered to black clergy in the Diocese of Pennsylvania, January 9, 1993.

57. Hayden, "From Holly to Turner," 4.

58. Sarah and Elizabeth Delany, *Having Our Say: The Delany Sisters' First 100 Years* (New York: Kodansha International, 1993).

59. The Reverend Harry Rahming, letter to the Reverend Canon Thomas W. S. Logan, May 10, 1978, 7 (Logan papers).

60. Michael J. Beary, "Birds of Passage: A History of the Separate Black Episcopal Church in Arkansas, 1902–1939," M.A. thesis, University of Arkansas, 1993, esp. chap. 2, "A Charter to Fail: The Election of Edward T. Demby."

61. Edwards, "Episcopal Church and the Black Man," 160.

62. The Reverend Harry Rahming, letter to the Reverend Canon Thomas W. S. Logan, May 10, 1978, 7. Father Rahming was ordained deacon in 1918, the year of Demby's consecration, and was the deacon of the mass at that service. After a brief ministry in Kansas City, Mo., he accepted a call to the Church of the Holy Redeemer, Denver, Colo., from which he retired in 1966, at the age of 72. He died twenty years later.

63. Bragg, *Afro-American Group,* 294.

64. As it turned out, Demby did indeed rock the boat in no uncertain terms. In 1932, he protested the election of the new bishop of Arkansas on the grounds that the bishop-elect had run on a racist ticket and that the black delegates to that convention had been subjected to overt discrimination, namely that they would have a separate celebration of the holy eucharist in the crypt of the church. An investigation followed, and the House of Bishops refused to confirm the election. Demby writes of the incident:

> On the arrival of the Negro clergy on the morning of the convention in conference it was decided, because of the condition of the place where we were told to celebrate the Body and Blood of Christ, and the uncatholic proceeding of the whole affair, and with justice to the race which we represent, it would not be wise for us to carry out the idea of the rector, and we did not.

Cf. Harold T. Lewis, "Archon Edward Thomas Demby, Pioneer of Social Justice," in *Boulé Journal* (Fall 1992); Michael J. Beary, "Up from the Basement: Bishop Demby's Struggle for a Catholic Church" in *Linkage,* no. 13 (1993); and Beary, "Birds of Passage."

65. Demby papers, National Archives of the Episcopal Church, Austin, Tex.

66. E. Thomas Demby, in his address to the Convention of the Diocese of Arkansas, 1918, in *Journal of the Convention of the Diocese of Arkansas* (1918). Cf. Harold T. Lewis, "Doing the Right Thing," *Linkage* no. 13 (1993).

67. *Journal of the Convention of the Diocese of Arkansas* (1919).

68. *Journal of the General Convention of the Episcopal Church* (1940). Also, see Reimers, "Negro Bishops and Diocesan Segregation," 237ff. It is interesting to note that Demby could not envision the day when blacks could be elected as diocesan bishops, with jurisdiction over white as well as black Episcopalians.

69. Four other blacks have since held diocesan bishoprics: John Thomas Walker, bishop of Washington, 1977–86; Orris George Walker Jr., bishop of Long Island, 1991– ; Herbert Thompson Jr., bishop of Southern Ohio, 1991– ; and Clarence N. Coleridge, bishop of Connecticut, 1993– . (John Walker and Coleridge had also served as suffragans in their respective dioceses before being elevated to diocesan.) Prior to Bishop Burgess, black diocesan bishops had been elected by the Episcopal Church, but to head overseas missionary jurisdictions. They were James Theodore Holly, as bishop of Haiti, 1874; Samuel David Ferguson, as bishop of Liberia, 1885; Bravid Washington Harris, as bishop of Liberia, 1945; and Dillard Houston Brown, as bishop of Liberia, 1961.

70. Canon Campbell was one of two priests elected as suffragan bishops for the Diocese of Virginia on May 1, 1993. Owing to unforeseen difficulties, Canon Campbell, at the request of the Standing Committee of the Diocese, withdrew from the election process. Canon Campbell, stating that he had "no intentions of harming the ministry of this church," complied with the request, citing his action as a "painful privilege."

71. Preston B. Hannibal, "Anglicanism's First Black Bishop: Pioneer or Experiment," *Linkage,* no. 10 (December 1988): 7.

72. David Hinderer, cited in ibid., 7, italics mine.

73. Henry Townsend, cited in ibid.

74. Cited in ibid., a reference to 1 Kings 4:25.

75. Williams, *Black Americans and the Evangelization of Africa,* 9.

76. Hayden, "Afro-Anglican Linkages," 31.

77. See Gregory U. Rigsby, *Alexander Crummell: Pioneer in Nineteenth-Century Pan-African Thought* (New York: Greenwood Press, 1987), esp. chap. 4, "Alexander Crummell, Missionary in Liberia," 71ff. In light of Bishop Payne's reputation, it is interesting to note that the seminary for black ordinands was named for him.

78. Ibid.

79. This in fact alters the historical understanding of the episcopate itself. The *Oxford Dictionary of the Christian Church* states that the understanding of the office of bishop is predicated primarily on election and mission (ed. F. L. Cross [New York: Oxford University Press, 1978], 176).

80. Hayden. "From Holly to Turner," 4.

81. Ibid.

82. Hayden, "Afro-Anglican Linkages."

83. Hayden, "From Holly to Turner," 4. It should be pointed out, however, that at least one of the church's bishops was supportive of black Episcopalians' efforts to secure men for the episcopate, and expressed the hope that the consecration of Bishop Ferguson would signal the removal of other racial barriers:

> Dr. [Samuel David] Ferguson was consecrated Missionary Bishop of Cape Palmas in Grace Church, New York on St. John Baptist's Day, June 24 [1885], on which occasion it was my privilege to act as one of the presenters. It was a memorable day, for it was the first consecration of a bishop of the African race for our own church, and now that a black man has a seat in our House of Bishops, I trust it will not be long before his right to a seat elsewhere may cease to be seriously challenged. We may well be watchful lest we admit to the Ministry, unfit men whether white or black; but when once we have given to one the Church's ordination, we may wisely consent to give him those other rights which ordinarily go with it. (The Right Reverend Henry Codman Potter, Address to the Convention of the Diocese of New York, 1885.)

Chapter 6. West Indian Anglicans: Missionaries to Black Episcopalians?

Epigraph: Charles E. Oakley, "Hills of the North, rejoice," No. 269 (hymn text, c. 1860), *Hymns Ancient and Modern* (Tiptree, Essex, 1982). The entire first verse reads as follows:

> Isles of the southern seas
> Deep in your coral caves,
> Pent be each warring breeze
> Lulled be your restless waves.

1. Cf. introduction, n. 11.

2. Interview between Bishop Primo and Dr. Randall Burkett, Chicago, December 12, 1984.

3. Philip Kasinitz, *Caribbean New York: Black Immigrants and the Politics of Race* (Ithaca, N.Y.: Cornell University Press, 1992), 19ff. According to Kasinitz, the first large wave arrived between 1900 and 1930, and "a somewhat more middle class group" arrived in the 1930s, as did another wave some three decades later.

4. Thomas Sowell, *Ethnic America* (New York: Basic Books, 1981), 216.

5. White, "Patriarch McGuire and the Episcopal Church:" "In 1930 there were 54,754 'foreign Negroes' in New York City, ten times the number found in Miami, which ranked next on the list. Those immigrants flocked in from all the islands of the Caribbean, but especially from the British West Indies, where Anglicanism was long established."

6. Burkett, *Garveyism as a Religious Movement,* 171. Cf. Bragg, in a letter to the *Living Church,* January 20, 1927, in which he reports that the increase in the number of black Episcopalians in seven Southern states had increased from 3,011 in the mid-1850s to 7,196 forty years later. The corresponding numbers for the six northern states cited were 1,975 and 19,511.

7. Cf. Harold T. Lewis, *The Recruitment of Black Clergy for the Episcopal Church: Some Biblical, Theological and Practical Considerations* (New York: Executive Council of the Episcopal Church, 1981), ii:

> There is a paucity of black clerical leadership in the church. A study recently conducted by Professor Robert Hood of General Seminary, and Mrs. Nell Gibson, a consultant on recruitment for the Office of Black Ministries, revealed that of the 350 or so predominantly black congregations in this country, 82 are vacant, and 82 more are staffed by white clergy. When these facts are seen in light of another — that there are currently only about 20 blacks enrolled in the church's seminaries (a figure which has remained virtually constant for the last several years) we realize at once that the five or six ordinations each year do not suffice in replenishing the ranks of black clergy.

8. Several congregations, especially along the eastern seaboard, are made up primarily of West Indian immigrants and their descendants. Among them are St. Ambrose, Harlem; All Souls, Harlem; St. Cyprian's, Boston; St. Augustine's, Brooklyn; St. Mark's, Brooklyn; and St. Agnes', Miami. St. Agnes' was named for St. Agnes', Nassau, Bahamas, the parish to which the congregation's founders originally belonged.

9. *Washington Post,* November 17, 1990, in a story about a gathering of West Indian clergy in the United States, reported that there were approximately 130 Caribbean clergy in the United States (according to Kortright Davis, this figure today is closer to 190). This compares to a total black Episcopal priest population of 545 (*Directory of Black Clergy in the Episcopal Church,* ed. Marc S. Jones [Executive Council of the Episcopal Church, 1991], 50). It should be noted that this figure includes only those who actually migrated from the West Indies. The number would increase significantly if it included first- and second-generation West Indians.

In several major dioceses, e.g., New York, Long Island, and Pennsylvania, the Caribbean clergy overwhelmingly outnumber American-born black clergy. In Pennsylvania, according to the bishop suffragan, the Right Reverend Franklin D. Turner, there are only four African American clergy, including himself. The Rev. Canon Thomas W. S. Logan in 1976 compiled a list of all black clergy who had served in the diocese over the past 200 years. Half of those listed (nine out of eighteen) at that time were West Indians.

Codrington College, the oldest Anglican theological college in the Western hemisphere, was founded in 1745 by the SPG as trustees for the estate of Christopher Codrington who had left his plantations for a school for the study of "physic, chirurgery and divinity." It was established primarily as a theological college by Bishop Coleridge of Barbados in 1829.

10. Cited in Hayden, "Black Ministry in the Episcopal Church," 2.

11. Burgess, sermon at Absalom Jones Theological Institute, 3.

12. George Alexander McGuire, in appendix to Brown, *Crucial Racial Question,* 276.

13. Although the colonial powers in the Caribbean islands, including the reverend clergy, were all white, virtually all of the communicants were black. Therefore, Anglicanism was seen as a religion to which black West Indians

could "naturally" belong. McGuire admitted later that his Caribbean experience of Anglicanism prevented him from understanding the need for a racial episcopate: "Baptised in the Church of England and reared in the West Indies where there was no need for racial episcopal supervision, I failed to fully appreciate the necessity for this movement." (Burkett, *Garveyism as a Religious Movement.*)

14. White, "Patriarch McGuire and the Episcopal Church," 122.

15. Edwards, "Episcopal Church and the Black Man."

16. The Anglo-Catholic mode of worship prevalent in the West Indies is attributable in large measure to the influence of the SPG. Colonies to which they had sent missionaries, especially in the West Indies and West Africa, were "high-church," while colonies missionized by the CMS (principally in East Africa) were "low-church."

17. Interview with Canon Logan, Yeadon, Pennsylvania, July 9, 1994.

18. Burgess, sermon at Absalom Jones Theological Institute, 4; Bennett, "Black Episcopalians," 243.

19. White, "Patriarch McGuire and the Episcopal Church," 122.

20. Hayden, "Overview," 1.

21. For a full discussion of African American missionaries to West Africa, see chapter 7.

22. Owing to the small pool of parishes and applicants, it was not always possible for the parties concerned to effect a mutually agreeable match. Alexander Crummell, for example, was turned down by the vestries of St. Luke's, New Haven, and St. Philip's, Harlem, and ousted by Christ Church, Providence.

23. Hayden observes:

> A general attitude on the part of white Episcopalians was that the diaconate should be the *normal* ministry for blacks and that the priesthood should be limited to those black men who were truly exceptional. In 1875 Benjamin Bosworth Smith, the Presiding Bishop, wrote that he encouraged "the training of young men for deacon's orders on a minimum qualification, encouraging the best and most gifted of them to look forward from three to five years to full priests' orders." This same attitude was expressed by the chairman of the Board of Examining Chaplains of the Diocese of Washington who wrote: "Our policy has been to be as easy with such candidates for the diaconate as the canons allow and to make it as hard for such deacons to get the priesthood as the canons fairly construed required." ("Overview," 7.)

24. White, "Patriarch McGuire and the Episcopal Church," 126. Hayden points out that of the 137 blacks ordained deacon between 1866 and 1900, only 86 were advanced to the priesthood.

25. Hayden, "Overview," 1.

26. Noel L. Erskine, *Decolonizing Theology: A Caribbean Perspective* (Maryknoll, N.Y.: Orbis Books, 1981), 71.

27. John Melville Burgess, in a letter to the Reverend Canon Harold T. Lewis, December 14, 1993.

28. Taylor, "Tensions and Opportunities between West Indian and American Blacks," 278.

29. Davis, *Emancipation Still Comin',* 61; J. E. Reece and C. G. Clark-Hunt, *Barbados Diocesan History* (London: West India Committee, 1925), 61; S. H. M. Jones, *Diocese of Gambia and the Rio Pongas, 1835–1951: Its Origins and Early History* (Banjul: Book Production and Material Resources Unit, Diocese of Gambia, 1966).

30. Jones, *Diocese of Gambia and the Rio Pongas,* 6.

31. Reece and Clark-Hunt, *Barbados Diocesan History;* Crummell, "The Regeneration of Africa," in *Africa and America,* 445.

32. Reece and Clark-Hunt, *Barbados Diocesan History,* 6, 7. According to Hayden, Rawle received a letter from Presiding Bishop Benjamin Bosworth Smith, requesting that he send Codrington students to the United States ("Overview," 2).

33. Minutes from a meeting at 79 Pall Mall, London, August 9, 1842, attended by Archdeacons Parry, Davis and Austin, cited in Sehon S. Goodridge, *Facing the Challenge of Emancipation: A Study of the Ministry of William Hart Coleridge, First Bishop of Barbados, 1824–42* (Bridgetown, Barbados: Cedar Press, 1981), 45.

34. Smith informs us that "the first white missionaries lived only six weeks; the second to arrive lived two years, but the next did not last more than four months. Consequently, from 1864 onwards, no European went to the Pongas" ("Overview").

35. Hayden, "Afro-Anglican Linkages," 27.

36. Bela Vasady Jr., "The Role of the Black West Indian Missionary in West Africa, 1840–1890," Ph.D. dissertation, Temple University, Philadelphia, 1972, 183.

37. Davis reminds us that John Mitchinson, bishop of Barbados, 1793–81, allowed for three classes of humankind. The highest, of course, was white Europeans. The lowest was, according to him, the savage pure and simple. Between both classes were those races who were inferior to the higher types of humanity but had come into contact with the higher races. Of these, said Mitchinson, the West Indian furnishes a good example, the more instructive because it is possible to compare the Negro who has lived thus under Christianity with his heathen congener in Africa (Davis, *Emancipation Still Comin',* 61).

38. Hayden, "Black Ministry in the Episcopal Church," 2.

39. Kortright Davis writes:

> I can well remember the days when as a young school-boy growing up in colonial Antigua, in the West Indies, we had to celebrate each May 24 as 'Empire Day.' After we had lustily sung:
>
> Rule Britannia
> Britannia rules the waves,
> Britons never, never, never,
> Shall be Slaves
>
> we would be rewarded with buns and lemonade.

("Afro-Anglicanism and the Ecumenical Imperative.")

40. Edwards, "Episcopal Church and the Black Man."

41. Lennox Raphael, "West Indians and Afro-Americans," *Freedomways* (3rd quarter, 1964): 441.

42. Taylor, "Tensions and Opportunities between West Indian and American Blacks," 277.

43. Ibid., 275–76.

44. Raphael, "West Indians and Afro-Americans," 442.

45. Clarence N. Coleridge, "Towards Effective Ministry in the U.S.," an address delivered at the Caribbean Anglican Consultation, Arlington, Va., November 1990, in Davis, ed., "Pilgrims and Not Strangers."

46. White, "Patriarch McGuire and the Episcopal Church," 123.

47. Henderson Brome, "A Study of the Assimilation of Barbadian Immigrants in the United States with Special Reference to the Barbadians in New York," Ed.D. dissertation, Columbia University, New York, 1978, 60.

48. Taylor, "Tensions and Opportunities between West Indian and American Blacks," 274.

49. Thomas Sowell, *Economics and Politics of Race: An International Perspective* (New York: Morrow, 1983) 104.

50. Taylor, "Tensions and Opportunities between West Indian and American Blacks," 274.

51. Raphael, "West Indians and Afro-Americans," 438.

52. Haynes, "West Indian-American Relations," 16.

53. Davis, *Emancipation Still Comin'.*

54. Kasinitz, *Caribbean New York,* 20.

55. Davis, *Emancipation Still Comin',* 126. Sowell suggests that the entrepreneurial spirit may have been due to a pronouncedly different economic climate in the West Indies:

> West Indian slaves and free Negroes together were major suppliers of food to the larger society. Barbados, for example, depended almost wholly on them for food, and huckstering was "deeply imbedded in the cultural system of non-whites" there. Thus, even during the era of slavery, West Indian Negroes — both slave and free — had economic incentives to exercise initiative, as well as experience in buying, selling and managing their own affairs. The experiences was usually denied slaves in the U.S. who were issued rations, and who were deliberately kept in a state of dependence which was not feasible under West Indian conditions. (Sowell, *Economics and Politics of Race,* 103.)

56. Raphael, "West Indians and Afro-Americans," 438.

57. The eight dioceses in the Province of the West Indies: Barbados, Belize, Guyana, Jamaica, Nassau and the Bahamas, North Eastern Caribbean and Aruba (formerly Antigua), Trinidad and Tobago, and the Windward Islands, are all headed by native West Indians. The last English bishop in the Province was the Most Reverend Alan Knight, bishop of Guyana and archbishop of the West Indies, who died in office in 1982. The Province includes two dioceses not geographically part of the West Indies — Guyana, formerly British Guiana, on the north coast of South America; and Belize, formerly British Honduras, on the east coast of Central America. Their ethnic makeup, however, is the same as the rest of the Province.

58. Ibid., 5. A generalization can be made that the NAACP stood for the American ideal of assimilation, whereas the UNIA advocated a black independence and self-determination.

59. Taylor, "Tensions and Opportunities between West Indian and American Blacks," 273.

60. Ira Reid, *The Negro Immigrant: His Background, Characteristics, and Social Adjustment, 1899–1937* (New York: AMS Press, 1939), 125.

61. In recent decades, the black ranks of the Episcopal Church have also been swelled by an influx of Anglicans from Africa, especially Nigeria, South Africa, Ghana, and Sierra Leone, but as this is a relatively recent phenomenon, we will not address the development here. Many such persons for many years did not affiliate with the Episcopal Church because they did not know that it was an Anglican church. Many churches now add "Anglican" to their notice boards, in order to attract such persons. There are perhaps thirty or forty African priests who currently serve in the Episcopal Church.

62. Taylor, "Tensions and Opportunities between West Indian and American Blacks."

63. The Bragg "pedigree" is traced back even further. George Sr. was confirmed by Richard Channing Moore, the second bishop of New York, at about the same time that the bishop had ordained Peter Williams Jr., the second black priest in the Episcopal Church:

> After Moore laid his hands on Bragg's father, the bishop remarked that someday he hoped there would be colored ministers in the South as there were in New York. When the Episcopal teachers came to Petersburg from Philadelphia in 1866 and began the mission school for freedmen, Caroline Bragg and her father were the first to welcome them, and the Bragg family took the leadership in establishing St. Stephen's Church. Bragg's father became senior warden; his uncle junior warden; another uncle the choir director, another uncle, the superintendent of the Sunday school; his first cousin, Thomas White Cain, became a priest and another first cousin, Robert Tabb, also became a priest. (Hayden, "Overview," 3.)

64. White, "Patriarch McGuire and the Episcopal Church"; Du Bois, *The Philadelphia Negro,* 217.

65. Information in this section gleaned primarily from William L. Quay, "Archdeacon Henry L. Phillips (1847–1947)," *Archives Newsletter* Diocese of Pennsylvania 1, no. 2 (February 1985).

66. Because of the lack of mobility in deployment, black clergy tended to serve long tenures. Only seven rectors have served St. Philip's, Harlem, in its 175-year history; N. Peterson Boyd and John Milton Coleman were the only rectors in the first sixty years of the history of St. Philip's, Brooklyn; F. A. I. Bennett, founding rector of Calvary Church, Washington, served from 1901 until his death forty years later, when he was succeeded by James O. West Jr., who was rector until his retirement in 1990.

67. Information obtained from Father Oxley's papers provided by his daughter, Elizabeth Oxley Hatcher, a member of St. Andrew's, Cincinnati.

68. Hayden, "Let My People Go."

69. For this section, we are indebted to Dr. Hayden's manuscript, "Arnold Hamilton Maloney, Priest and Scientist, 1888–1955," n.p., 1994.

70. White, "Patriarch McGuire and the Episcopal Church," 132.

71. *Afro-American Group,* 42 *et passim;* address to the Convention of the Diocese of Arkansas, 1919.

72. Cf. Burkett, *Black Redemption,* esp. chapter 11, "George Alexander McGuire."

73. *Divine Liturgy and Other Rites of the African Orthodox Church* (1945), 48; White, "Patriarch McGuire and the Episcopal Church," 134; Bragg, *Richard Allen and Absalom Jones,* 4. McGuire, as noted below, served as rector of St. Thomas from 1900 to 1905.

74. From a letter by McGuire to the bishop of Massachusetts, requesting that St. Bartholomew's, Cambridge, be admitted as a parish church, cited in Burkett, *Black Redemption,* 160.

75. Cited in White, "Patriarch McGuire and the Episcopal Church," 116ff.

76. For this section, we are especially indebted to two works by Randall Burkett: "George Alexander McGuire," in *Black Redemption,* 157ff.; and "Sect or Civil Religion: The Debate with George Alexander McGuire," in *Garveyism as a Religious Movement,* 71ff.

77. St. Ambrose, c. 339–97, is said to have been elected bishop of Milan in 374, when a boy in the crowd at the cathedral yelled out "Ambrose for bishop!" Ambrose, a Roman governor with his seat in Milan, was only a catechumen; upon his election, he was baptized, and ordained deacon and priest within a few days before his consecration as bishop. Cf. *Oxford Dictionary of the Christian Church.*

78. Burkett, *Black Redemption,* 159. In his book *The Catholic Church and the Color Line* (1907), Brown wrote: "A God-implanted race prejudice makes it impossible, absolutely so, that Afro-Americans and Anglo-Americans should ever occupy the same footing in a dual racial church" (cited in White, "Patriarch McGuire and the Episcopal Church," 113). Brown referred to himself as *"episcopus in partibus Bolshevikium et Infidelium,"* and wrote: "I consider going to a church and praying to a God to be bad habits and if I would live my life over, I would not allow myself to become addicted to them" (*Communism and Christianism* [1920], 144, cited in White, "Patriarch McGuire and the Episcopal Church").

79. White, "Patriarch McGuire and the Episcopal Church," 115–16. Brown had espoused the "Arkansas Plan" providing for Negro bishops and jurisdictions.

80. Cited in White, "Patriarch McGuire and the Episcopal Church," 115.

81. In a letter to *The Church Advocate* 17, no. 5 (March 1908): 3.

82. Cited in Raphael, "West Indians and Afro-Americans."

83. McGuire's appendix to Brown, *Crucial Race Question,* 280ff.

84. Edwards, "Episcopal Church and the Black Man."

85. White, "Patriarch McGuire and the Episcopal Church," 116.

86. In a comment that could be made about the founding of most black congregations, the Reverend Kenneth Hughes, a Jamaican priest who was rector of St. Bartholomew's in the 1950s, wrote:

> These churchmen of colour, forever hating segregation but denied fraternity with their fellow churchmen *were driven into segregation* because, as their initiating petition said, they wanted to worship in freedom, peace and harmony, without any limitation as to numbers, rights and privileges, which conditions were denied them in neighboring congregations. (*History of St. Bartholomew's P.E. Church* [Cambridge, Mass., 1958].)

87. White suggests that the fact that McGuire was suspect among the overwhelmingly low-church Boston clergy for his high-church practices may have had some small part in the diocesan decision. But it is widely believed that the primary motivation was racial.

88. This experience, according to White, afforded him the opportunity to preach at various places throughout the country, and was "an invaluable experience in seeing the Episcopal Church as a whole, and there was no better place for discovering what the Episcopal Church thought was good for its Negro members" (117). For a full discussion of the ACIN, see chapter 8.

89. Burkett, *Black Redemption,* 6

90. For a complete discussion of the issue of the validity of McGuire's orders, see White, "Patriarch McGuire and the Episcopal Church," 129ff. It should be pointed out that although inspired by Garvey, the AOC, with its distinctive Anglican ethos, survived both Garveyism and the UNIA.

91. Bragg and Frazier, in terms of their outspokenness, were atypical. As Burkett observes:

> Black Episcopalians generally (as was probably the case with most blacks during the 1920s in predominantly white religious denominations) would not be noted for the militancy of their social protest concerning the racial question. There were exceptions of course, such as George Freeman Bragg Jr., and George Frazier Miller, but they were clearly in a minority. (*Garveyism as a Religious Movement,* 172.)

92. G. Moore, in *Life* magazine, June 30, 1967, cited in White, "Patriarch McGuire and the Episcopal Church."

93. White, "Patriarch McGuire and the Episcopal Church," 133.

94. The ecclesiology espoused by Maloney, a Trinidadian (see introduction) while it bore some similarity to later black and Third World ecclesiologies, would not have been shared by most black Episcopalians of his vintage, who were wedded to a theology of assimilation. Black Episcopal theologians of the 1960s and after, however, who stress self-determination and empowerment, espouse an ideology and ecclesiology very much akin to Maloney's thought. It should also be mentioned that an outward manifestation of the West Indian's ecclesiology was his "churchmanship." It was a more natural transition for the high-church West Indian to adjust to the liturgical practices of the AOC than for the American black, more at home with "low" to "middle-of-the-road" churchmanship of the South.

95. White, "Patriarch McGuire and the Episcopal Church," 123. While we understand and accept the gist of White's observation, it is somewhat misleading, as it does not take into account the fact that black Americans were prodigious in the establishment of social and religious structures, e.g., black fra-

ternal organizations and the predominantly black denominations such as AME, AMEZ, and CME.

96. Cf. Taylor, "Tensions and Opportunities between West Indian and American Blacks."

97. Burgess, sermon at Absalom Jones Theological Institution.

98. Coleridge, "Towards Effective Ministry in the U.S."

99. Taylor, "Tensions and Opportunities between West Indian and American Blacks," 273.

100. White, "Patriarch McGuire and the Episcopal Church," 123

101. Other highly publicized racial incidents during the period in which the Episcopal Church was implicated strengthened the West Indian belief that American society and its Episcopal Church were inimical, resulting in their determination to close ranks, either within or without the Episcopal Church (see White, "Patriarch McGuire and the Episcopal Church," 132ff.).

102. Davis, "Afro-Anglicanism and the Ecumenical Imperative," 2

103. Enrique Brown, "Ministry to Caribbean Persons," address delivered at the Caribbean Consultation, Arlington, Va., 1990, in Davis, ed., "Pilgrims and Not Strangers."

104. Reported in Davis, ed., "Pilgrims and Not Strangers."

Chapter 7. Black Episcopalians as Missionaries to Africa

Epigraph: Heber, "From Greenland's icy mountains."

1. Of the first twenty-five black Episcopal clergy (between the ordination of Absalom Jones in 1795 and the end of the Civil War) those appointed as missionaries to Africa were Jacob Oson (1828; died before departure), Gustavus V. Caesar (1830), Edward Jones (1830), Alexander Crummell (1842), Augustus Hanson (1842), Eli Stokes (1843), William Munroe (1846), Thomas Pinckney (1852), Garretson Gibson (1854), Alfred Russell (1854), Hezekiah Greene (born in the West Indies) (1854), Thomas J. Thompson (1858), Joseph Wilcox (1861), and Samuel Ferguson, 1865.

Two clergymen who went as missionaries to the West Indies were Isaiah DeGrasse (1838), and James Theodore Holly (1855).

The remaining black clergymen of the period exercised their ministries in the United States: Absalom Jones (1795), Peter Williams (1820), William Leavington (1824), James Ward (born in the West Indies) (1825), William Douglas (1834), Samuel Berry (1847), Harrison Webb (1853), William Alston (1859), and John Peterson (1865). Based on data compiled by Randall K. Burkett, College of the Holy Cross, Worcester, Mass., 1980.

2. A similar experiment, the African School, had been founded by the Presbyterians in New Jersey in 1816. The Presbyterians also operated the Ashmun Institute in Pennsylvania, which prepared men for missionary work in Liberia. In 1829, the African Education Society of the United States was established in Washington, D.C. Like the AMS, it was short-lived.

3. *African Repository* 6, no. 9 (November 1830): 263.

4. Jonathan Wainwright, "Address to the Executive Committee of the African Mission School Society, together with the records of the proceedings at the formation of said society" (Hartford: H & F. J. Huntington, 1828), 3.

5. The Domestic and Foreign Missionary Society is the official, corporate name of the Episcopal Church in the U.S.A. It was formed at the 1820 meeting of the General Convention, at the urging and with the financial support of the CMS, whose secretary suggested to the Episcopal Church "that the most effectual way of raising missionary zeal in America would be the formation of a missionary society in the Episcopal Church of the United States." (Cited in D. Ellwood Dunn, *A History of the Episcopal Church in Liberia, 1821–1980* [Metuchen, N.J.: Scarecrow Press, 1992], 34.)

6. Wainwright, "Address to the Executive Committee."

7. Cited in *African Repository* (1827): 348.

8. Wainwright, "Address to the Executive Committee," 3–4.

9. Grace Church played a prominent role in the Episcopal Church's missionary endeavor during the nineteenth century. It was there that James Theodore Holly and Samuel David Ferguson were consecrated.

10. Jonathan Wainwright, "A Discourse," 19–20, in Wainwright, "Address to the Executive Committee."

11. Ibid., 5.

12. Randall K. Burkett, "Elizabeth Mars Johnson Thomson, 1807–1864: A Research Note," *Historical Magazine of the Episcopal Church* 55, no. 1 (March 1986): 24.

13. Report of the Trustees of the African Mission School (1830), 21.

14. Bishop Brownell, in *Journal of the Convention of the Diocese of Connecticut* (1829).

15. Burkett, "Elizabeth Thomson," 24. Mrs. Thomson initially worked in Liberia under the auspices of the Ladies Liberian School Association of Philadelphia, founded in 1831 to promote education in Liberia through the establishment of schools and the support of competent teachers (Dunn, *History of the Episcopal Church in Liberia,* 40–41).

16. Burkett, "Elizabeth Thomson," 23.

17. Dunn, *History of the Episcopal Church in Liberia,* 44.

18. Cf. *Episcopal Watchman* 2.45 (January 24, 1829): 358: "It is reasonable to presume that the people of color are as yet generally uninformed of the existence of the institution, nor will the knowledge of it reach them, until the clergy will take the pains to communicate it from the desk [i.e., the pulpit]." It is interesting to note that later, when blacks were still not forthcoming, it was suggested that "coloured members of the Church whose situation renders them competent to the task be asked to assist in the choice of fit candidates." ("Rights of All," *African Repository* [August 7, 1829]: 29.)

19. Clifton Brewer, *A History of Religious Education in the Episcopal Church to 1835* (New York: Yale University Press, 1924), 52.

20. Vincent P. Franklin, *Black Self-Determination: A Cultural History of African-American Resistance* (Brooklyn, N.Y.: Lawrence Hill Books, 1992), 96.

21. Jonathan Wainwright, "A Plea for Missions," a sermon preached before the Board of Directors of the Domestic & Foreign Missionary Society of the Protestant Episcopal Church in the U.S., in St. James' Church, Philadelphia, May 13, 1828.

22. Franklin, *Black Self-Determination,* 100.

23. Bettye J. Gardner, "Opposition to Emigration: A Selected Letter from William Watkins, a Colored Baltimorean," *Journal of Negro History* (1978): 155.

24. Franklin, *Black Self-Determination,* 99.

25. Burkett, "Elizabeth Thomson," 24.

26. P. J. Staudenraus, *The African Colonization Movement, 1816–1865* (New York: Columbia University Press, 1961), i.

27. *African Repository* 8 (1832): 170–71, cited in Franklin, *Black Self-Determination.* It should be noted that Silliman's speech was delivered in 1832, a year after Nat Turner's slave rebellion took place in Virginia.

28. Wood, *Arrogance of Faith,* 294.

29. Franklin, *Black Self-Determination,* 97.

30. Gardner, "Opposition to Emigration."

31. Wainwright, "Address to the Executive Committee," 20.

32. See Wood, *Arrogance of Faith,* 294.

33. James Habersham, quoted in Edwards, "Episcopal Church and the Black Man," 5, italics mine.

34. Wainwright, "Discourse," 23, italics mine.

35. *The Episcopal Watchman* 4, no. 18 (September 1830).

36. Heber, "From Greenland's icy mountains."

37. W. L. Williams, *Black Americans and the Evangelization of Africa, 1877–1900* (Madison: University of Wisconsin Press, 1982), 11ff.

38. *Proceedings of the Board of Missions of the Protestant Episcopal Church* (New York, 1837), 101.

39. Dunn, *History of the Episcopal Church in Liberia,* 44, 49.

40. Burkett, "Elizabeth Thomson," 27.

41. *Spirit of Missions* (1864), 214–15.

42. Burkett points out that Thomson's tenure was matched by Edward Jones in Sierra Leone, and approximated by Bishop John Payne in Liberia (cf. "Elizabeth Thomson").

43. Dunn, *History of the Episcopal Church in Liberia,* 50.

44. Cited in ibid., 55.

45. Savage served in Liberia intermittently between 1836 and 1847. After the failure of his own health and the death of two wives, he returned to the United States. Minor worked faithfully in Liberia for six years, and died there in 1843 at the age of 29.

46. A letter from Payne to Vaughan, January 17, 1842, cited in Dunn, *History of the Episcopal Church in Liberia,* 58. Emphasis added.

47. Dunn, *History of the Episcopal Church in Liberia,* 88.

48. J. Carleton Hayden, "Alexander Crummell, Afro-Anglican Pioneer in the United States, England, and Liberia, 1819–1898," *Linkage,* no. 5 (January 1986): 16. Crummell, of course, was a staunch abolitionist, and therefore did not concur with the ACS's proslavery stance.

49. Lukson E. Ejofodomi, "The Missionary Career of Alexander Crummell in Liberia: 1853–1873," Ph.D. diss., University of Michigan at Ann Arbor, 1974.

50. Alexander Crummell, *Africa and America,* cited in Williams, *Black Americans,* 11.

51. Hayden, "Alexander Crummell."

52. Alexander Crummell, address to the Pennsylvania Colonization Society, Church of the Epiphany, Philadelphia, October 1865.

53. "The Episcopal Church in Liberia: On Laying the Cornerstone at St. Andrew's," in Crummell, *Africa and America,* 463.

54. Cited in Dunn, *History of the Episcopal Church in Liberia,* 93.

55. D. Ellwood Dunn, "George Daniel Browne (1933–1993): Architect of West African Indigenization," *Linkage,* no. 13 (June 1993): 28.

56. Cf. Dunn, *History of the Episcopal Church in Liberia,* 280.

The last African American Episcopal priest who served as a missionary to Liberia was the Reverend Paul Washington, 1948–54. The Episcopal Church in the twentieth century reversed its previous missionary policy, and began to discourage black clergy from going to the mission field, under the guise that they would not be accepted by Africans or other people of color. One suspects that another motivation was that it wanted to keep the mission field, where missionaries "fared sumptuously every day," as the preserve of white clergy. Since Father Washington, the only black clergy to serve as missionaries outside the continental United States were the Reverend Thomas W. Gibbs to the Virgin Islands in 1958; the Reverend Harold T. Lewis to Honduras, 1971–72; and the Reverend Canon George Brandt, as provincial secretary in the Province of Central Africa, 1983–86.

57. Davis, *Emancipation Still Comin',* 62.

58. Lewis, *The Recruitment of Black Clergy,* iii.

59. The presiding bishop of the Episcopal Church wrote in 1986:

> I applaud the work the Task Force for the Recruitment, Training and Deployment of Black Clergy. The intentionality which it has shown in seeking out and encouraging Black men and women to offer themselves for the sacred ministry, and providing a support system for them during and after the process between aspiration and ordination, is sorely needed, as it provides a corrective to the practices of a previous age, when minority vocations were often discouraged.

The Most Rev. Edmond Lee Browning, in *Report of the Task Force for the Recruitment, Training and Deployment of Black Clergy,* ed. Stephen Scott Kirk (New York: Executive Council of the Episcopal Church, June 1986).

Chapter 8. Renewed Efforts to Evangelize African Americans

Epigraph: Doane, "Fling out the banner."

1. An official document of the ACIN reads:

> The Episcopal Church . . . relatively to its size the wealthiest of ecclesiastical bodies in this country, has been expending for work among Negroes only $60,000 a year, a sum utterly inadequate both to the needs of the Negroes and to the financial ability and the moral position of the church. (Records of the ACIN, Archives RG61.1.3.)

2. Samuel Bishop, "The Church among the Negroes," ACIN publication (February 1907), 2, Archives RG61.1.4.

3. Hayden reports:

> In 1886, the conference of churchworkers memorialized General Convention to re-constitute a special commission to replace the Freedman's Commission which had been discontinued in 1877. The Commission on Work Among the Colored People was created the next year but was composed of a majority of southerners and headquartered in Washington, D.C. to allay white southern misgivings. The conference workers then concentrated on getting black input on the commission and on the board of St. Augustine's School. When the Commission was reorganized in 1895, Dr. Crummell was appointed as one of 21 members. John Henry Pollard, archdeacon for colored work in North Carolina, became a board member at St. Augustine's and Henry Beard Delany vice-principal. The conference's request of 1898 that a black priest be appointed as the Commission's field agent was never granted and in 1904 the Commission, embroiled in controversies, was dismantled. ("Let my people go," Archives RG159.1.)

4. "Historical Background" [of the ACIN], Archives RG61.1.3., italics mine.

5. Bishop, "The Church among the Negroes." The founders of the ACIN attributed the lack of success among black Episcopalians to the facts that it was

> a national church, with a democratic form of government; and national action on difficult and perplexing questions is always a compound of varying and possibly of antagonistic sectional needs, motives and forces. Another is that certain racial facts and necessities have flung our Church machinery out of gear. (Archives RG61.1.3.)

6. Ibid., 2.

7. Ibid.

8. ACIN Annual Report (New York: Office of the General Agent, 1912), Archives RG61.1.5.

9. "The American Church Institute for Negroes" (1950), Archives RG61.2.31, italics mine.

10. Pamphlet published by ACIN (1910), Archives RG61.1.4.

11. Ibid.

12. "The American Church Institute for Negroes," publicity brochure (1958), Archives RG61.3.8.

13. "Religious life on the campus receives high priority in aiding students to prepare themselves for living worthy lives," ACIN brochure, Archives RG61.2.31. Indeed, in this connection, Kenneth Hughes would later report that

"converts to the Church in college, on returning to their own communities, often find only a 'white' church into which they are not welcome." ("Problems of Minorities Discussed by Negro Church Leaders," 6.)

14. Hayden. "Let My People Go," 26, italics mine. These "employable skills" fell basically into two types: those that befitted blacks to function within the segregated institutions of their own community, notably the school and the church; and those positions, such as nursing, cooking, and so on, which prepared blacks for service of whites. In neither case, therefore, did the ACIN attempt to enable blacks to enter the mainstream of the workplace.

15. Archives RG61.1.3.

16. ACIN annual report, italics mine.

17. Ibid., 9–10.

18. Burgess, "The Role of ESCRU in the Life of the Church."

19. "American Church Institute for Negroes," 4.

20. Bishop, "The Church among the Negroes."

21. Such a view, of course, is reflective of the way blacks were perceived by the general population. As early as 1875, Crummell states:

> We are living in this country, a part of its population, and yet in divers respects, we are as foreign to its inhabitants as though we were living in the Sandwich Islands. It is this our actual separation from the real life to be nation, which constitutes us "a nation within nation." (Thanksgiving sermon, November 25, 1875.)

22. Cooper, "Womanhood."

23. Records of the ACIN, Archives, RG61.1.3.

24. The change in name was made to avoid a confusion between the Episcopal Church's governing body and the National Council of Churches. General Convention is the supreme authority of the Church; between its triennial meetings, the Executive Council acts in its stead.

25. *Journal of the General Convention* (1943), 551.

26. Ibid. (1919), 228.

27. Ibid. (1934), 348, italics mine.

28. Ibid.

29. Ibid. (1943), 477–78.

30. Ibid. (1934), 478. See chapter 3 for our discussion of the white and black understandings of "catholic."

31. Such a conclusion could be reached because the committee chose to base its findings on those dioceses where there was *de jure* discrimination against blacks, and chose to ignore the *de facto* discrimination that existed throughout the Church.

32. *Journal of the General Convention* (1934), 476.

33. Ibid., 477.

34. Ibid. (1940), 343. It should be noted that the 1955 General Convention was originally scheduled to take place in Houston, but because nonsegregated accommodations could not be guaranteed, the Church decided, under pressure from the CCWACP, Dr. Caution, and Associate Justice Thurgood Marshall (an Episcopalian) to move the Convention to Honolulu (see chapter 9).

35. *Journal of the General Convention* (1940), 501.

36. The black members of the group were Bishop Demby, Archdeacon Bravid Washington Harris of Southern Virginia, the Reverend Edmund Oxley of Cincinnati, and his son, Lt. Lawrence Oxley; the Venerable George Plaskett of Newark, N.J., and Mr. Henry Craft of New York. The Bi-Racial Committee on Negro Work was later formed, drawing largely on the same membership. Archdeacon Harris was appointed to the post of Secretary for Negro Work.

37. *Journal of the General Convention* (1943), 549–50.

Chapter 9. The Witness of the Conference of Church Workers among Colored People and the Secretaries for Negro Work

Epigraph: Karl Heinrich von Bagatzky, "Awake thou spirit of the watchmen," no. 255 (hymn text, 1749), trans. Winfred Douglas and Arthur Farlander, *The Hymnal 1940.*

1. Memorial to the 1919 General Convention, cited in the *Church Advocate* (November 1919).

2. *Church Advocate* (October 1908), 3.

3. CCWACP memorial to the 1907 General Convention, cited in the *Church Advocate* (October 1907), 3.

4. Ibid.

5. *Church Advocate* 30, no. 10 (August 1922).

6. J. C. Hayden, "'For Zion's Sake I will not hold my peace': George Freeman Bragg, Jr., Priest, Pastor and Prophet," *Linkage* 6 (Oct. 1986): 10.

7. Ibid.

8. Records of the ACIN, Archives, RG61.1.

9. Edwards, "Episcopal Church and the Black Man," 139.

10. John M. Burgess, *Bravid Washington Harris of Liberia* (New York: National Council of the Episcopal Church, 1965), 8.

11. Walter D. Dennis, "Tollie LeRoy Caution: Forerunner, Pathfinder, Prophet," *Linkage,* no. 9 (June 1988): 8.

12. Franklin D. Turner, "Tollie LeRoy Caution: A Man of Faith, Scholarship and Service," *Linkage,* no. 9 (June 1988).

13. Minutes of the Bi-Racial Sub-Committee on Negro Work, November 6–7, 1945, Archives RG159.1.

14. David E. Sumner, *The Episcopal Church's History: 1945–1985* (Wilton, Conn.: Morehouse-Barlow, 1987), 31, 16.

15. Minutes, Special Meeting of the Triennial Conference of Episcopal Church Workers (Logan papers).

16. "Social Relations: Not Just a Watch-dog," *Living Church,* May 16, 1954, 6.

17. Minutes, Special Meeting of the Triennial Conference of Episcopal Church Workers (Logan papers).

18. Ibid.

19. *Living Church,* May 16, 1954. St. Luke's never had the opportunity to carry out its decision, since the Church's black leadership, as we have indicated,

was successful in convincing Presiding Bishop Sherrill to move the Convention to Honolulu.

20. Letter from Dade to Logan, March 15, 1961.

21. Bragg, *Afro-American Group*, 165.

Chapter 10. The Episcopal Church and the Civil Rights Movement

Epigraph: George Wallace Briggs, "Christ is the world's true light," no. 258 (hymn text, 1933), *The Hymnal 1940.*

1. Harold T. Lewis, "Behold a Dreamer," a sermon preached on the commemoration of Martin Luther King Jr.'s birthday, in the Cathedral Church of SS Peter and Paul, Washington D.C., January 19, 1992:

> The Church has for too long been a non-*prophet* organization. We have often exercised a ministry, not "with the cross of Jesus going on before," as the hymn reminds us, but "with the cross of Jesus bringing up the rear!" According to an apocryphal tale, the founding fathers, having drawn up the Constitution, went across the street and founded the Episcopal Church. Ever since, the church, by and large, has been a mirror of the society at large. We have been a chaplaincy to the status quo, and not a champion of the oppressed. A prophetic church is not one which looks into a crystal ball and tells the future; rather it is a church which reads the signs of the times, interprets them, and charts a course of action, even if it be an unpopular one.

In Harold T. Lewis, *In Season, Out of Season* (New York: Executive Council of the Episcopal Church, 1993), 83.

2. John Kater, "Experiment in Freedom: The Episcopal Church and the Black Power Movement," *Historical Magazine of the Episcopal Church* (March 1979): 68, italics mine.

3. Ibid., 68–69.

4. In *Brown v. Board of Education* (Topeka, Kansas) the Supreme Court ruled that segregation of public schools was unconstitutional. It struck down the "separate but equal" rule that had dominated American jurisprudence since *Plessy v. Ferguson* in 1896. It is interesting to note that owing to similar pressures, the Episcopal Church felt "compelled" to come out in favor of racial equality during World War II (Hayden, "Let My People Go," 27).

5. Sumner, *Episcopal Church's History*, 37.

6. *Journal of the General Convention* (1955). It should be noted that while the Church declared that black Episcopalians would be welcome in the pews in any congregation, there is no suggestion that the altars and pulpits of those congregations would be open to them.

7. Burgess, "The Role of ESCRU in the Life of the Church."

8. John Booty. *The Episcopal Church in Crisis* (Cambridge, Mass.: Cowley Publications, 1988), 55.

9. Kater, "Experiment in Freedom," 69.

10. The Vietnam War was seen as exacerbating racial tension in the United States, partly because a disproportionately high number of that war's casualties

were African Americans, who, according to one Vietnam veteran, were "black men sent by white men to kill yellow men." The irony of black men who were sent to fight for the rights of an oppressed minority on the other side of the world, but who returned to a country in which their own rights were denied, was not lost on civil rights activists.

11. Booty, *Episcopal Church in Crisis*, 57.

12. Statement by the presiding bishop of the Episcopal Church, May 26, 1963, Archives, PP7.

13. "A Statement on the Church and the Racial Crisis," adopted by the bishop and chapter of the Diocese of Southern Ohio, October 12, 1963 (ESCRU papers, Archives). Hayden observes that as a result of such self-examination, many dioceses became painfully aware of the lack of black clerical leadership and proceeded to elect several black bishops, among whom were Richard Beamon Martin (Long Island, 1967) and John Thomas Walker (Washington, 1971). See Hayden, "From Holly to Turner."

14. H. Irving Mayson, minutes of the meeting of the ad hoc committee concerned with racial inequities existing in the Protestant Episcopal Church with the presiding bishop, April 18, 1967, 1 (Cooper papers).

15. Ibid.

16. The founding proposal believed its unofficial nature to be an asset:

> Enjoying a status similar to that of other independent societies in the Church, this association would work cooperatively with the national and diocesan departments of Christian social relations, but would be free to affirm policy and develop program in a way that official agencies are not always able.

The Executive Council of the Episcopal Church sent two members to the inaugural meeting as observers, the Reverend Arthur Walmsley, Executive Secretary, Division of Christian Citizenship (later bishop of Connecticut) and the Reverend Tollie L. Caution, Secretary for Negro Work (Archives, PP7).

17. While "widely based" geographically, and biracial, ESCRU's membership, black and white, was made up of what could be called the "liberal establishment" of the Episcopal Church. Four of the participants at the organizational meeting in Raleigh later became bishops well known for their forthrightness on matters relating to civil rights: Kilmer Myers (California) and Paul Moore Jr. (suffragan of Washington, later translated to New York), who are white; John Burgess (Massachusetts) and Walter Dennis (suffragan, New York), who are black.

18. Interview with Bishop Walter Dennis, New York City, June 17, 1994.

19. John B. Morris and Cornelius Tarplee, "A Proposal: Formation in the Episcopal Church of a Church Society for Racial Unity," November 18, 1959, Archives, PP7.

20. *Living Church*, January 10, 1960, 6.

21. Although blacks were elected to the presidency of the board of ESCRU, the position of executive director was held by two white clergy from the South, John Morris and Richard Dreisbach. But it should be noted that in 1966, the first executive director wrote:

> Many of us have acknowledged for some time that the more color visible at the helm of ESCRU, the better. With ten out of 23 Directors being Negro, and seven of the 23 Chapter Chairmen, we actually show a much higher proportion of Negro leadership than is found elsewhere in the Episcopal Church, which is overwhelmingly white. Accepting, as I do, that our chief role is to cause the whole Church to move some, I am not compulsively concerned — and indeed, welcome white leadership. At the same time, I have been long persuaded that it would be advantageous tactically or strategically for ESCRU's Executive Director to be black. White bishops can't respond to a Negro and write him off as being some sort of guilt-ridden grandson of a slave owner. (John B. Morris, "Responsible Militancy and the Way Ahead — Part II"-December 6, 1966. Papers, Archives. PP7.)

22. The Rev. Joseph A. Pelham, director of the Department of Christian Social Relations of the Diocese of Michigan, in a letter to prospective members of ESCRU, December 7, 1959, Archives, PP7.

23. Among those was the Lovett School, run by the Episcopal Diocese of Atlanta, to which the children of the Reverend Dr. Martin Luther King Jr. had been denied admission because of their race.

24. Resolutions from first annual meeting, Williamsburg, Va., January 8–11, 1961, Archives, PP7.

25. The ashes from the burned books were then imposed on the foreheads of participants in the demonstrations. Several white members of ESCRU, sympathetic to the cause, but opposed on principle to the burning of books as a form of protest, resigned from ESCRU in the wake of the book-burnings.

26. Hayden, "Let My People Go," 28.

27. Kater, "Experiment in Freedom," 69–70.

28. In this connection, it is interesting to note that four years after *Brown vs. Board of Education,* at the 1958 General Convention, a deputy from the diocese of North Carolina introduced a resolution that "a sincere belief in the rightness of segregation is not incompatible with a belief in the dignity of all men and their equality before God" ("House of Deputies Has Conflict over Resolutions on Race," *The Witness,* October 16, 1958, 5).

29. Indeed, the emergence of "Black Power" and the slogan "Black Is Beautiful" were seen by most blacks as correctives to this period of blacks' cultural captivity. At the same time they were seen to many in the white community as "red flags," indeed as signs of "reverse racism."

30. Thus, in its 1967 "Self-Study," ESCRU attempted to reflect a new consciousness by promulgating a statement vastly different in its theology from that which it had espoused at is founding: "'Cultural and racial unity' are taken to mean that we are for free interchange between cultural and racial groups which may or not lead to one race and one cultural world" (Archives, PP7).

31. Burgess, "The Role of ESCRU in the Life of the Church," italics mine.

32. Hayden, "Let My People Go," 28.

33. There are some notable exceptions to this "rule." As we have pointed out, in cases where "white flight" was a factor, i.e., the abandonment of the city on the part of whites, many such merged parishes, usually housed in the larger facility previously occupied by the white parish, became flourishing black con-

gregations. Trinity Cathedral, the result of a merger between it and St. Philip's, Newark; St. Matthew's and St. Joseph's, Detroit, and St. Luke's, Germantown, Philadelphia (a merger of St. Luke's and St. Barnabas') are prominent examples.

34. Cf. Introduction. It should also be pointed out that since black clergy were almost always deployed to black congregations, and were seen to have little function outside of this arena, the death of black congregations would also mean that black clergy would find themselves unemployed. Since assimilation was always on white terms, it was not within the realms of possibility that black priests would be called to lead the congregations made up of their former parishioners and a majority of whites.

35. The Reverend Kenneth de Poullain Hughes, rector of St. Bartholomew's, Cambridge, Mass.; the Reverend Jesse F. Anderson Sr., rector of St. Thomas', Philadelphia; the Reverend Henri A. Stines, Southern field representative for ESCRU; the Reverend Quinland R. Gordon, rector of the Church of the Atonement, Washington, D.C.; the Reverend Robert E. Hood, rector of St. Augustine's, Gary, Ind.; and the Reverend James P. Breeden of the National Council of Churches.

36. "A Declaration of Concern," presented by Negro priests at 1965 meeting of the House of Bishops, Glacier National Park, Montana, italics mine (Archives, PP7). The comment in this document anent the white domination of the overseas mission field is worthy of note in light of our previous discussion about ACIN's lament that the church had done little for blacks but had been enormously successful in missionary work overseas.

37. Resolution at 1966 Annual Meeting of ESCRU, New York City, Archives, PP7.

38. Ibid. ESCRU responded to the challenge and in a resolution passed at its 1967 annual meeting voted to "support, in appropriate ways, the attempt of the black community to organize for the achievement of a power of self-determination" ("Advisory statements and directions adopted by the Annual Meeting of ESCRU," September 15–17, 1967, Seattle, Wash., Archives, PP7.

39. Minutes of the Black Caucus of the eighth annual meeting of the Episcopal Society for Cultural and Racial Unity, November 16, 1968, submitted by Betty Howard, secretary pro tem, Archives, PP7.

40. Barbara Harris is now bishop suffragan of Massachusetts. She is the first woman bishop in the Anglican Communion.

41. Letter from the executive director of ESCRU to its membership, dated November 4, 1970, Archives, PP7.

42. Ibid.

43. According to the melting-pot theory, each ethnic or racial group sacrifices its individual identity in order to contribute to the "sauce," which draws from the flavors of each group. According to the salad-bowl theory, each group contributes its taste to the new creation, but retains its own identity. It has recently been suggested, tongue-in-cheek, that new emphases on racial and ethnic distinctiveness, resulting at times in racial fragmentation, even separation,

should be dubbed the "salad-bar theory." It is interesting to note that a famous sociological study pointed out that the idea of the melting pot was specious *ab initio:*

> It is striking that in 1963, almost forty years after mass immigration from Europe to this country ended,... the notion that the intense and unprecedented mixture of ethnic religious groups in American life was soon to blend into a homogeneous end product has outlived its usefulness and also its credibility. In the meantime, the persisting facts of ethnicity demand attention, understanding and accommodation. The point about the melting pot is that it did not happen.

Nathan Glazer and Patrick D. Moynihan, *Beyond the Melting Pot* (Cambridge: MIT Press, 1974), 5.

44. Burgess, "The Role of ESCRU in the Life of the Church."

45. Edward W. Rodman, *Let There Be Peace among Us: A Story of the Union of Black Episcopalians* (Boston: Union of Black Episcopalians, 1989), 5.

46. James F. Findlay Jr., *Church People in the Struggle: The National Council of Churches and the Black Freedom Movement, 1950–1970* (New York: Oxford University Press, 1993), 213.

47. Rodman, *Let There Be Peace among Us,* 4. GCSP met with resistance from many quarters.

> Controversial from its inception in October 1970, opposition from bishop and local church people [principally because grants recipients were not church related and were often perceived as holding views incompatible with those of the Episcopal Church] led to major restrictions in the functioning of the fund. Three years later, it disappeared entirely in an internal bureaucratic merger. John Hines, from the beginning one of the strongest supporters of the Special Program, was replaced as Presiding Bishop by John Allin... Bishop of the Diocese of Mississippi. (Findlay, *Church People in the Struggle,* 220.)

48. ESCRU *Newsletter,* September 14, 1969, 1, Archives PP7.

49. *Journal of the Special Convention of the General Convention 1968,* 206.

50. In a meeting with black clergy on January 17, 1968, Presiding Bishop Hines

> stated that Mr. Leon Modeste, who has been named to direct the new General Convention Special unit (i.e., the urban crisis program) has been given free reins in choosing his staff. According to the Presiding Bishop, Mr. Modeste did not choose Dr. Caution. Thus, the painful task remained to call Dr. Caution in and inform him of the same. Inasmuch as many of the duties performed by Dr. Caution would be taken over by the new unit, this necessarily meant an end to his position and he had to be so informed. (H. Irving Mayson, "Minutes of a meeting of Negro Priests with the Presiding Bishop re: 'Retirement of Tollie L. Caution,' Episcopal Church Center, New York City, January 17, 1968; Cooper papers.)

In a letter to Bishop Primo, Bishop Corrigan, who at the presiding bishop's behest had actually executed Caution's dismissal, wrote: "Dr. Caution's function was properly transferred to the new unit under Mr. Modeste. We did not deem it advisable to transfer Dr. Caution into the new unit" (minutes of January 17, 1968 meeting between black clergy and Bishop Hines; Cooper papers).

According to Bishop Primo, however, Dr. Caution, a quintessential churchman, and a faithful and influential member of the staff for many years, posed a threat to Leon Modeste, the director of GCSP, and the Reverend Quinland

Gordon, a member of his staff. They thought he might be a hindrance as they sought to interface with segments of the black community that Caution might find objectionable.

51. Letter from Bishop Burgess to Bishop Corrigan, cited in Cooper, Minutes of Ad Hoc Committee of Negro Clergy, February 7, 1968, 1; Cooper papers.

52. For information in this section, the author is indebted to comments made by Bishop Primo, obtained during an interview in Wilmington, Delaware, on June 7, 1994.

53. The full name of the group was "The Ad Hoc Committee concerned with racial inequities existing in the Protestant Episcopal Church."

54. Among those present were the Reverend Messrs. Jesse F. Anderson Sr., rector, St. Thomas', Philadelphia; Austin Cooper, rector, St. Philip's, Jacksonville, Fla.; Walter Dennis, canon of the Cathedral of St. John the Divine, New York City; Kenneth Hughes, rector, St. Bartholomew's, Cambridge, Mass.; Clifford Lauder, rector, All Souls, New York City; Shelton Pollen, curate, St. Luke's, Washington, D.C.; Quintin E. Primo Jr., rector, St. Matthew's, Wilmington, Delaware ; Warren Scott, chaplain, Morehouse College, Atlanta; St. Julian Simpkins, rector, St. Simon's, Rochester, New York; William A. Van Croft, rector, St. Luke's, Washington, D.C.; John Thomas Walker, canon of Washington Cathedral.

55. Primo maintains that Dr. Caution in many ways was not appreciated for the work he had done on behalf of the national church. "He certainly should have become a bishop," Primo opined. "When the House of Bishops elected Dillard Brown [rector of St. Luke's, Washington, D.C.] as Bishop of Liberia, that was the time to have appointed Tollie." Upon Dr. Caution's retirement, according to Bishop Walter Dennis, "Tollie was made a consultant who was never consulted."

56. At this meeting, held in New York on April 18, 1967, Primo presided. The other black priests present were the Reverend Messrs. Jesse F. Anderson Sr., James Breeden, Denzil Carty, Tollie L. Caution, Austin Cooper, Jeffrey Cuffee, John Davis, Walter Dennis, James Edden, Quinland Gordon, Kenneth Hughes, Robert Hood, Ellsworth Jackson, John Johnson, Irving Mayson, Harry Nevels, Joseph Nicholson, William O'Neal, Dillard Robinson, St. Julian Simpkins, Henri Stines, John Walker, Donald Wilson, Frederick Williams, and Harold Louis Wright. (Of these priests, Primo, Dennis, Mayson, Walker, and Wright later became bishops.) (H. Irving Mayson, Minutes of the "Meeting of the Ad Hoc Committee concerned with racial inequities existing in the Protestant Episcopal Church" with the presiding bishop, April 18, 1967.)

In addition to Bishop Hines, bishops in attendance were John Burgess, suffragan of Massachusetts (at the time the only black bishop from a U.S. diocese in the House of Bishops); Gerald Burrill, Chicago; Girault Jones, Louisiana; Leland Stark, Newark; and George Barrett, Rochester. Horace W. B. Donegan of New York had been invited, but was unable to be present (Minutes of Ad Hoc Committee with the Presiding Bishop, April 18, 1967).

57. At the meeting held on June 27, 1967, at the Episcopal Church Center in New York, black clergy present were the Reverend Messrs. Tollie Caution, Austin Cooper, Quinland Gordon, Robert Hood, Joseph Nicholson, Quintin Primo, and Harold Wright. White clergy in attendance were the Reverend Messrs. John Krumm, rector of Ascension, New York City, later bishop of Southern Ohio; David Collins, dean of Atlanta; and Gordon Charlton, rector of St. Andrew's, Wilmington, Del., later dean of the Episcopal Seminary of the Southwest and bishop suffragan of Texas. Bishops in attendance were Hines, Burgess, Jones, Stark (who had attended the previous meeting), and James Winchester Montgomery, who had succeeded Burrill as bishop of Chicago. (Bishop Montgomery is the grandson of Bishop James Winchester, bishop of Arkansas, under whom Bishop Demby had served as suffragan for colored work.) (Austin Cooper, Minutes of the Second Meeting of Negro Clergy with the Presiding Bishop and other Bishops and Priests, Tuesday, June 27, 1967, Episcopal Church Center, New York City; Cooper papers.)

58. Ibid., 4.

59. The resolution, adopted by Executive Council on February 16, 1967, read:

> Resolved, That the Executive Council pledge itself to constructive efforts to assure that Negro churchmen attain positions of leadership within the life of our own Church, . . . that to this end the Presiding Bishop is requested, in the responsible selection of qualified personnel to continue his efforts to appoint Negro clergymen and other professional persons to top executive positions on the staff of the Executive Council . . . and to establish means whereby Negroes may advise in the selection of, as well as appointment to, advisory bodies and other positions of national scope . . . and that the officers of the Council be requested to offer cooperation to diocesan bishops in developing means of securing the placement of a significant number of Negro clergymen in major parishes. (Cited in Minutes of meeting, June 27, 1967; Cooper papers.)

60. Interview with Bishop Primo, June 7, 1994.

61. The Reverend Austin Cooper, in a telephone interview on June 17, 1994. After serving as secretary of the ad hoc committee, he was elected secretary of the Union. Father Cooper is now the rector of St. Andrew's Church, Cleveland, Ohio.

According to Father Cooper's minutes of the meeting, at least two other factors affected the celerity which attended the motions to organize the Union. One was the report of Mr. Leon Modeste, head of the GCSP program (who had been invited to the meeting) who

> (quite in contrast to what the committee which met with the Presiding Bishop on January 17th was told) said that he had been approached by the Home Department (he preferred not to name persons) concerning whether or not Dr. Caution should remain. He stated that he told the Home Department of the need for Dr. Caution's continued employment and that the onus of discharging Dr. Caution would have to be on the Home Department, not on himself.

The other factor was Dr. Caution's reading of the duties he performs. In recording the observation that "few, if any of these duties could and would be formed by the new General Convention Special Unit," the UBCL founders expressed the belief that their interests would not be adequately addressed in the new structure; the UBCL, therefore, decided that it should provide the advocacy role for black Episcopalians now lost due to Dr. Caution's untimely departure.

62. Ibid. (Father Cooper's minutes), 5.

63. "Negro Episcopal Priests Form Union," *New York Times*, February 9, 1968. The article makes clear allusions to the Caution incident.

64. Primo was prevented from attending the organizational meeting due to illness, but was elected president *in absentia.* Those in attendance were Jesse F. Anderson Sr., rector of St. Thomas', Philadelphia; Tollie L. Caution, former secretary for racial minorities at the Episcopal Church Center; Austin R. Cooper, rector of St. Philip's, Jacksonville, Fla.; Walter Dennis, canon of the Cathedral of St. John the Divine in New York City, later bishop suffragan of New York; James Edden, rector of St. Thomas', Chicago; Thomas Gibbs, a member of the presiding bishop's staff (later dean of the Virgin Islands); Quinland Gordon, a member of the GCSP staff at the Episcopal Church Center; Kenneth Hughes, rector of St. Bartholomew's, Cambridge; H. Irving Mayson, rector of St. Andrew's, Cleveland (later bishop suffragan of Michigan); Henry Parker, director of the Delta Ministry in Mississippi; Shelton Pollen, curate, St. Luke's, Washington, D.C.; St. Julian Simpkins Jr., rector of St. Simon of Cyrene, Rochester, N.Y.; William A. Van Croft, rector of St. Luke's, Washington, D.C.; John T. Walker, canon of Washington Cathedral (later suffragan, then bishop of Washington); M. Moran Weston, rector of St. Philip's, Harlem; Frederick Williams, rector of St. Clement's, Inkster, Mich.; Harold Louis Wright, rector of the Church of the Resurrection, E. Elmhurst, N.Y. (and later bishop suffragan of New York). (Austin Cooper, Minutes of Ad Hoc Committee of Negro Clergy, St. Philip's Church, Harlem, February 7, 1968.)

65. At the February 7 meeting, the Reverend Kenneth Hughes moved that an association of black clergy be formed (per the recommendation of a subcommittee that had met during the Washington meeting on January 5). At that time, a paper was presented by the Reverend Austin Cooper entitled "Concerning an Association of Negro Priests." But at the February meeting, "Irving Mayson felt that there should be a Union of Black Clergy and Laymen of the Episcopal Church." Upon Hughes' withdrawal of his motion, Mayson made his, and "Thus, 'the Union of Black Clergy and Laymen' of the Episcopal Church came into being" (Cooper, Minutes of Ad Hoc Committee meeting). The union's guidelines, drawn up at that meeting, indicated that "the membership shall invite laymen to join the organization who have shown interest, or whose interest has been aroused, or who have been recommended by clergy or other lay persons."

66. Cooper, Minutes of Ad Hoc Committee meeting.

67. Primo explained that the decision to place ads instead of sending a story to the publications, or a press release, was that through the ads, they could have control over what was said, and would not have to run the risk of their copy being altered.

68. *The Witness* is known principally for its liberal views; and *The Living Church* for its conservative slant. *The Episcopalian* (now *Episcopal Life*) is the official monthly publication of the Episcopal Church and, as a house organ, has been middle-of-the-road.

69. Primo, interview, June 6, 1994. Primo chose the Reverend Edward Rodman to function as a UBE "ambassador," who staffed the majority of the regional conferences.

70. Interview with Bishop Dennis, New York City, June 17, 1994.

71. Bishop Charles Carpenter of Alabama, acting on information received from parishioners of St. Mark's, Birmingham, a black congregation, issued the ultimatum to the vicar of St. Mark's. (N.B.: A vicar is the priest-in-charge of a mission, i.e., a congregation financially dependent on the diocese; the vicar is appointed by the bishop, and not, as in the case of rectors of parishes, elected by the congregation. The vicar, therefore, serves at the pleasure of the bishop. The bishop could not have issued such a threat to the rector of a parish.)

72. Rodman, (*Let There Be Peace among Us,* 5, 6) in echoing the "social order" theme as articulated by Kater, observes: "It is important to note here that the Episcopal Church was not immune to the dynamics affecting the entire society, and therefore, it is not surprising that a Black Caucus emerged with or without the impetus of the actions of Bishop Hines."

73. Rodman attributes the longevity of the UBE to the fact that while black caucuses in other mainline denominations

> sought financial resources to implement a new program, or a response to some version of the reparations demand... to the UBE... money was never the issue, but rather respect for the role of Blacks within the Episcopal Church, and their access to and participation in the decision-making process of the Church. I believe that, in retrospect, this clarity of purpose originally perceived by the founders of the Union and essentially adhered to by their successors, is a primary reason why the organization continues to this day while many of its counterparts in other denominations have changed form, or have ceased to exist. (Ibid., 5).

74. Ibid., 9. CCWACP's last president was the Reverend Donald Wilson, rector of St. James', Baltimore.

75. Among these were Jesse Anderson Jr., Lee Benefee, Robert Hood, Edward Rodman, Frederick Williams, and James Woodruff.

76. Rodman, *Let There Be Peace among Us.*

77. Booty, *Episcopal Church in Crisis,* 55.

78. Rodman (*Let There Be Peace among Us,* 16) points out that the efforts of the UBCL bore some fruit:

> A black priest was added to the staff of the GCSP to open up a dialogue with the Black Church regarding our participation in this empowerment program. Funds were mysteriously found for a recruitment program directed toward Blacks to enter the ordained ministry. Conversations were begun which were ultimately to lead to the creation of a Black Episcopal presence at the Interdenominational Theological Center in Atlanta [the Absalom Jones Theological Institute].

For a full discussion of Presiding Bishop Allin's acceptance of the UBE's demands, see the conclusion.

79. Harold T. Lewis, "I see a plumb line," a sermon preached during the 70th General Convention of the Episcopal Church, St. Mary's Church, Phoenix, Ariz., July 14, 1991, in *In Season, Out of Season,* 111.

Conclusion

Epigraph: John Oxenham, "In Christ there is no East or West," no. 263 (hymn text, 1908), *The Hymnal 1940.* The first (and more popular) tune to which the hymn is sung is, according to the hymnal, "a Negro Melody adapted by Harry T. Burleigh, 1939." Burleigh, an accomplished musician, was a soloist in the choir of St. George's Church, New York City. According to the parish's current rector, the Reverend Thomas Pike, Burleigh was in his own way a pioneer in the arena of civil rights. Many of the parishioners objected, in the 1890s, to Burleigh's appointment as a soloist, and threatened to withdraw their pledges if he was hired. One of the parish's vestrymen, the financier J. P. Morgan, announced that he would increase his own pledge to compensate for the losses realized through withdrawn pledges. The parishioners' bluff was called, and Burleigh sang in St. George's choir for 50 years.

1. Du Bois, *The Negro Church,* 139.

2. The Reverend Dalton Downs, in a letter to the Reverend Joseph Green, August 7, 1973, Collection of the records of the Office of Black Ministries, Archives RG159.1.20.

3. Archdeacon John Culmer of South Florida was, in the 1940s, the first black priest elected to the House of Deputies. It is interesting to note in this regard that it was not until 1970 that the House voted to seat *women* deputies. (This was the same year at which General Convention voted to approve the ordination of women to the diaconate.)

4. Cf. Bishop Gibson's letter to Virginia Planters, chap. 2.

5. It is instructive perhaps to note that the Episcopal Church has employed similar strategies with other minority groups. In 1976, in an attempt to placate homosexuals, the General Convention passed a resolution proclaiming that "homosexual persons are children of God who have a full and equal claim with all other persons upon the love and acceptance and pastoral concern of the Church." The Church did not anticipate that the gay community would later use the same resolution as grounds for petitioning for approval of the blessing of same-sex unions and the ordination of avowed homosexuals.

In 1977, the year following the General Convention's decision to allow the ordination of women to the priesthood and episcopate, the House of Bishops, meeting in Port St. Lucie, Florida, passed a resolution, later known as the "conscience clause," which provided canonical protection for those bishops, clergy, and laypersons (who at the time constituted a significant minority in the Church) who because of their theological convictions were unable to accept the ordination of women. This was a stopgap measure designed to keep within the fold Episcopalians of differing persuasions. The resolution did not, however, consider its long-tern ramifications, namely, that it has given bishops who refuse to ordain women the right to disregard the canons of the church, which specifically provide for the admission of women to all the orders of the church. Bishop Dennis calls the conscience clause a "gentlemen's agreement" that should not be binding because it places reconciliation before justice, a strategy that has long characterized the Episcopal Church's approach to its social policy (see Kater's comments, chapter 10). In response to those who maintain that the traditionalist stance of an all-male priesthood is the "catholic" position, Bishop Dennis quips: "You cannot be more catholic than the church you belong to!"

6. Cited in Hayden, "Overview," 15.

7. See report of protest presented to the House of Bishops in chapter 7.

8. Robert Hood, "The Placement and Deployment of Negro Clergy in the Episcopal Church," a report compiled for the Episcopal Society for Cultural and Racial Unity, September 1967, Archives PP7.

9. See chapter 10.

10. "A Declaration, by Priests who are Negroes, on the Personnel Policies and Practices of the Protestant Episcopal Church in the U.S.A," cited in Nicholson, *What Is Happening to the Negro in the Protestant Episcopal Church?*

11. Edwards, "Episcopal Church and the Black Man," 151.

12. Adair Lumis, *Black Clergy in the Episcopal Church: Recruitment, Training and Deployment* (New York: Executive Council of the Episcopal Church, 1979), 39.

13. Letter from the Reverend Canon Edward W. Rodman, canon missioner, Diocese of Massachusetts, to the presiding bishop and black bishops of the Episcopal Church, June 1992.

14. The study, conducted by Dr. Leroy Wells, was entitled "Black Male Participation in the Leadership of the Episcopal Church: A Call for Action."

15. Rodman, *Let There Be Peace among Us,* 38.

16. The Reverend Canon Edward B. Geyer was soon thereafter named executive assistant to Bishop Allin.

17. Funding to the black colleges has been significantly reduced. The funding capacities of all of the ethnic desks has been removed. There is, on the books, an affirmative action policy at Executive Council, but given the ethnic composition of the staff, has proved to be totally ineffective. The number of black deputies has decreased, as has the number of black appointments of standing committees. There are no black clergy, or clergy of any race, on the presiding bishop's senior staff.

18. Strictly speaking, the vice-president is elected by the House upon the presiding bishop's nomination.

19. Wells, "Black Male Participation in the Leadership of the Episcopal Church."

20. The three black males on the appointed staff are Caribbean-born.

21. "A Historical Tragedy in the Life of the Church" (a story about the embezzlement of $2.2 million from the Church's trust funds by former treasurer Ellen F. Cooke), *Living Church,* May 21, 1995, 7.

22. Between 1981 and 1993, thirteen black priests were consecrated as bishops in both domestic and overseas jurisdictions of the Episcopal Church. Thirty-two black priests have been elevated to the episcopate between 1884, when James Theodore Holly was consecrated first bishop of Haiti, and 1993, when Zaché Duracin was consecrated sixth bishop of Haiti. In his sermon at the consecration of Barbara Harris in 1989, the Reverend Paul Washington correctly observed that in the history of the Episcopal Church there have not been as many black rectors of white congregations.

23. For example, although the bishop possesses *potestas* by virtue of office to ordain, his or her *auctoritas* to do so is conferred by the Standing Committee of the diocese. It can be said that earlier efforts on the part of blacks to be consecrated as bishops was a quest for *potestas;* seeking of rectorships a quest for *auctoritas.* They can be seen as two sides of the ecclesiastical coin: one theological, the other political.

24. *Book of Common Prayer,* 1979, 855.

25. NTL Institute for Applied Behavioral Science, *Overview of Race and Ethnic Relations in the Episcopal Church,* 1991.

26. Interview with Bishop Primo conducted by Dr. Randall Burkett, December 12, 1984.

27. Interview with Bishop Dennis, New York City, June 16, 1994.

28. Sara Lawrence-Lightfoot, *I've Known Rivers: Lives of Loss and Liberation* (Reading, Mass.: Addison-Wesley, 1994), 10. Ms. Lawrence-Lightfoot's grandfather was the Reverend Sandy Alonzo Morgan, who served several parishes in the South. Her father, Charles Radford Lawrence, was the first black president of the House of Deputies of the Episcopal Church.

29. "The Sin of Racism," a Pastoral Letter from the House of Bishops of the Episcopal Church, March 1994, 1, italics mine. Parish clergy, upon receipt of pastoral letters, are canonically bound to read them during public worship on an appointed Sunday.

30. Ibid., 6.

31. It is interesting to note in this regard that Tollie Caution's job description was changed from Secretary for Negro Work to Secretary for the Division of Racial Minorities. One of the demands of black deputies to the 1973 General Convention was that the "black desk" be restored in its own right. In 1994, as part of the restructuring of the national Church, the ethnic desks will again function under a multicultural umbrella.

32. *Journal of the General Convention of the Episcopal Church,* 1961, italics mine.

33. Ibid., 7.

34. In the national church structure, in addition to an office for Black Ministries (formerly "Negro Work") there are offices for Asianamerican, Native American, and Hispanic ministries. Bishop Dennis comments:

> My enthusiastic support for the proposed covenant committing us to break down every barrier that separates God's people and to develop strategies for the recruitment, deployment and support of persons of color . . . forces me to inject a somber note: this task will become infinitely more difficult if the Convention approves

the Executive Council's [proposal] eliminating the several ethnic desks and their experienced staff officers. (Dennis, "Preview of General Convention," 291.)

35. Monica, her son Augustine, bishop of Hippo, and Cyprian, bishop of Carthage, were African saints. Simon of Cyrene is the one who was compelled to carry Jesus' cross, whom tradition has always depicted as a black man. St. Philip the Evangelist was, according to the Book of Acts, the one, who through baptizing the Ethiopian eunuch, was the first person to bring the Gospel to African soil. There are more black congregations under St. Philip's patronage than any other saint.

36. "'But We See Jesus': A Pastoral Letter from the Black Episcopal Bishops to Black Clergy and Laity in the Episcopal Church" (New York: Executive Council of the Episcopal Church, 1990), 1.

37. "The Codrington Consensus," Agreed Statement from the Conference on Afro-Anglicanism Held in Barbados, June 17–22, 1985, sec. 4.1, *Linkage,* no. 5 (December 1985): 11.

38. Frances Ellen Watkins Harper, "Full of Hope for the Future," *Church Advocate* 32, no. 8 (January 1924).

39. David Bosch, *Transforming Mission* (Maryknoll, N.Y.: Orbis Books, 1992), 447–48.

40. Gray, *Black Christians and White Missionaries,* 1.

41. George Freeman Bragg Jr., *How the Black Man Found the Church* (Baltimore: Church Advocate Press, 1917).

42. The Reverend Joseph Green, cited in Rodman, *Let There Be Peace among Us,* 52.

43. George Freeman Bragg Jr., "God's Black Man," *Church Advocate* 28, no. 11 (September 1920).

44. Codrington Consensus 7.1.

45. Briggs, "Christ is the world's true light."

46. Wilfred Wood, bishop of Croydon, speech to the General Synod of the Church of England, November 10, 1988, in *Keep the Faith, Baby!* (London: Bible Reading Fellowship, 1994), 18–19.

47. This echoes Ann Lammers's observation. Cf. introduction.

48. Oxenham, "In Christ there is no East or West."

49. See introduction, n. 60.

50. See introduction.

51. Tweedy, "Eternal God, whose power upholds."

52. See introduction.

Bibliography

N.B.: In references to records held in the Records of the American Church Institute for Negroes, National Archives of the Episcopal Church, Austin, Texas, the words "Box" and "folder" will be omitted. The alphanumeric code preceding the first decimal point will refer to the catalog number; the number preceding the second decimal will refer to the box number; and the number after the second decimal point will be the folder number. Records of the Episcopal Society for Cultural and Racial Unity are classified under a different system, whose common catalog number is PP7. Bishops' papers are classified under "Bishops' Biographical Files," which have no catalog numbers.

Archival and Nonpublished Materials

American Church Institute for Negroes, *Negro Education in Wartime,* 1942. Archives RG61.1.14.

Beary, Michael J. "Birds of Passage: A History of the Separate Black Episcopal Church in Arkansas, 1902–1939." M.A. thesis, University of Arkansas, 1993.

Birch, Adolphus A. Minutes of the Twelfth Triennial Conference of the Conference for Church Workers among Colored People, Washington, D.C., May 11–12, 1955. In the private papers of the Reverend Dr. Thomas W. S. Logan Sr., Philadelphia; hereafter Logan Papers.

———. Summary, Special Meeting of the Triennial Conference of Episcopal Church Workers (Conference of Church Workers among Colored People), St. George's Church, Washington, D.C., April 28, 1954. Logan Papers.

Bishop, Samuel H. "The Church and the Negroes: A Statement Concerning Our Work within the Borders of the United States." New York: Board of Missions, 1945. Archives RG61.1.4.

———. Letter to the Executive Committee of the American Church Institute for Negroes, December 13, 1913. Archives RG61.1.6.

Brome, Henderson LaVere. "A Study of the Assimilation of Barbadian Immigrants in the United States with Special Reference to the Barbadians in New York." Ed.D. dissertation, Columbia University, New York, 1978.

Caution, Tollie L. "A Decade of Progress in Negro Work 1941–1951." Records of the Episcopal Commission for Black Ministries, Archives RG159.

———. Minutes of Meeting of Bi-Racial Sub-Committee on Negro Work, November 6–7, 1945. Archives RG159.

———. Minutes of Meeting of Bi-Racial Sub-Committee on Negro Work, April 9–10, 1946. Archives RG159.

Cooper, Austin R. "Minutes of a Meeting of Negro Priests with the Presiding Bishop [John Hines] Re 'Retirement' of the Reverend Doctor Tollie L. Caution." Episcopal Church Center, New York City, January 17, 1968. Private papers of the Reverend Dr. Austin R. Cooper Sr., Cleveland, Ohio; hereafter "Cooper Papers."

———. "Minutes of a Meeting of the Ad Hoc Committee of Negro Clergy." St. Philip's, Episcopal Church, Harlem, New York, February 7, 1968. Cooper Papers.

———. "Minutes of the Second Meeting of Negro Clergy with the Presiding Bishop [John Hines] and other bishops and priests." Episcopal Church Center, New York, June 27, 1967. Cooper Papers.

Crowder, James W., et al. Resolutions Presented by the Committee on Resolutions at the Episcopal Society for Cultural and Racial Unity Annual Meeting, Washington, D.C., November 14–16, 1963. Logan Papers.

Dade, Malcolm. Letters to the Reverend Thomas Logan, March 15 and May 4, 1961. Logan Papers.

Davis, Kortright, ed. "'Pilgrims and Not Strangers': Report of the Caribbean Anglican Consultation, Arlington, Virginia, November, 1990." Washington, May 1991.

Downs, Dalton. Letter to the Reverend Joseph Green, August 7, 1973. Archives 159.1.20.

Edwards, John Henry. "The Episcopal Church and the Black Man in the United States." Archives RG159.1.17.

———. "The Story of a Negro Parish," 1936. Archives of St. Luke's Church, New Haven, Conn.

Ejofodomi, L. E. "The Missionary Career of Alexander Crummell in Liberia, 1853–1873." Ph.D. dissertation, University of Michigan, Ann Arbor, 1974.

Gross, Fannie P. "The Value and Function of an Executive Secretary for a Division on Negro Work," submitted to Dr. Weiand of the ACIN, 1942. Archives RG159.

Harris, Bravid W. Minutes, Bi-Racial Sub-Committee Meeting, November 10, 1944. Archives RG159.

———. Minutes, "Second Annual Report of the Secretary for Negro Work to the Bi-Racial Committee," November 10, 1944. Archives RG159.

Harrison, Eleanor S. "'One, Holy, Catholic and Apostolic Church?' The African American Struggle for Incorporation in the Episcopal Church:

A Case Study of St. John's Church, Savannah, Georgia." B.A. thesis, Princeton University, 1992.

Hayden, J. Carleton. "Different Names but the Same Agenda." 1968. Archives RG159.1.

———. "Let My People Go: The Role of Blacks in the Episcopal Church." 1975. Archives RG159.

———. "Reading, Religion, and Racism: The Mission of the Episcopal Church to Blacks in Virginia, 1865–1877," Ph.D. dissertation, Howard University, Washington, D.C., 1972.

Hood, Robert E. "The Placement and Deployment of Negro Clergy in the Episcopal Church." A report compiled for the Episcopal Society for Cultural and Racial Unity, 1967. Records of the Episcopal Society for Cultural and Racial Unity. Archives PP7.

Hughes, Kenneth deP. *History of St. Bartholomew's P.E. Church.* Cambridge, Mass., 1958.

———. Letter to the Reverend Thomas W. S. Logan, March 21, 1960. Logan Papers.

Logan, Thomas W. S., Sr. Letters to the Members of the Conference of Church Workers among Colored People, March 13, 1954; March 1960. Logan Papers.

———. "Memorial to Black Negro Clergymen who served within the Diocese of Pennsylvania, within the last Two Hundred Years," March 28, 1976. Logan Papers.

Martin, Richard Beamon. Letter to the Reverend Thomas W. S. Logan, April 12, 1960. Logan Papers.

Mayson, H. Irving. Minutes of a meeting of the Ad Hoc Committee Concerned with Racial Inequities Existing in the Protestant Episcopal Church with the Presiding Bishop [John Hines] Episcopal Church Center, New York City, April 18, 1967. Cooper Papers.

Morgan, Hera Phyllis. "Special Meeting of the Triennial Conference of Episcopal Church Workers," St. George's Church, Washington, D.C., April 28, 1954. Logan Papers.

Morris, John B. (president of ESCRU). Letters to the Reverend Thomas S. Logan, June 16, July 7, and August 1, 1960. Logan Papers.

Oxley, Lt. Lawrence A. Letter to the Reverend Thomas W. S. Logan, March 21, 1960. Logan Papers.

Parker, Henry. Letter to the Reverend Thomas Logan, March 1960. Logan Papers.

Parker, Walter P. H. Minutes of the Meeting of the Conference of Church Workers among Colored People, St. Matthew's Church, Detroit, September 13–15, 1961. Logan Papers.

Penick, Edwin A., et al. Report of the Special Committee on Temporary Missionary Districts (originally "Racial Episcopate Jurisdiction"), 1929. Archives RG61.
Quay, William L. "Archdeacon Henry L. Phillips (1847–1947)," *Archives Newsletter* 1, no. 2 (Diocese of Pennsylvania), February, 1985.
Rahming, Harry E. Letter to the Reverend Canon Thomas Logan, May 10, 1978. Logan Papers.
Samuelson, Clifford L. Minutes, First Meeting of Committee on Negro Work, February 8, 1943. Archives RG159.
Summer School of Religious Education. Recommendations made at a meeting, June 10–14, 1963. Logan Papers.
Trigg, Dr. Harold L. "Through a Negro Layman's Eyes." An address to the Joint Session of the General Convention, Cleveland, Ohio, October 3, 1943. Logan Papers.
Vasady, Bela. "The Role of the Black West Indian Missionary in West Africa, 1840–1890," Ph.D. dissertation, Temple University, Philadelphia, 1972.
Wells, Leroy, Jr. "Black Male Participation in the Leadership of the Episcopal Church: Issues and a Call for Action." June 1993.
Winchester, James, Bishop of Arkansas. "A Pastoral Experience #11: God's Faithful Servant." Bishops' Biographical Files, Archives.

Official Publications of the Episcopal Church (published by the Executive Council of the Episcopal Church, New York, unless otherwise noted)

Book of Common Prayer. New York: Church Hymnal Corporation, 1979.
Burgess, John M., Clarence N. Coleridge, Walter D. Dennis, et al. "'But We See Jesus': A Pastoral Letter from the Black Bishops to Black Clergy and Laity in the Episcopal Church," 1990.
Episcopal Church Annual. Ridgefield, Conn.: Morehouse Publishing, 1994.
Episcopal Clerical Directory. New York: Church Hymnal Corporation, 1993.
House of Bishops of the Episcopal Church. "The Sin of Racism." Pastoral letter promulgated March 1994.
Hymnal 1940. New York: Church Hymnal Corporation.
Hymnal 1940 Companion. New York: Church Hymnal Corporation.
Jones, Marc S., ed. *Directory of Black Clergy in the Episcopal Church, 1993.*
Journals of the General Convention of the Episcopal Church.
Kirk, Stephen S., ed., *Report of the Task Force for the Recruitment, Training and Deployment of Black Clergy.* 1985.
Lesser Feasts and Fasts. New York: Church Hymnal Corporation, 1980.
Lewis, Harold T., ed. *The Recruitment of Black Clergy for the Episcopal Church: Some Biblical, Theological, and Practical Considerations.* New York: Executive Council of the Episcopal Church, 1981.

Linkage. Official journal of the Office of Black Ministries, nos. 1–13, 1984–93.

Lumis, Adair. *Black Clergy in the Episcopal Church: Recruitment, Training, and Deployment.* 1979.

NTL Institute for Applied Behavioral Science. *Overview of Race and Ethnic Relations in the Episcopal Church, 1991.*

Books

Addison, James Thayer. *The Episcopal Church in the United States, 1789–1931.* New York: Scribner's, 1951.

Albright, Raymond W. *A History of the Protestant Episcopal Church.* New York: Macmillan, 1964.

Aptheker, Herbert, ed. *Writings by W. E. B. Du Bois in Non-Periodical Literature edited by others.* Millwood, N.Y.: Kraus Thompson, 1982.

Bardolph, Richard. *The Negro Vanguard.* New York: Random House, 1961.

Booty, John. *The Episcopal Church in Crisis.* Cambridge, Mass.: Cowley Publications, 1988.

Bosch, David. *Transforming Mission.* Maryknoll, N.Y.: Orbis Books, 1992.

Bragg, George Freeman, Jr. *Afro-American Church Work: Historical Addresses.* Baltimore: Church Advocate Press, 1918.

———. *The Attitude of the Church Workers among Colored People Towards the Adaptation of the Episcopal Church to the Needs of the Colored Race.* Baltimore: Church Advocate Press, 1906.

———. *The Episcopal Church and the Black Man.* Baltimore: Church Advocate Press, 1908.

———. *First Negro Priest on Southern Soil.* Baltimore: Church Advocate Press, 1909.

———. *History of the Afro-American Group in the Episcopal Church.* Baltimore: Church Advocate Press, 1922.

———. *How the Black Man Found the Church.* Baltimore: Church Advocate Press, 1917.

———. *Richard Allen and Absalom Jones.* Baltimore: Church Advocate Press, 1915.

———. *Story of Old St. Stephen's Church, Petersburg, Va., and the Origin of the Bishop Payne Divinity School.* Baltimore: Church Advocate Press, 1917.

Brewer, Clifton. *A History of Religious Education in the Episcopal Church to 1835.* New York: Yale University Press, 1924.

Brown, William Montgomery. *The Crucial Race Question.* Little Rock: Arkansas Churchman's Publishing, 1907.

Burgess, John Melville, ed. *Black Gospel/White Church.* New York: Seabury, 1982.

———. *Bravid Washington Harris of Liberia.* New York: National Council of the Episcopal Church, 1965.

Burkett, Randall K. *Black Redemption: Churchmen Speak for the Garvey Movement.* Philadelphia: Temple University Press, 1978.

———. *Garveyism as a Religious Movement: The Institutionalization of Black Civil Religion.* Metuchen, N.J.: Scarecrow Press, 1978.

Cheshire, J. Blount. *The Church in the Confederate States.* New York: Longmans Green, 1912.

Cone, James. *A Black Theology of Liberation.* Philadelphia: Lippincott, 1970.

Crummell, Alexander. *Africa and America: Addresses and Discourses.* 1891; Miami: Mnemosyne Publishing, 1969.

Cyprian, St., Bishop of Carthage. *De Unitate Ecclesiae Catholicae.* Edited by M. Bévenot, S.J. Oxford: Clarendon Press, 1971.

Davis, Cyprian. *The History of Black Catholics in the United States.* New York: Crossroad, 1993.

Davis, Kortright. *Emancipation Still Comin'.* Maryknoll, N.Y.: Orbis Books, 1990.

Dawley, Powel Mills. *Our Christian Heritage: Church History and the Episcopal Church.* New York: Morehouse Gorham, 1959.

Delany, Sarah, and A. Elizabeth Delany. *Having Our Say: The Delany Sisters' First 100 Years.* New York: Kodansha International, 1993.

Du Bois, W. E. B. *The Negro Church.* Atlanta: Atlanta University Press, 1903.

———. *The Philadelphia Negro: A Social Study.* 1898; New York: Schocken Books, 1969.

———. *The Souls of Black Folk.* Chicago: A. C. McClurg & Co., 1931.

Dunn, D. Ellwood. *A History of the Episcopal Church in Liberia, 1821–1980.* Metuchen, N.J.: Scarecrow Press, 1992.

Edwards, John Henry. *The Negro Churchman's Upward Climb.* Hartford, Conn.: Church Missions Publishing, 1936.

Erskine, Noel L. *Decolonizing Theology: A Caribbean Perspective.* Maryknoll, N.Y.: Orbis Books, 1981.

Findlay, James F., Jr. *Church People in the Struggle: The National Council of Churches and the Black Freedom Movement, 1950–1970.* New York: Oxford University Press, 1993.

Franklin, John Hope. *From Slavery to Freedom.* 7th ed. New York: McGraw-Hill, 1994.

Franklin, Vincent P. *Black Self-Determination: A Cultural History of African-American Resistance.* Brooklyn, N.Y.: Lawrence Hill Books, 1992.

Frazier, E. Franklin. *The Negro Church in America.* New York: Schocken Books, 1963.

Gatewood, Willard. *Aristocrats of Color: The Black Elite, 1880–1920.* Bloomington: University of Indiana Press, 1990.

George, Carol V. R. *Segregated Sabbaths: Richard Allen and the Rise of Independent Black Churches, 1760–1840.* London: Oxford University Press, 1973.

Goodridge, Sehon. *Facing the Challenge of Emancipation: A Study of the Ministry of William Hart Coleridge, First Bishop of Barbados, 1824–1842.* Bridgetown, Barbados: Cedar Press, 1981.

Gray, Richard. *Black Christians and White Missionaries.* London: Yale University Press, 1990.

Hacker, Andrew. *Two Nations: Black, White, Separate, Hostile, Unequal.* New York: Scribner's, 1992.

Harris, Odell Greenleaf. *A History of the Seminary to Prepare Black Men for the Ministry of the Protestant Episcopal Church.* Alexandria: Virginia Theological Seminary, 1980.

Hodges, George. *Three Hundred Years of the Episcopal Church in America.* Philadelphia: George W. Jacobs & Co., 1906.

Hoskins, Charles. *Black Episcopalians in Georgia: Strife, Struggle and Salvation.* Savannah: St. Matthew's Episcopal Church, 1980.

Jakobson, Stiv. *Am I Not a Man and a Brother?* Uppsala: Almqvist & Wiksell, 1972.

Jones, S. H. M. *Diocese of Gambia and the Rio Pongas, 1835–1951: Its Origins and Early History.* Banjul: Book Production and Material Resources Unit, Diocese of Gambia, 1966.

Kasinitz, Philip. *Caribbean New York: Black Immigrants and the Politics of Race.* Ithaca: Cornell University Press, 1992.

Konolige, Kit, and Frederica Konolige. *The Power of Their Glory — America's Ruling Class: The Episcopalians.* New York: Wyden Books, 1978.

Lawrence-Lightfoot, Sara. *I've Known Rivers: Lives of Loss and Liberation.* Reading, Mass.: Addison-Wesley, 1994.

Lincoln, C. Eric, and Lawrence H. Mamiya. *The Black Church in the African-American Experience.* Durham, N.C.: Duke University Press, 1993.

Manross, William Wilson. *A History of the American Episcopal Church.* New York: Morehouse-Gorham, 1950.

Nicholson, Joseph. *What Is Happening to the Negro in the Protestant Episcopal Church?* St. Louis: Ad Hoc Clergy Committee, 1968.

Niebuhr, H. Richard. *The Social Sources of Denominationalism.* New York: World Publishing, 1957.

Pennington, Edgar L. *Thomas Bray's Associates and Their Work among Negroes.* Worcester, Mass.: American Antiquarian Society, 1939.

Prichard, Robert W. *A History of the Episcopal Church.* Harrisburg, Pa.: Morehouse, 1991.

———. *Readings from the History of the Episcopal Church.* Wilton, Conn.: Morehouse-Barlow, 1986.

Raboteau, Albert J. *Slave Religion: The "Invisible Institution" in the Antebellum South.* New York: Oxford University Press, 1978.

Reece, J. E., and C. G. Clark-Hunt. *Barbados Diocesan History.* London: The West India Committee, 1925.

Reid, Ira. *The Negro Immigrant: His Background, Characteristics, and Social Adjustment, 1899–1937.* New York: AMS Press, 1939.

Rigsby, Gregory U. *Alexander Crummell: Pioneer in Nineteenth-Century Pan-African Thought.* New York: Greenwood Press, 1987.

Rodman, Edward W. *Let There Be Peace among Us: A Story of the Union of Black Episcopalians.* Boston: Union of Black Episcopalians, 1989.

Sowell, Thomas. *Economics and Politics of Race: An International Perspective.* New York: Morrow, 1983.

———. *Ethnic America.* New York: Basic Books, 1981.

Staudenraus, P. J. *The African Colonization Movement, 1816–1865.* New York: Columbia University Press, 1961.

Sumner, David E. *The Episcopal Church's History: 1945–1985.* Wilton, Conn.: Morehouse-Barlow, 1987.

Sykes, Stephen, and John Booty. *The Study of Anglicanism.* Philadelphia: SPCK/Fortress, 1988.

Taylor, Blanche Mercer. *Plenteous Harvest: The Episcopal Church in Kansas, 1837–1972.* Topeka: Diocese of Kansas, 1973.

Thurman, Wallace. *Negro Life in New York's Harlem.* Kansas City: Girard, 1928.

Weatherford, W. D. *The American Church and the Negro.* Boston: Christian Publishing House, 1957.

Weston, M. Moran. *Social Policy of the Episcopal Church in the Twentieth Century.* New York: Seabury, 1964.

Wilberforce, Samuel (Lord Bishop of Oxford). *A History of the Protestant Episcopal Church in America.* 2nd ed. London: Francis & John Rivington, 1846.

Williams, Walter L. *Black Americans and the Evangelization of Africa, 1877–1900.* Madison: University of Wisconsin Press, 1982.

Wilmore, Gayraud. *Black and Presbyterian: The Heritage and the Hope.* Philadelphia: Geneva Press, 1983.

Wood, Forrest G. *The Arrogance of Faith: Christianity and Race in America from the Colonial Era to the Twentieth Century.* New York: Knopf, 1990.

Wood, Wilfred. *Keep the Faith, Baby!* London: Bible Reading Fellowship, 1994.

Woodson, Carter G. *History of the Negro Church.* Washington, D.C.: Associated Publishers, 1921.

Articles

Barr, Phyllis. "Learning the Lessons of Freedom: Black History at Trinity Church [New York City]." *Trinity News,* Lent 1992.

Beary, Michael J. "Up from the Basement: Bishop Demby's Struggle for a Catholic Church." *Linkage,* no. 13 (1993).

Bennett, Robert A. "Black Episcopalians: A History from the Colonial Period to the Present." *Historical Magazine of the Episcopal Church* 43 (September 1974): 231–45.

Bird, Van S. "Christian Witness and Social Transformation — I." *St. Luke's Journal of Theology* 22, no. 4 (September 1979): 284–96.

Bragg, George Freeman, Jr. "Beginnings of Negro Work in the South." *The Living Church,* August 20, 1921, 505.

———. "Christian Statesmanship." *The Church Advocate* 19, no. 7 (May 1910).

———. "God's Black Man." *The Church Advocate* 28, no. 11 (Sep. 1920).

———. "South Carolina: A Good Field for the Negro Missionary Bishop." *The Church Advocate* 22, no. 12 (April 1913).

———. "The Episcopal Church and the Negro Race." *Historical Magazine of the Episcopal Church* 4, no. 1 (March 1935): 47–52.

Burkett, Randall K. "Elizabeth Mars Johnson Thomson, 1807–1864: A Research Note." *Historical Magazine of the Episcopal Church* 55, no. 1 (March 1986).

Crummell, Alexander. "The Best Methods of Church Work among the Colored People." *The Church Magazine* (June 1887): 555–56.

Davis, Kortright. "Afro-Anglicanism and the Ecumenical Imperative." *Linkage,* no. 6 (October 1986): 2–4.

———. "Bilateral Dialogue and Contextualization." *Journal of Ecumenical Studies* 23, no. 3 (1986): 387–99.

Dennis, Walter D. "A Personal Preview of the 71st General Convention of the Episcopal Church." *Sewanee Theological Review* 31, no. 3 (1994): 286–308.

———. "Tollie LeRoy Caution: Forerunner, Pathfinder, Prophet." *Linkage,* no. 9 (June 1988): 8.

Dunn, D. Ellwood. "George Daniel Browne (1933–1993): Architect of West African Indigenization." *Linkage,* no. 13 (June 1993): 28.

Franklin, John Hope. "Negro Episcopalians in Ante-Bellum North Carolina." *Historical Magazine of the Episcopal Church* 13 (1944): 217–34.

Gardner, Bettye J. "Opposition to Emigration: A Selected Letter from William Watkins, a Colored Baltimorean." *Journal of Negro History* 110 (1978): 265ff.

Hannibal, Preston B. "Anglicanism's First Black Bishop: Pioneer or Experiment?" *Linkage,* no. 10 (December 1988): 7–9.

Hayden, J. Carleton. "Afro-Anglican Linkages, 1701–1900: Ethiopia Shall Soon Stretch Out Her Hands Unto God." *Journal of Religious Thought* 44, no. 1 (1987): 25–34.

———. "After the War: The Mission and Growth of the Episcopal Church among Blacks in the South, 1865–1877." *Historical Magazine of the Episcopal Church* (1972): 4ff.

———. "Alexander Crummell, Afro-Anglican Pioneer in the United States, England, and Liberia, 1819–1898." *Linkage,* no. 5 (January 1986): 16–17.

———. "Arnold Hamilton Maloney, Priest and Scientist, 1888–1955." n.p., 1994.

———. "Black Episcopal Preaching in the Nineteenth Century: Intellect and Will." *Journal of Religious Thought* 39 (1982): 12–30.

———. "Black Ministry in the Episcopal Church: An Overview." In Adair Lumis, ed., *Black Ministry in the Episcopal Church: Recruitment, Training and Deployment* (New York: Executive Council of the Episcopal Church, 1979), 1–19.

———. "Conversion and Control: Dilemma of Episcopalians in Providing for the Religious Instruction of Slaves, Charleston, South Carolina, 1845–1860." *Historical Magazine of the Episcopal Church* (1972): 143–68.

———. "'For Zion's Sake I will not hold my peace': George Freeman Bragg, Jr., Priest, Pastor and Prophet." *Linkage,* no. 6 (October 1986): 10ff.

———. "From Holly to Turner: Black Bishops in the American Succession." *Linkage,* no. 10 (December 1988): 4–6.

———. "James Solomon Russell (1857–1935): Missionary and Founder of St. Paul's College." *Linkage* (March 1987): 10–11.

———. "James Theodore Holly: Pioneer Bishop." *Linkage* (March 1985): 11.

Haynes, Samuel. "West Indian-American Relations." *The African,* August 1945, 5, 16.

Hughes, Kenneth de P. "Problems of Minorities Discussed by Negro Church Leaders." *The Witness,* October 23, 1958, 6ff.

Kater, John L. "Experiment in Freedom: The Episcopal Church and the Black Power Movement."*Historical Magazine of the Episcopal Church* (March 1979): 66–81.

LaBar, Thomas, and Mary S. Wright. "The New Citizen: A Progress Report on the Negro and the Episcopal Church." *The Episcopalian* (October 1957): 20–27.

Lammers, Ann C. "The Rev. Absalom Jones and the Episcopal Church: Christian Theology and Black Consciousness in a New Alliance." *Historical Magazine of the Episcopal Church* 51 (1982): 159–84.

Lewis, Harold T. "Archon Edward Thomas Demby, Pioneer of Social Justice." *Boulé Journal* (Fall 1992): 8–9.

———. "Black and Anglican Traditions: How Can They Co-exist?" *College of Preachers Newsletter* 23, no. 3 (Fall 1977): 1–2.

———. "Centenary of a Black Caucus." *Ministry Development Journal* (1983): 19–21.

Pobee, John. "Afro-Anglican: Meaning and Movement." *Journal of Religious Thought* 44, no. 1 (1987): 35–44.

———. "Newer Dioceses of the Anglican Communion — Movement and Prospect." In Sykes and Booty, eds., *The Study of Anglicanism.*

Raphael, Lennox. "West Indians and Afro-Americans." *Freedomways* (3rd quarter, 1964), Special issue on the people of the Caribbean area, 438–45.

Reimers, David M. "Negro Bishops and Diocesan Segregation in the Protestant Episcopal Church: 1870–1954." *Historical Magazine of the Episcopal Church* 31 (September 1962): 231–42.

Taylor, E. Don. "Tensions and Opportunities between West Indian and American Blacks in the Episcopal Church — II." *St. Luke's Journal of Theology* 22, no. 4 (September 1979): 272–84.

Traynham, Warner. "A Theological Perspective on the Last Two Hundred Years of the Black Presence in the Episcopal Church." *Journal of Religious Thought* 50, nos. 1 and 2 (Fall-Spring 1993–94).

Turner, Franklin D. "Tollie LeRoy Caution: A Man of Faith, Scholarship and Service." *Linkage,* no. 9 (June 1988): 9–10.

White, Gavin. "Patriarch McGuire and the Episcopal Church." *Historical Magazine of the Episcopal Church* 38 (1969): 109–41.

Sermons and Addresses

Brown, Enrique R. "Ministry to Caribbean Persons." Address delivered at the Caribbean Consultation, Arlington, Va., November 1990. In Davis, ed., "Pilgrims and Not Strangers."

Brown, J. Henry. "The Task of the Church among Negroes." Commencement address to the faculty and graduates of the Bishop Payne Divinity School, May 22, 1945. Archives RG61.

Burkett, Randall K. "The Reverend Harry Croswell and Black Episcopalians in New Haven, 1815–1860." Paper delivered at the Biennial Convention of the American Studies Association, San Diego, Calif., November 1, 1985.

Burgess, John Melville. "The Character of the Black Witness." In Burgess, ed., *Black Gospel/White Church.*

———. Opening address delivered before the Convocation of Black Episcopalians, 1979. *St. Luke's Journal of Theology* 22, no. 4 (September 1979): 245–47.

———. "The Role of ESCRU in the Life of the Church." Keynote address delivered at the opening of the second annual meeting of the Episcopal Society for Cultural and Racial Unity, Chicago, June 22, 1962.

The Records of the Episcopal Society for Cultural and Racial Unity, Archives PP7.

———. A sermon delivered at the Institution of the Very Rev. Quinland Gordon as Dean of the Absalom Jones Theological Institute, Atlanta, April 11, 1972. Archives PP7.

Coleridge, Clarence N. "Towards Effective Ministry in the U.S." Address delivered at the Caribbean Anglican Consultation, Arlington, Va., November 1990. In Davis, ed., "Pilgrims and Not Strangers."

Cooper, Anna Julia. "Womanhood: A Vital Element in the Regeneration and Progress of a Race." Address read before the convocation of colored clergy of the Protestant Episcopal Church at Washington, D.C., 1886, in Cooper, *A Voice from the South,* Schomburg Library of Nineteenth-Century Black Women Writers (New York: Oxford University Press, 1988).

Cooper, Austin R., Sr. "Concerning an Association of Negro Priests." Paper delivered at a meeting of Negro clergy in St. Luke's Church, Washington, D.C., January 5, 1968. Cooper Papers.

Davis, Kortright. "A West Indian Bridge to Solidarity." Paper delivered at the Caribbean Anglican Consultation, Arlington, Va., November 1990. In Davis, ed., "Pilgrims and Not Strangers."

Gailor, Thomas F., Bishop of Tennessee. "Qualifications of Christian Leadership." Sermon preached at the Consecration of Bishop Demby, September 29, 1918, All Saints Church, St. Louis, Mo. In "Facts Associated with the Ordination and Consecration of Edward Thomas Demby," Bishops' Biographical Files, Archives.

Harris, Bravid W. "A Study of Our Work." Paper delivered at the St. Augustine's Conference, St. Augustine's College, Raleigh, N.C., June 1, 1939. Archives RG159.

Lewis, Harold T. "Behold a Dreamer." Sermon delivered at a service commemorating the birthday of the Reverend Dr. Martin Luther King Jr., Washington Cathedral, January 19, 1992, in *In Season, Out of Season: A Collection of Sermons* (New York: Executive Council of the Episcopal Church, 1992).

———. "Doing the Right Thing." Sermon preached at a service of solemn evensong following the dedication of a tombstone for the Right Reverend Edward Thomas Demby, in St. Andrew's Church, Cleveland, Ohio, May 17, 1992, in *Linkage,* no. 13 (1993).

———. "I See a Plumb Line." Sermon preached during the 70th General Convention of the Episcopal Church, in St. Mary's Church, Phoenix, Ariz., July 14, 1991, in *In Season, Out of Season: A Collection of Sermons* (New York: Executive Council of the Episcopal Church, 1992).

Maloney, Arnold Hamilton. "Whites Strive to Keep the Colored Race Divided." *Negro World* (July 1922).

Miller, George Frazier. "The Missionary Episcopate as a Method of Evangelism." In Burgess, ed., *Black Gospel/White Church,* 31–35.

Potter, Henry Codman, Assistant Bishop of New York. Address to the Convention of the Diocese of New York. *Journal of the Diocese of New York* (1885), 89.

Rodman, Edward W. "Walk about Zion." Address delivered to a black clergy conference in the Diocese of Pennsylvania, January 9, 1993.

Wainwright, Jonathan Mayhew. "Address to the Executive Committee of the African Mission School Society, together with the records of the proceedings at the formation of said society." Hartford: H & F. J. Huntington, 1828.

———. "A Plea for Missions." Preached before the Board of Directors of the Domestic & Foreign Missionary Society of the Protestant Episcopal Church in the U.S., in St. James' Church, Philadelphia, May 13, 1828.

Index